Contents

Preface

This book originated at a conference held in the spring of 1999 at the John Jay College of Criminal Justice in New York City. The aim of the conference was to look at three points of a triangular arrangement: *crime,* a changing *liberalism,* and a related something we called *the risk society.* In fact, things did not work out with quite as much symmetry as the image of the triangle suggests. The real problem of the conference was considerably weighted in the direction of crime, or rather, crime and criminal justice agencies. They were looked at against the political and social background of the two largest Anglo-Saxon democracies. That background had itself changed radically over the past two decades with the rise of a new market-oriented liberalism and a new society keyed to the de-centring of risk, changes introduced by Margaret Thatcher and Ronald Reagan but confirmed by Bill Clinton and Tony Blair. The question concerned how crime and especially criminal justice agencies had fared in this new milieu.

Most of the papers in this book were presented in preliminary form at that conference, and for the most part the three-day event was a success. A number of debts were incurred, and the editors of this volume are keenly aware of them and would like to say thank you where it is due. We are grateful to President Gerald W. Lynch, Provost Basil Wilson, Vice President Mary Rothlein and the Alumni Association, Dean James Levine, and to the Student Government of the College. We are also grateful for the creative energies of the Bursar's Office at John Jay College and especially to Robert Sermier and Angela Martin. We also owe thanks to Ms Venezia Michelsen who acted as the student aide to the conference. She tended to the details and made everything work smoothly.

We are grateful to the following for providing excellent feedback in their roles as commentators and panel chairs: Ron Clarke, Burton Zweibach, John Kleinig, Michael Jacobson, Lynn Chancer, Adina Schwartz, Kitty Helland, Jerome Skolnick, James Levine, Rainer Kroll, and Justin Sullivan. We thank *Dissent,* in which an earlier version of Philip Green's chapter appeared and we thank our long-suffering partners who endured the inevitable stress that such occasions bring. But, most of all we thank our busy and eminent colleagues who made the event so stimulating, exciting and worthwhile and then wrote the essays that make up this book.

The book is the conference's final record, and if it makes even a small contribution to understanding the perplexing problem of crime and criminal justice arrangements in contemporary Anglo-Saxon societies, then it will have redeemed itself. We will leave it to the reader to answer the question as to whether it has.

Kevin Stenson and Robert R. Sullivan
London and New York, September 2000

Biographical details of contributors

Jessica Allen, having previously worked at the London School of Economics, is currently a researcher and evaluator at the American Museum of Natural History, New York. Publications include (with Sonia Livingstone and Robert Reiner) 'True lies: changing images of crime in British post-war cinema' *European Journal of Communications*, 1998.

Eric Cadora is Director of the Community Justice project at the Center for Alternative Sentencing and Employment Services, New York.

Todd Clear is Distinguished Professor, John Jay College of Criminal Justice, City University of New York. His publications include *The Community Justice Ideal*, Westview Press, 1999 (with David R. Warp).

Adam Edwards is senior lecturer in criminology at the Nottingham Trent University, UK. His publications include, 'Networking and Crime Control at the Local Level'. In M. Ryan, S. Savage and D. Wall (eds), *Criminal Justice Networks*, Macmillan, 2000.

Philip Green is Emeritus Professor of Government at Smith College, USA. His publications include *Cracks in the Pedestal: Gender and Ideology in Hollywood*, University of Massachusetts Press, 1998.

Barbara Hudson is Professor of Law at the University of Central Lancashire. Her publications include *Understanding Justice*, Open University Press, 1996.

Sonia Livingstone is Professor of Social Psychology at the London School of Economics. Her publications include *Making Sense of Television*, Routledge, 1998.

Eugene McLaughlin is senior lecturer in criminology and social policy at the Open University, UK. His publications include (co-edited with John Muncie) *The Sage Dictionary of Criminology*, Sage Publications, 2001.

Karim Murji is senior lecturer in the faculty of social science at the Open University, UK. His publications include *Policing Drugs*, Ashgate, 2000.

Pat O'Malley is Professor of Law and Legal Studies at LaTrobe University, Australia. His publications include *Crime and the Risk Society*, Dartmouth, 1998.

Robert Reiner is Professor of Criminology at the London School of Economics. His publications include *The Politics of the Police* (third edition), Oxford University Press, 2000.

Jonathan Simon is Professor of Law at the University of Miami, USA. His publications include *Poor Discipline: Parole and the Social Control of the Underclass, 1890–1990*, University of Chicago Press, 1993.

Richard Sparks is Professor of Criminology at Keele University, UK. His publications include (with Evi Girling and Ian Loader) *Crime and Social Change in Middle England*, Routledge, 2000.

Kevin Stenson is Professor of Criminology and Social Policy at Buckinghamshire Chilterns University College, UK. His publications include (edited with David Cowell), *The Politics of Crime Control*, Sage Publications, 1991.

Robert R. Sullivan is Emeritus Professor of Political Science at John Jay College of Criminal Justice, City University of New York. His publications include *Political Hermeneutics*, Penn State University Press, 1989.

Introduction: a guide to the chapters

Kevin Stenson and Robert. R. Sullivan

This book assembles a cast of theoretically diverse and eminent criminologists from anglophone countries in three continents to explore the implications of the increasing salience attributed to crime, law, and order in the advanced liberal democracies. It explores the links between neo-liberal policies, increasing inequalities that have accompanied them and the tensions between the growing use of actuarially based, risk management approaches to crime control, as in other areas of government, and a complex spread of other approaches. These range from a growing use of harsh, 'zero tolerance' approaches to policing and harsh punishments, including the death penalty, to community-based forms of crime prevention, mediation and informal justice. The essays here also reflect the faltering attempts to contest these priorities and the ways in which they focus on the crimes of the poor and marginalized groups in the population, rather than those of the powerful and privileged and the agents of the state. In this book the focus remains on the debates that have had greatest political impact: what to do about mainstream rather than 'elite' crime – a topic that also deserves sustained scrutiny.

The book is structured in terms of five broad themes. The first two chapters by Stenson and Sullivan set the debates within a broader understanding of the links between crime, the shifting forms of liberalism and the risk society. The second theme, pursued by Stenson and Edwards and Clear and Cadora's chapters, focuses on the 'turn to the local': the new emphasis on local strategies of crime control and community justice. The third theme, developed in the two chapters by O'Malley and McLaughlin and Murji, focuses on the problematic relationship between neo-liberalism, managerialism and policing. The fourth theme, developed in the chapters by Simon and Hudson, explores the tensions between rationalist and risk management approaches, and on the other hand the increasingly retributive and even cruel and vengeful tendencies in approaches to criminal justice. The fifth and final theme, explored by the three chapters by Reiner, Livingstone and Allen, by Sparks and by Green, is the crucial links between crime and the mass media in shifting political, economic and cultural contexts. The remainder of this introduction and Stenson's Chapter One will provide a more detailed guide to the reader of the key issues raised in the chapters.

1   The new politics of crime control, by Kevin Stenson

This chapter sets the issues raised in this book in a wider political context, providing working definitions of key terms like liberalism, politics, government, and governance. It firstly unpacks the new political saliency accorded to crime. Secondly, it analyses the retreat from 'liberal' approaches to crime control fashionable in the high period of the welfare states between 1945 and the late 1970s. Thirdly, it analyses the shifts in liberal society in the broadest sense of the term as associated with the post-monarchical liberal democracies. It highlights the changes from 'social' modes of government characteristic of the welfare states to 'advanced liberal' modes of government that were associated with the rise of New Right intellectuals and regimes in the 1980s and 1990s. They involved a mixture of neo-liberal, free market philosophies and traditional conservative values that prioritised the defence of hierarchy and the attempt to restore traditional morality. Fourthly, the chapter records the struggle to construct approaches to crime control under the auspices of 'third way' or, as it is also termed, 'progressive governance' rationalities of government. These try to integrate tough policies associated with the Right with those that attempt to deal with underlying crimogenic conditions. It would be premature to describe these developments as constituting a new phase of liberal government. Rather, they embody a stage of political experiment and re-emphasis within the broad terrain of advanced liberal government. Fifthly, the chapter highlights the vital importance of social scientists as liberal – in the widest sense – critics of power.

2   The schizophrenic self: neo-liberal criminal justice, by Robert R. Sullivan

From a political philosophical perspective, Sullivan argues that through their various phases of development, liberal states from the eighteenth century have practised what he describes as 'schizophrenic' forms of criminal justice. Despite the rhetoric of impartial universal law, in the language of one of liberalism's founding architects, John Locke, there has been one law for the 'rich, enlightened and blessed' and another for the 'noxious' and 'degenerate' underclasses. For Locke, the liberal social contract required an uncompromising war on the criminal as the archetypal 'other', who by his actions threatens the integrity of the contract. This anticipates the recent ongoing 'wars' on drugs and crime. The necessary response to this threat must be, through the vehicle of punishment, a relationship of absolute power between the mighty state and the criminal. This demonised 'other' may be somewhat confused with the racialisation of the perceivably threatening outsider.

Yet, Sullivan argues, the form and complexity of this duality has varied. Since the rise of Reagan and Thatcher's regimes in the 1980s with neo-liberal agendas to roll back their respective welfare states, there has been a growing reliance on the self-policing of the new middle classes. On the other hand, the policing of the poor and rebellious has involved a complex mix of what may at times function as socially inclusive neo-liberal techniques, together with mere repressive technologies of control. The technologies made possible by neo-liberal reforms employ actuarial and managerial practices to control criminals, deemed to be rational actors just like the respectable. However, neo-liberalism co-exists with more traditional, punitive and repressive, residually conservative logics of control. These include the reliance on popular zero tolerance approaches to policing, the use of militarized SWAT (Special Weapons and Tactics) squads and harsh punishments. It is argued that it is misleading to exaggerate the tension between the faces of this penal duality since, in combination, they effectively secure stable sovereign state power in both the US and UK.

3   Risk and community practice, by Todd Clear and Eric Cadora

Clear and Cadora argue that risk, defined as the probability that some undesirable event will occur, and its artefacts may be found in just about every aspect of the correctional apparatus. The prison wall is response to the risk that a confined person may prefer not to stay inside; the razor wire atop a cyclone fence is meant to affect the calculation of the costs of freedom for those behind the fence. The probation officer's recommendation to the court is a venture into probable futures and an assessment of likelihood of their coming about. Wherever one looks in the world of penality, the traces of risk are found. In part this has been highlighted in Feeley and Simon's influential thesis that modern criminal justice is increasingly actuarial in character, prioritizing risk analysis and management over other goals like just desserts and rehabilitation.

   This chapter has two purposes. The first is to provide an essay on 'risk' as it concerns penology. The purpose of this first objective is to hone the contemporary critical analysis of the new penology prioritising risk assessment and management, with a grounded, demystified understanding of risk. Risk is not a recent idea, but has always been a central feature of post-monarchy penal systems and practice. Hence, making risk a centrepiece in portraying present penal practice may over-emphasize its role in producing whatever change may be afoot in penal thought and activity. It follows that the impetus for change in contemporary penal activity lies less in the shifting distribution of risk than in other forces, though we await a full analysis of those other forces.

   The second purpose of the chapter is to hold up this sharpened understanding of risk against the 'community justice movement', a range of initiatives at local level, including restorative justice and related strategies of problem solving, community policing and regeneration, and to examine the ways in which the inescapable reality of risk might be purposefully manifested in particular strategies of community justice. Some of the finer elements of risk are unpacked and there is an attempt to go beyond the more general arguments about actuarial justice and penality. The chapter differentiates three main action purposes to which calculation of risk may be directed: risk control, emphasized by political elites, directly responsive to electorates; risk management, favoured by penal managers and risk reduction, including rehabilitative measures to tackle the wellsprings of offenders' motivations, favoured by front line personnel.

4   Crime control and liberal government: the 'third way' and the shift to the local, by Kevin Stenson and Adam Edwards

This chapter notes the growing centrality of crime, and surrounding fears, as a political issue in Western liberal democracies and emphasises the uneasy tension between three broad strategies of crime control. Firstly, *punitive sovereignty* prioritizes the struggle by official agencies to regain control over public spaces through technologies of control that try to improve 'quality of life'. Secondly, *target hardening*, or situational crime control measures, through environmental redesign and other measures, attempt to reduce the opportunities for crime. Thirdly, strategies of *community security* attempt, at local levels, to weed crimogenic people and conditions from troubled neighbourhoods, seed and encourage informal family and community controls and virtuous spirals of social and economic regeneration. This sphere includes a series of overlapping innovations, including problem-solving policing, community/restorative justice initiatives and community safety strategies.

These crime control strategies can no longer be viewed as the province of 'expert' professionals, buffered from the political process in their administration of law and the delivery of mandated programmes. Rather, their knowledge bases, while drawn from social science, have become key intellectual instruments of government. They are what Michel Foucault describes as governmental *savoirs*. These embody governmental philosophies, or rationalities, together with the policy strategies and technologies (instrumental means) which they deploy or with which they become aligned. They forge new ways to make populations thinkable and measurable for the purposes of liberal government: what Foucault described as *governmentality*. These do not simply describe the world, they also create their own regimes of what counts as the accredited 'truths' about the nature, causes and remedies for crime. These governmental *savoirs* take the form of general theories of risk and also more specific theories and strategies of crime control.

The chapter describes the key role these strategies play in the reconstruction of liberal government against the back-cloth of the great pressures associated with an increasingly interdependent global political economy and related demographic and other social changes. In particular, political movements of the centre ground have tried to articulate policies of the third way, beyond social democracy and the fragmentation and dislocations associated with neo-liberal administrations. In the sphere of crime control this is associated with a new emphasis on local, holistic, partnership policies targeted to high-risk neighbourhoods and groups. Given the declining faith and participation in the old, remote, commercially dominated institutions and practices of liberal democracy, these developments can be seen as methods which try to reconnect the poor and the marginalised to the democratic mainstream. This operates via more fluid, participatory involvement in community-responsive, public institutions. While the jury remains out on the longer-term prospects, it is nonetheless possible to identify certain key strategic dilemmas confronting the third way project at different spatial scales in the effort to balance the provision of universal services with the increasing emphasis on the need to target resources and services towards those areas and population groups defined as 'high risk'. This is undertaken by drawing on empirical research on local modes of crime control in two English cities.

5   Policing crime risks in the neo-liberal era, by Pat O'Malley

The nexus between risk-based models of government and neo-liberal politics has been explored extensively in recent years, in the field of criminal justice and crime control possibly further than elsewhere. Yet in some ways analyses have taken for granted a fairly uniform and straightforward nexus between risk-based approaches and neo-liberalism. This chapter will explore some of the subtleties that emerge when crime prevention and related policing and criminal justice programmes are examined not so much for their evincing of the risk/neo-liberal nexus, but for light they cast on variations that appear within its field of play. In particular, it will be argued that we may think of neo-liberalism as providing a political lexicon in terms of which programmes with other origins and agendas are being expressed and given form. Often these programmes are associated with 'welfare' and 'social' frameworks that have been targeted by neo-liberalism, but also much more traditionally conservative programmes are gaining (or retaining) currency. This is not to suggest that it is business as usual for such approaches, and that neo-liberal talk has really changed little. In part this is because language has key effects, and in part it is because the terms are often linked with transformative techniques of governance. In particular, the emphasis on agendas of individual responsibility and 'empowerment', and of evaluation and impact, effect significant changes. The result, as we might expect, is that neo-liberal approaches to governing crime risks are in some respects unstable, forming hybrids with other approaches. These do not simply reflect the foot-dragging resistance of welfare and 'the social', but rather signal transformations that may move us beyond 'neo-liberalism'.

6   Lost connections and new directions: neo-liberalism, new public managerialism, and the 'modernization' of the British police, by Eugene McLaughlin and Karim Murji

For many commentators one of the defining features of conservative, neo-liberal administrations has been the rise of managerialism as a source of market-based regulatory discipline in both private and public sectors. The mantra of economy, efficiency and effectiveness, operationalized in the emphasis placed on downsizing, performance indicators, pervasive auditing and so on, have created a new hegemony of the mentalities and practices of the accountancy industry. Where full-scale privatisation of public sector agencies like schools, hospitals and the police is deemed impractical, then the new market-style disciplines are introduced by central state ministries through a plethora of circuitous devices that challenge the powers of traditional professional and occupational cultures and elites. They also strengthen the power of a new class of managers and administrators who progressively eat away at roles and responsibilities hitherto assumed to be the preserve of the established professions.

The ultimate sanction used by central government to enforce conformity with centrally set policy goals, benchmarks of good practice and performance indicators is 'market testing', leading to privatisation of the work of the agency. This is termed, in the UK, the new public managerialism (NPM). In this chapter, McLaughlin and Murji identify two broad theoretical models that highlight the link between neo-liberalism and the NPM. First there is a social democratic model with Durkheimian roots. This sees the NPM as undermining the roots of the British, liberal/social democratic traditions of 'policing by consent', with its values of local autonomy and an emphasis on the symbolic role of the police in constructing a national solidarity. It cannot therefore be characterised narrowly as a body that delivers a service like any other commodity.

The second, 'governmentality', model highlights changes in the organisation of policing, with the new emphasis on partnership between agencies and the public in undertaking crime control and forging new forms of accountability, as indicative of the new modes of advanced liberal government ushered in by the neo-liberal transformation in governance. This chapter challenges both these theoretical models by arguing that NPM has a relative autonomy from neo-liberalism and has had a profound and pervasive impact on public services that extends into the period of New Labour, 'third way' government. It represents a powerful impetus for accelerating organisational change. In any case, the differences between the 'third way project' and conservative rule are too significant for the term neo-liberalism to be meaningfully applied to both. The changes already wrought in policing by NPM are messy, uneven and often contested, yet their effects have done much to reveal nostalgic illusions and consoling fictions about the liberal and consensual nature of the old cultures of previous models of British policing.

7   'Entitlement to cruelty': neo-liberalism and the punitive mentality in the United States, by Jonathan Simon

According to Simon, much of the current discussion of penal practices in the US presumes that political support for harsh, cruel measures, like the revival of the death penalty, the introduction of modern versions of the chain-gang and boot camps reflects a belief by ordinary citizens, manipulated or otherwise, that crime is out of control and that the past failure of government to impose certain and stiff penalties is to blame. Some, especially critics of punishment policies, see that instrumental rationality as deeply compromised by other ideological agendas, including class- and ethnicity-based conflicts and their resulting tensions. But overall, in this sense, the sociology of punishment parallels the sociology of deviance in presuming that the repulsion or attraction towards crime is basically a displacement of other deeper social objectives.

Jack Katz argued against the view that crimes were best seen as displacements for normal objectives of economic and social advancement. Rather, crime is attractive to many offenders because it is fun, expressive and satisfying. It is argued that the sociology of the punitive mentality might try its own version of Katz's post-Mertonian turn. As a preface to this, consideration is given to whether it is possible to understand current trends towards cruel punishments as a reversal of the long-term transition to less cruel modes of punishment identified in influential theses by Durkheim and Elias. These theorists understood these shifts as manifestations of deeper changes in social structure and the psychic economy of the individual. By contrast, it is argued here that attention should be focussed on mapping the more surface ways in which punishments, and the legal structures of assigning and imposing punishments, provide satisfaction to those authorising them, exercising them, watching them, or merely acting in the highly charged atmosphere that some punishments create. The benefits provided by punishment here may range from instrumental, to ideological, to emotional.

This chapter offers some preliminary reflections on the re-emergence of a public role for cruelty. Cruelty in this sense means satisfaction at the suffering implied by or imposed by punishments on criminals, and this public satisfaction breaks through some of the restraints on the public and officially sanctioned expression of these feelings imposed by earlier liberal values and sensibilities. The new questions posed are: what does the cultural production of cruelty do? What kinds of things does it make visible as a form of knowledge? What strategies does it invite? Cruelty can be viewed as a resource for communities, political authorities and individuals as they seek to establish a new moral economy.

The risk society creates conditions where cruelty may become a resource for self-fashioning. For example, the radical decomposition of the community and class contexts in which individualism was held in check during the first, industrial phase of modernity leaves a self largely responsible for its own rituals of sancti-fication. In this context it may be useful that the suffering of others can be made to reflect the value and esteem of those for whom the suffering is enacted. The current invocation of vengeance reflects not only a hardening of attitude against offenders but also a sense of entitlement to the death penalty as a satisfying personal experience for victims and a satisfying genre for the rest of the community. To this end the role of the state is rather different from that which characterized it in the old patriarchal monarchies, when a key function of cruel punishment was to demonstrate a fearful and awesome presence of the state and majesty. Rather, the new penal state is a 'buddy state'. Its role is to be a buddy or friend to the victim, being a reliable provider of that lawfully consecrated but privately consumed entitlement to cruelty that a conviction for serious crime produces.

8   Punishment, rights and difference: defending justice in the risk society, by Barbara Hudson

The author traces the changing patterns of penality in the UK in the 1980s and 1990s. While the fashion for diversion had reduced rates of incarceration of juvenile offenders in the 1980s, a growing punitiveness in the treatment of adult offenders had created a record high point in 1988 and growing concerns about riots and deteriorating prison conditions. This created the conditions favouring a revival of the 'justice model', with its emphasis on the need for 'due process' and introducing clear principles for the allocation of penal sanctions. This was crystallised in the Criminal Justice Act of 1991, encouraging penal bifurcation, with prison intended for serious offences and non-custodial sanctions developed and strengthened to provide appropriate penalties for less serious offences. However, the policy climate soon shifted in a punitive direction. Hence, prison numbers have increased steadily through the 1990s, accompanied by a major programme of prison expansion in both state and commercial sectors, a trend maintained by the New Labour administration.

The shift away from the due process justice model has been joined by a renewed, 'actuarial' emphasis on risk assessment and management. However, there have been significant shifts in the meanings of risk. Earlier notions of risk had focused on defining the dangerousness of the individual and the prevention and management of criminal acts. The new priority placed on public protection and the needs of victims broadened the definitions of risk to emphasize the assessment of the potential for recidivism and shifted the focus away from the criminal act to the need to protect against the dangerous offender. These are manifested, for example, in new measures introduced in the UK to broaden the scope for preventive detention of the mentally ill who may be thought likely to commit an offence. Such policy measures are responsive to politicians' sensitivities to public campaigning on behalf of victims.

In assessing the interpretive models for explaining these shifts, the author criticises those perspectives on governance that downplay the role of sovereign state control, since most of the changes noted have been accompanied by growing Home Office control and co-ordination of institutional shifts in policing and crime prevention and control. The best interpretive model remains that which demonstrates the link between the introduction of neo-liberal economic and social reforms, growing inequalities and the strengthening of state apparatuses to cope with the problems of dissent and social dislocation thrown up by these changes. The growing, illiberal emphasis on crime control as risk management, with its potential for wholesale miscarriages of justice, highlights the need to restate the arguments for an updated justice model. This would shift focus away from universalist models of justice that downplay individual and group differences to one that recognises the crucial differences of class, race and gender in understanding both crime and appropriate levels of punishment.

9 Casino culture: media and crime in a winner-loser society, by Robert Reiner, Sonia Livingstone and Jessica Allen

In this chapter, the authors argue that mass media representations of crime are central to the competing accounts of changing patterns, trends and rates of crime and fear of crime since the Second World War. Although there is a huge literature on the relationships between media representations, crime, and fear of crime, hardly any of this examines change over long periods of time. This is particularly important for theoretical explanations of the risk society and late or postmodernity. The concept of the risk society connotes not only a shift in the nature of risk but also an alteration in cultural sensibilities and strategies for dealing with risk. In this perspective, problems and solutions are de-moralised, de-mystified and secularised. Furthermore, individuals are held to be responsible for their fates in an increasingly unequal, deregulated 'winner-loser', or 'casino' culture. These perspectives accord a key role to the media in constructing dominant images of reality and indeed helping to blur older assumed boundaries between what is considered to be real and that which is representational or fictional. The media also play a pivotal role in reproducing the 'casino culture', celebrating the winners as celebrities and devaluing any styles of life other than spectacular consumerism.

This chapter explores the way that shifting media depictions of social reality over time have moved towards this cultural frame via reference to a historical content analysis of changing film, press and TV media representations of crime in Britain since 1945, together with a study of audience interpretations of these. The study of audience interpretations employed a focus group methodology, emphasising age differences in response.

The data demonstrate a shift in media and popular discourse about crime and criminal justice, indicating a demystification of authority and law. In Durkheimian terms, early post-war images of crime and justice tended to depict society in consensualist terms. Crime was seen as a violation of social order and criminal justice was depicted in 'sacred' terms as a social mechanism ensuring solidarity, intrinsically deserving of respect. Crimes were seen therefore as wrongs against a social, legal or moral order, which must be condemned *ipso facto*. By contrast, more recent images and popular discourse tends to replace this view with a view of crimes as contestable harms by individuals against other individuals, the moral status of which is not given but has to be established by particular, individualised narratives, and is not inscribed by official status. This is related to increasing anxiety about personal victimisation by crime, as well as concern about law and order as a policy issue. It is not suggested that there is a mechanistic causal relationship between media images and 'objective' patterns of crime, shifting forms of policy and criminal justice and the wider features of the 'risk society'. Rather, it is argued that it is more useful to envisage a dialectical interaction between these elements.

10   'Bringin' it all back home': populism, media coverage and the dynamics of locality and globality in the politics of crime control, by Richard Sparks

Sparks argues that in our understandings of the place of crime and punishment in the culture and politics of 'risk societies', the mass media plays a vital role. However, it would be too simplistic to lapse into deterministic accounts of the role of the media that exaggerate its capacity to shape the thoughts, attitudes, and feelings of audiences. Like other authors in this book, he notes the tension between, on the one hand, rationalist tendencies in punishment and control, including, for example, technologies of situational crime prevention and actuarial technologies of risk assessment and management and, on the other hand, the increasingly emotive, punitive rhetoric employed by the media and seemingly 'populist' politicians. It may be tempting to view the role of the media principally as a demagogic tool used by opportunistic politicians to make false representations about risks of crime and inflame the passions and fears of a gullible public, ignorant about the objective statistical 'risks' of criminal victimisation.

However, the lines of influence are more complex and multi-directional and Sparks argues against a simplistic polarity between risk-as-calculation and risk-as-representation. Drawing on a range of empirical examples, including his own research into local perceptions of risk, fear and crime in an English town, he emphasises the need to focus on how these troubling questions and information conveyed by the media are received and used by people in the everyday settings of their lives. A more anthropologically sophisticated conception of risk transcends classifications of risk as rational or irrational and explores how the identification of particular sources of threat and blame refracts a given community's dispositions towards order and authority. It also involves ways in which the bewildering global changes which affect people's lives materially and through media images are appropriated and made relevant to the local contours of place and everyday life. Beyond the local level, in a mobile and fragmented society news about crime and the talk it occasions remains among the few topics that are emotive and graspable enough to enable people to make connections across the social and geographical divides.

11   American television, crime and the risk society, by Philip Green

According to Green, the mass media provide a crucial cultural underpinning to the consumerist individualisation and market dependency that characterises risk societies. Green's perspective on the role of the media differs significantly from those of Reiner *et al* and Sparks, in his developing an updated version of the 1950s mass society thesis. He stresses the vital role of the economic and social structures of the media in governing the ideological frame for the depiction of human experience and emphasises the significant differences between the US and the UK in that respect. American network television epitomises the market-oriented social arrangements promoted by neo-liberalism. The disciplines of market competition foster, in shows about police and criminal justice, a bland caution and avoidance of uncomfortable moral ambiguities.

By isolating people from local, particularistic cultures, television homogenizes knowledge and experience through the consumption of morally and ideologically uniform cultural product. Despite minor concessions to naturalism, in the main narratives are subordinated to the dominant cultural myths that emphasize the virtues of the American way of life, the triumph of good over evil and justice over the criminal. It is claimed that the technological change and the marketization of the media in the UK are pushing the media in the same direction. Yet, through illustrative analyses of British TV shows covering similar themes to their US counterparts, Green argues that the traditional, paternalist British public service ethos provided a degree of protection to the BBC and Channel 4 from market pressures. This created the space to depict more naturalistic representations of moral ambiguity and hence provide a more mature and enriching contribution to public discourse about crime, justice and the other great political issues facing complex, conflictual market societies.

1

Crime, liberalism and risk

The new politics of crime control

Kevin Stenson

Introduction

This chapter will set the issues raised in this book in a wider political context, providing working definitions of key terms like liberalism, politics, government, and governance. It firstly unpacks the new political saliency accorded to crime. Secondly, it analyses the retreat from 'liberal' approaches to crime control fashionable in the high period of the welfare states between 1945 and the late 1970s. Thirdly, it analyses the shifts in liberal society in the broadest sense of the term as associated with the post-monarchical liberal democracies. It highlights the changes from 'social' modes of government characteristic of the welfare states to 'advanced liberal' modes of government. These were associated with the rise of New Right intellectuals and regimes. Their mixture of neo-liberal, free market philosophies and traditional conservative values prioritised the defence of hierarchy and the attempt to restore traditional morality. Fourthly, the chapter records the struggle to construct approaches to crime control under the auspices of 'third way' or, as it is also termed, 'progressive governance' rationalities of government. It would be premature to describe these developments as constituting a new phase of liberal government. Rather, they embody a stage of political experiment and re-emphasis within the broad terrain of advanced liberal government. These try to integrate tough policies associated with the Right with those that attempt to deal with underlying crimogenic conditions. Fifthly, the chapter highlights the vital importance of social scientists as liberal – in the widest sense – critics of power.

The salience of crime control

The focus for the saliency placed on law and order lies in, *inter alia*, long-term trends towards increasing levels of officially recorded crime, especially crimes of violence and drug-related crime, growing legal recognition of hitherto neglected areas of crime like domestic violence, rape, hate crimes against minorities and growing concerns over fear, insecurity and a retreat from the open public sphere into heavily guarded zones of surveillance and security. In addition, in an increasingly interdependent world, where boundaries between nation states are blurring, there are concerns about the challenges to law, order and governmental legitimacy posed by the spread of transnational modes of criminal organization and the influx into richer countries of people fleeing war, poverty and the cataclysmic changes in the post-communist societies. In the latter countries organised crime, underpinned by ruthless violence, has become a mainstream feature of economic life. There is increasing concern in the richer countries that this virus could spread and threaten the integrity of western banks and industrial corporations (Sheptycki, 1995; Rawlinson, 1998; Taylor, 1999).

Hence, during a period of enormous global, political, economic and cultural change, crime is emerging as an issue at the very core of government in societies marked by increasing demographic diversity, mobility and inequalities, and within which the news and entertainment media have become increasingly focussed on crime. A central theme of this book is that the media are not (not that they ever were) simply neutral conduits of information about crime. The institutional arrangements that organise the media and rhetorical forms through which crime is represented can play a vital role in shaping and reflecting our deepest personal and cultural fears and sensibilities about crime and insecurity. Moreover, in an increasingly fragmented world marked by mutual distrust and suspicion in public spaces, the media become increasingly important as a source of information about crime. Furthermore, where other sources of solidarity have become tenuous, we can at least be united in our ghoulish fascination for the reported shadowy worlds of death, violence and the anarchic and carnivalesque flouting of the rules that still constrain most of our lives (see chapters by Reiner *et al*, Green and Sparks in this volume).

This politicization of crime control, echoing a deeply ingrained, profound dread of crime and related social and spatial polarization in many poor countries, is also now increasingly a feature of France, Germany, Austria and other West European countries (Stenson, 2000a). Even the Netherlands, for long viewed in England as a beacon of progressive penal practice, has responded to rising public anxiety about crime with a growing use of imprisonment. Since 1975 its prison capacity has increased fivefold (van Swaaningen, 2000). Concerns about crime, especially the routine 'volume', acquisitive crimes and crimes against the person, join a series of other anxieties about environmental and other risks created by the effects of a new industrial order, increasingly resistant to the control of politicians. However, among progressive politicians and social scientists, there is concern that the responses made to trends and public fears highlight a drift towards an emotionally fuelled, vengeful approach to crime control that can threaten the delicate cultural foundations of both liberalism and democracy.

Retreat from liberalism?

It is now common among politicians of the centre, as well as those on the right, to avoid describing themselves as 'liberal' about crime. In the UK, for example, the

New Labour Home Secretary Jack Straw was involved in a bidding war before the 1997 election with the punitive Tory Home secretary Michael Howard over how tough they would be on criminals and how much they both wished to import Mayor Giuliani's 'zero tolerance', quality of life approach to policing. Notwithstanding barely audible dissenting academic voices, striking claims were made about the success of these strategies in New York's war on the criminal classes in the 1990s, a city that feels palpably more secure to outsiders who have known it over many years. Straw has consistently claimed that a tough approach chimes with the needs and wishes of Labour's core working-class constituents who suffer directly from crime, far more than middle-class 'liberals' and leftists (including criminologists). Their credibility is said to be undermined by their refusing to live in rundown areas or send their children to crime-prone schools in such neighbourhoods.

In short, middle-class progressives, living in their distinct cultural and geographical spheres, are accused of displaying a patrician disdain for the justifiable anxieties of poor and working-class people, groups with whom they have less and less in common. There was no discernible shame in the Government admitting that in June 2000 the British prison population had, since the election, risen by 4,500 prisoners (and set to increase rapidly), often living in overcrowded conditions and with little scope for rehabilitation or education. This was despite, under an administration famed for its fiscal prudence, the fact that it cost £25,000 per annum to keep a prisoner, in contrast to £16,000 for a boy at Eton, one of Britain's most exclusive schools. Ironically, in the same month CBS News in the USA (in a report widely publicised in the UK) warned vacationing Americans that – leaving aside murder and rape – Britain was a more crime-ridden and dangerous society than the US (*The Guardian*, 30 June 2000).

The meaning of 'liberal' in this context echoes its common American meaning. It is associated with a 'bleeding heart' perspective that is sympathetic to the offender rather than the victim, indeed views the offender as a victim of injustice and inequality. Moreover, it is associated with social science theories and the expertise of the welfare professions developed during the high period of the post-war welfare states. At least in the minds of their critics, these now deeply unfashionable approaches avoided recognizing the personal agency and moral responsibility of the criminal and saw crime as the outcome not, as on the Right, of a pervasive collapse of authority and morality, but of personal and social pathologies, deprivation and inequalities. Humane social engineers in the offender-oriented social service and criminal justice professions would properly deal with these problems. In echoing these critiques and sharing some intellectual ground with the right, New Labour has faithfully followed the electorally successful path forged by Clinton and Gore in the US; they distanced the New Democrats from old Rooseveltian, 'liberal' policies. This refers particularly to the New Democrats' removal of rights to welfare and the introduction of workfare policies, the defence of the burgeoning use of imprisonment (now over 2 million Americans), the death penalty, boot camps, 'three strikes and you're out' sentencing policies and the 'war against drugs' in the African-American and Hispanic ghettos (see chapters by Simon, Hudson, Stenson and Edwards in this volume).

As in the UK, a strong democratic case can be made to argue that such policies suit the feelings and wishes of the majority. Yet the targets of these policies are disproportionately poor whites and the visible ethnic minorities. Hence, building a consensual community among the majority comes at the price of ghettoizing expanding sections of the population into desolate urban zones that are inhabited by the poor, the addicted, the homeless, the mentally and physically ill. Along with the expanding prisons these spaces segregating the perceivably disreputable from the respectable increasingly function as vast human garbage dumps, where survival, excitement and success and opportunities for entrepreneurship depend increasingly on involvement in illegal economies (Hobbs, 1995). The crucial test of the dismantling of the welfare safety nets will come in the troughs of economic cycles that few economists believe have been abolished by the deregulation of markets.

In harder economic times, particularly, reliance on these dumping grounds risks further weakening the connections between the poor and the damaged with the labour market, now the only acceptable and realistic route to the good life, or even to a reasonably civilized lifestyle. During the 1990s and into the new millennium, the centre left administrations of the New Democrats in the US, New Labour in the UK and their counterparts in Australasia have signally failed to halt the drift towards widening inequalities opened up by the policies of the Right. This is not alleviated by the fact that the majority of people have become better off. This, in effect, signals a reversal of the struggles to broaden the scope of inclusive formal and substantive rights of citizenship that was one of the hallmarks of welfare states (Currie, 1997; Taylor, 1999; Young, 1999). Furthermore, it is tempting to view their reliance on harsh methods of crime control as proof that they are simply conservatives in disguise. However, I will shortly argue that this view is an over-simplification and we need to recognise significant shifts introduced under centre left governments in the area of crime control as in other spheres of government.

However, if Straw denies being a liberal in the 'bleeding heart' sense, it is less clear that he would, as a parliamentarian, lawyer, and stout advocate of anti-racism, deny being a liberal in the wider and deeper sense. This broader meaning of liberalism involves a commitment to the principles and values laid down by Locke, Jefferson, and the other great Enlightenment architects of liberal, constitutional, representative democracies in the eighteenth and nineteenth centuries. These basic principles and values include, for example: the valorisation of the rights and expression of the individual; the separation of powers; a respect for procedural and substantive justice (the rule of law); democratic representation; the need for checks and balances against centralised state tyranny; and the need for tolerance towards minorities. It is clearly difficult for mainstream politicians seeking election to disavow liberal principles and values in this broader sense. Yet capturing the broader sense of liberalism is awesomely difficult for the social scientist and certainly beyond the grasp of parsimonious philosophical lists.

Liberal societies tend to be easily recognisable when you experience and contrast them with the many authoritarian societies that, as Amnesty International reminds us, are ruled by the routine, unaccountable use of violence and terror.

However, boiling them down to an easy essential definition is difficult, given the considerable variety between countries, regions, and local politico-cultural traditions. Hence, liberalism is not simply a bundle of ideas, the province of political philosophers. It is best understood in social science terms, as a set of linkages between abstract political rationalities, policy programmes and visions and local cultures of political institutions and practices. Furthermore, the problems of maintaining sovereign legal and military authority over geographical territory are not just historical leftovers from monarchical regimes. These issues have always posed crucial questions for liberal regimes given that in practice they usually operate in hybrid relation to forms of nationalism, the articulation of which liberals have always had to compete with ideologues of the Right. The centrality of the struggle for sovereign control in an inherently plural and unequal polity has ensured that despite the benign rehabilitation rhetoric of welfare state penology, at every stage in the history of liberal societies it has been possible to identify a dark underbelly of repressive policing and criminal justice in dealing with recalcitrant, alienated and rebellious sections of the population (Sim, 1990; see Sullivan in this volume; Stenson, 1998, 1999, 2000b).

This should also remind us of the philosophical truism that although historically liberalism and democracy were mutually constituted and close soul mates, they have often been in tension with each other. This is particularly so in the case of crime control. In this sphere, giving the people (or at least large constituencies with clout) what they want can mean tossing them the red meat of revenge with liberal values of justice the principal casualties. There are serious concerns that the hyperbole surrounding the identification of individuals and groups as representing 'high risk' criminal threats can be a warrant for and a prelude to withdrawing from them the (liberal) rights to rigorous 'due process' of law and a fair trial (see Hudson, Chapter 8, this volume). However, in order to understand the ebb and flow of current trends and debates we need to examine more deeply the nature and transformation of liberal polities.

Transforming liberal society: from welfarism to advanced liberalism

Hence, liberalism in the wider and deeper sense refers to the broad range of post-monarchist societies in Europe and its colonies that have developed from the late eighteenth century. These emerged in the wake of the attempts in the eighteenth century to create a more civilized alternative model of governance to the familiar aristocratic tyrannies, with their arbitrary forms of justice and policing, vague legal codes and cruelty to minorities (Stenson, 1998, 2000a). However, as critics on the leftist radical edge of liberalism remind us, liberalism and hypocrisy are close bedfellows. Throughout the chequered history of liberal polities, adherence to the (liberal) niceties of due process of law has always been a privilege accorded more to the middle and respectable working classes (Sim, 1990). Rougher and harsher codes and practices usually ruled the poor and also subject colonial populations.

Mindful of the above, and despite some continuity since the eighteenth century, we have witnessed major transformations in modes of liberal *government* (the exercize of public, collectively authorized political power). The early forms of market liberalism unleashed productive forces and generated a plurality of commercial, religious and other sites of non-state *governance* (those more or less rational attempts to shape human subjectivity and conduct), but at enormous costs to the well being of the poor. While they may be rather amnesiac about those costs, more recent liberals, in the tougher economic sense, seek to rediscover the virtues of early forms of liberalism.

A key concern of this book is to uncover how the new politics of crime control in the latest phase of advanced liberalism reflect the rise since the late 1970s of a dominant approach to government that is based on a thorough-going critique by politicians and intellectuals of the neo-liberal and neo-conservative New Right of the various welfare state versions of liberal government. The great political compromises with organized labour and other sites of institutional power within the liberal polity created the various state-centred approaches to government that attempted through social and economic policies to moderate the effects of unconstrained markets. They also provided safety nets and tutelage in the arts of family management for the poor and the weak. And they crystallized in the 'social' governmental ethos of welfare states created in the wake of Roosevelt's New Deal in the 1930s and the post-war European welfare states. Welfarism reflected a prevailing optimism that gradually the 'goods' of life would be brought within the reach of all and the assumption that the role of the state was to try to realize a more just, equitable and inclusive society. It was characterized by the pursuit of social justice, full, secure employment, and the promotion of solidarity through the provision of universal services.

Moreover, the 'tax and spend', Keynesian policies of welfarism involved attempts by the state to maintain full employment through provision of public sector jobs. It also involved the use of fiscal and monetary policy at the level of the nation state to manipulate demand so as to maintain employment during down periods of economic cycles. Welfarism usually involved complex linkages between institutions of penality and welfare (Garland, 1985). It was accompanied by a belief held by at least some sections of those in public service, that social workers and other professionals in agencies of criminal justice, armed with social science based expertise, could rehabilitate those embroiled in deviant lifestyles and who were suffering from personal and social pathologies. One of the consequences of this link between penality and welfare, together with the lower electoral political saliency accorded crime control, was that, at least outside the US, in most jurisdictions in the advanced democracies between 1945 and 1980 the business of crime control and criminal justice was buffered from significant, *publicly visible* interference from politicians. This was so despite wide variations in organizational and legal cultures. In the advanced democracies crime control and criminal justice were seen to be jobs requiring the expertise of the professionals. Hence, they were seen as issues of routine government and administration rather than an occasion for the mayhem of public *politics*, in the sense of public forms of contest about how –

in this case – to conceptualise and manage crime (Stenson, 2000a and b).

New Right intellectuals and politicians sought to revive the risk-loving enterprise spirit of the early forms of economic liberalism, before the effects of the sclerotic, risk-averse 'nanny' state's protection of people from the rigours of market competition had taken root. This approach views markets and market disciplines as superior to the institutions and practices associated with the twentieth century welfare states. New approaches to crime control and government more generally have been particularly marked in the Anglophone democracies of the USA, UK and Australasia. In these countries politicians of the neo-liberal Right have mounted the most powerful assault on the intellectual culture, institutions and Keynesian social and economic policies of the post-war welfare states (see O'Malley, Chapter 5 in this volume and Rose, 1996). With the legacy of the New Right regimes of the 1980s and early 1990s which combined free market neo-liberal ideologies with elements of traditional conservatism, the welfarist, paternalist approach gave way to a new agenda.

More broadly, in the new agenda, the state assists in the distribution of the 'bads' of modern civilization (Ericson and Haggerty, 1997). Inequality and poverty are accepted as given features of modern life, providing a source of criminal and other risks. Nevertheless, this acceptance of inequality is tempered by the utopian, neo-liberal belief that unfettering the markets accelerates the forces of economic, political and cultural globalization and the erosion of the boundaries between nation states. The consequent economic growth that this entails will increase global wealth, some of which (hopefully) trickles down to the grateful poor. With tax and spend and the techniques of protective Keynesian demand management ruled out, a key role of the nation state is to improve the economic 'supply side', to help citizens and corporations equip themselves with the knowledge, skills and infrastructure that will enable them to compete more effectively in the global market place. With the collapse of communism in 1989 and the weakening of trade unionism in western countries, neo-liberals claim that there is no governmental alternative.

These political and economic shifts have been accompanied by major cultural and social changes that have impacted on the texture of everyday family, community, and working life. These include, in most of the advanced liberal democracies, the growth of individualism and consumerism, with their elevation of the needs and choices of the individual over those of corporate bodies ranging from the family to the state. This in turn has been accompanied by rising divorce rates, increasing numbers of single person- and single-parent households and rising demographic mobility. This climate has also fostered the growth of large numbers of feminist, ethnic and other rights-based social movements. It is small wonder that in these conditions there has emerged an 'intrinsic heterogeneity, contestability and mobility in practices for the government of conduct' (Rose, 2000: 323). These governmental developments have crystallized into what Nikolas Rose has termed the phase of 'advanced liberalism'. In this phase, for the majority of the population, the older, vast 'top-down' forms of bureaucracy in governmental, political and business organizations have given way increasingly to network-based, indirect forms of control. In essence people are encouraged to be more entre-preneurial and self-governing, but according to criteria and performance measures set by central policy makers, whether in government or on the company board.

The forms of advanced liberal government ushered in by the administrations of the conservative Right in the 1980s, particularly in the US, the UK, Australia and New Zealand, involved also a new governmental hybrid of neo-liberalism and neo-conservatism (Cruikshank, 1998). The latter is based on nostalgia for hierarchy, social discipline, and moral re-armament through a revitalisation of the role of organized religion and encourages greater personal and local communal responsibility for security against life's risks. The New Right hybrid also favours redistributing the tasks of government beyond the state to include new partnerships of statutory, not-for-profit and commercial institutions and citizen action initiatives. The new lexicon manifests a preference for free market solutions to human ills and the servicing of needs, for example: downsizing, deregulation, labour flexibility, privatisation, welfare reform, workfare and the introduction of performance measures and other commercial, managerial disciplines into police, criminal justice and other remaining public agencies (see McLaughlin and Murji, Chapter 6 in this volume).

Crime control in advanced liberalism

What are the implications of these shifts towards advanced liberalism? Changes in the patterns of family, community and commercial life diminish the insulating factors - not least the daily guardianship of home and street – which may in earlier times have provided a degree of protection to the better-off from everyday anxieties about routine property crime and crimes against the person. These anxieties create a new common sense that requires all of us to remain vigilant against the risks of crime. These concerns and the enormous networks of commercial and political interests they have spawned have settled into a 'crime complex', now deeply embedded and reproduced and manifested in public opinion and the crime obsessions of the mass media and populist politicians (Garland, 2000). This is most visibly indexed in the dramatic expansion of (increasingly commercialised) prisons in the anglophone countries of the advanced world (Matthews, 1999). The new commercial agencies of security and incarceration are no longer mere adjuncts to the work of public agencies but are major innovators of the technologies of crime control and drive the agendas of state policy makers.

The transformations of government associated with this 'crime complex' can be seen not simply as attempts to govern crime and criminals but also involve 'government through crime'. The introduction, *inter alia,* of CCTV, new insurance technologies, new means to assess and manage 'dangerousness' and other risks of crime, the notification of the public about the whereabouts of paedophiles and in the UK the new statutory requirement for local community safety partnerships to undertake crime audits, are among the host of ways in which new powers have, to use Michel Foucault's term, created a new 'governmentality'. This refers to the new means to render populations thinkable and measurable, through categorisation, differentiation, and sorting into hierarchies, for the purposes of government (Stenson, 2000a: 236). In the complex mix of these technologies of rule, the struggle to govern the soul of the criminal has not disappeared. These developments do allow the retention of some individually oriented work with offenders. Probation officers, for example, can mentor the deviant, as long as they foster more rational and morally reflective patterns of thinking among those in trouble with the law and living chaotic lifestyles (Rose, 2000). Hence, in the new workfare states the *moral engineer replaces the social engineer.*

Though the multiplicity of forms of governance, scope for individual freedoms and checks on central authorities have always been hallmarks of liberal polities, the new anxiety about crime, the prioritisation of the needs and feelings of victims and a growing punitiveness towards offenders, manifested in 'zero tolerance' policies to drive petty offenders from the central public spaces and attendant championing of victims, can generate policies and emotional climates that further jeopardise liberal values and institutions. This is so even though the threats of crime can be viewed – at least for the more comfortable classes – as often disproportionate to the statistical likelihood of victimisation. Nevertheless, concerns about crime involve more than dry calculations about the risk of victimhood (see Sparks, Chapter 10 in this volume).

Mavericks against the mainstream

This pro-market creed has been promulgated internationally through a host of organizations from the acronym soup, including the UN, the OECD (Organization for Economic Cooperation and Development), IMF (International Monetary Fund), G7, the WTO (World Trade Organization) and the WB (World Bank). It was crystallized in a major UN congress on crime prevention in Vienna in April 2000. The message to poorer countries is clear. Their richer brethren will view poor countries with favour to the extent that they are able to contain corruption, money laundering, organized crime and street crime, sufficiently to create a stable and welcoming enough environment for investments by international corporations. This is the route towards obtaining economic aid, debt relief, or assistance with the development of policing and criminal justice. However, belief that there is no alternative to this complacent neo-liberalism was rudely shattered at the international convention of the World Trade Organisation in Seattle in 1999. Loose alliances of discordant groups, critical of the untrammelled powers of the international corporations and their allies in the major western parties and state administrations, staged violent protests and achieved enormous media success in publicizing their causes. These protests and a plethora of others in their wake have been forged largely, in anarchistic style, through the Internet.

Hence, feminist, ethnic, ecological, religious and other new social movements in civil society constitute sites of governance in their own right, all of which generate their own conceptions of the nature of 'crime', or social harm more generally conceived, and the agenda for its control. With their own governmental visions, they have flowered beyond the orbits of nation states and major corporations. There are affinities between these 'maverick' voices and movements and the theoretical vision of the libertarian/anarchistic, abolitionist school in criminology. Sceptical of the overweening power of state, law, and repressive criminal justice, abolitionists provide radical alternatives to narrow legal conceptions of 'crime' as defined by the law and dominant corporate interests. They also reject the banal, neo-liberal tendency to view the human subject in narrowly economic terms as a consumer/non-consumer or wealth creator/drone (Muncie, 2000).

The 'third way' of progressive governance, risk and reconstituting the social

However, back in the political 'mainstream' of debate about crime and social problems and increasingly goaded by the mavericks on the fringes (Stenson, 1991), the emerging new parties of the centre left are struggling to integrate neo-liberal and neo-conservative policy themes with those which might create a measure of inclusiveness for the most marginalized groups. However, to repeat the point made in the introduction, it is better to view these experiments as occurring within the overall terrain of advanced liberalism, rather than as constituting a radically new stage of development. This centre ground of the 'third way' or 'progressive governance' as it is now more usually termed, is sufficiently broad to facilitate considerable debate, for example about the relative merits of the use of state power. This field includes, for example, Clinton's 'New Democrats' and their UK allies in 'New Labour'. It also includes Gerhard Schröder's new Social Democrats in Germany and Lionel Jospin's revamped French Socialist party. Jospin enunciates statist socialist rhetoric while pursuing an agenda, including the wholesale privatization of state assets, that would bring a triumphant smile to Mrs Thatcher's face (Lloyd, 2000).

At a more abstract level these middle-ground political discourses often incorporate elements of social science analysis, notably selective versions of the theories of the 'risk society' and 'globalization' in an effort to provide a new intellectual consensus for progressive policy makers. They can hence serve as governmental *savoirs*, or intellectual instruments of government. The new forms of risk have been described by Ulrich Beck and Tony Giddens, intellectuals with the ear of the newly ascendant centre-left politicians in the US and Europe, as manifestations of the humanly 'manufactured uncertainty' of late modernity. This is a feature of societies marked by accelerating technological change and globalisation: by increased economic, political and cultural interdependence on a global scale (Beck, 1992; Giddens, 1998).

These risks are allegedly of a different order to the older risks inflicted by nature on technologically more primitive societies. According to this perspective, risks like pollution, global warming, traffic gridlock, and the risks of crime are the result of how human activity has created huge, unintended negative effects on both the natural and social environment. Escalating fear and paranoia about risks creates demand for increasingly more sophisticated technologies of risk information. The resulting dissemination of information about risks increases fear and thus demand for yet further information about risk in a spiral of anxiety. Risks must be contained and managed collectively where possible, but for the most part remain the responsibility of families, firms and other bodies beyond the remit of the state (Stenson, 1999; Rose, 2000).

Generalised characterization of the 'risk society' involves perhaps an unduly selective focus on some features of modern life. In the sphere of crime control, while many commentators may not be comfortable with such labels, there is a widely shared criminological view that the new lexicon of risk has downplayed older conservative and classical liberal concerns with justice as retribution or just desserts and also the welfarist concern with rehabilitation through criminal justice dispositions. The rise of managerialism, the belief that innovative, faddish management theories are the key to economic efficiency and success, has allied with the dissemination of the amoral actuarial mentalities and calculative technologies of the insurance and accountancy industries. For example, older individualized 'case-work' methods for understanding offenders in their quirky uniqueness have lost ground in favour of statistically based risk-assessment technologies. Through these means individuals and social categories are reconstituted as bundles of scores on risk assessment charts (Feeley and Simon, 1994). In this view, in response to rising fears about crime and insecurity, the role of the police and partner regulatory agencies is increasingly to act as producers and brokers of information about risk. The principal goal of professional practice, consequently, is to keep the lid on problems through pragmatic risk assessment and management policies and practices geared to individuals and to social collectivities and 'problem' areas – the latter largely through the pervasive practices of situational crime prevention and environmental redesign (Ericson and Haggerty, 1997; Hudson, Chapter 8 in this volume).

However, beyond the growing use of technologies of risk management in crime control the distinctive feature of the new 'progressive governance' administrations is, by contrast with their conservative predecessors, in every case, the attempt to link 'tough on crime' policies with those which are 'tough on the causes of crime'. The goal of these approaches is to rescue the casualties of – those 'socially excluded from'– a more brutally open and competitive market society. Even in France, where the commitment to welfarism remains stronger than in the Anglophone world, a growing public punitiveness, and the huge problems in managing disaffected ethnic minority youth living in bleak housing projects, have put severe strains on the welfarist system of juvenile justice (Crawford, 2000). In Jospin's phrase, the challenge for the new progressive governance is to 'bring politics back in' to the regulation of chaotic markets and their social effects.

However, as has already been argued, the conservative and 'social' themes in government have not been wholly displaced and some commentators argue that a key challenge is to unpack the hybrid forms of government through crime control.

Rational, actuarial risk management practices interact with revamped welfarist technologies in probation and social work and also with the use of punitive, emotionally driven measures in complex mixtures (see the chapters by Simon, Sullivan, O'Malley, Sparks, Hudson and Stenson and Edwards in this volume). However, against the downbeat Cassandras of risk, it is argued that risk management is not a recent invention but has always been a feature of criminal justice. Indeed innovations in risk management may offer considerable progressive potential for the development of locally responsive and empowering modes of crime control and criminal justice (Clear and Cadora, Chapter 3 in this volume).

These policies often embody the struggle to forge a communitarian, duty-oriented, more socially aware morality that could replace the rampant, criminogenic, selfish individualism fostered by the right-wing obsessions with markets and consumerism. These policies range from parent support programmes, educational and retraining programmes to get people from welfare into work to a 'turn to the local'. This takes the form of restorative/community justice movements, community policing, and local urban regeneration strategies (Hughes, 1998; see Chapters by Clear and Cadora and Stenson and Edwards in this volume). These local and, it is claimed, holistic approaches to crime control, justice and regeneration operate in uneasy tension with harsher, punitive approaches and the increasingly sophisticated technologies for environmental redesign and situational crime prevention. They indicate that claims about the 'death of the social' have, as Oscar Wilde may have said, been somewhat exaggerated. The universalist framework of law and social policy, the continuing need in liberal orders to secure sovereign rule over geographical territory from internal and external enemies, and the priority on the political right as much as on the political left for the promotion of an organic social solidarity ensures that, in a host of ways, 'social' modes of government are likely to be reconstituted (Stenson, 1998; Stenson and Watt, 1999; Crowther, 2000; O'Malley. Chapter 5 in this volume).

Conclusion: critique, democracy, and crime control

There are dangers in prematurely foreclosing debate about these issues. Well-meaning politicians – especially those on the new centre ground of 'progressive governance' – may view the role of the social scientist as principally that of the policy technician, advising on how best to implement manifestly sensible agendas. Now it is possible to develop social science theories that offer both explanations of crime and control and also help to underpin normative theories for the policy maker and professional practitioner. They can, hence, function as *governmental savoirs,* that is intellectual tools of government at policy-making and front-line levels. For example, the 'routine activities', control and labelling theories produced by criminologists have been adopted by policy makers and practitioners, and some of the authors in this book would endorse that role for social science. Nevertheless, it is dangerous to confine the social scientist to this problem-solving role on behalf of authorities.

Public intellectuals who are liberal in the broadest, if not necessarily the narrow, sense, must resist this narrowly drawn role. This is because at the heart of liberal orders is the possibility, indeed necessity, of critique. It is essential, for the reproduction of liberal democracy, that the academy, like journalism, remains free to pose questions and set limits to those with power. Hence, the health of democracy requires ongoing debate about ends as well as means and, more profoundly, about how to make sense of the shifting contexts within which policies are developed and implemented. In order to help maintain open dialogue the book will provide a guide to facilitate the unpicking of the complex and contradictory meanings of these institutional, intellectual and policy developments. Despite coming from diverse theoretical perspectives, these authors are united in challenging the view that the definition, diagnosis and management of crime are issues best left to politicians and experts in the public agencies mandated with the tasks of crime control. A key premise of this book is that it is the duty of leading public intellectuals with expertise in this field to promote and help inform democratic debate about these issues and to help safeguard inclusive liberal freedoms into the new millennium.

References

Beck, U. 1992. *Risk Society*. London: Sage.

Crawford, A. 2000. 'Why British criminologists lose their critical faculties upon crossing the channel: some thoughts on comparative criminology from an empirical investigation in France and England', *Social Work in Europe*, 7, 1: 122–30.

Crowther, C. 2000. 'Thinking about the underclass: towards a political economy of policing', *Theoretical Criminology*, 4, 2: 149–167.

Cruikshank, B. 1998. 'Moral disentitlement: personal autonomy and political reproduction'. In Häninnen, S. (ed) *Displacement of Social Policies*. Jyvaskyla: SoPhi Publications.

Currie, E. 1997. 'Market, crime and community: towards a mid-range theory of post-industrial violence', *Theoretical Criminology*, 1, 2: 147–172.

Ericson, R. and Haggerty, K. 1997. *Policing the Risk Society*. Toronto: University of Ontario Press.

Feeley, M. and Simon, J. 1994. 'Actuarial justice: the emerging new criminal law'. In Nelken, D. (ed) *The Futures of Criminology*. London: Sage.

Garland, D. 1985. *Punishment and Welfare*. Aldershot: Gower.

Garland, D. 2000. 'The culture of high crime societies: some preconditions of recent "law and order" policies', *British Journal of Criminology*, 40, 3 (forthcoming).

Giddens, A. 1998. 'Risk society: the context of British politics'. In Franklin, J. (ed) *The Politics of the Risk Society*. Cambridge: Polity.

Hobbs, D. 1995. *Bad Business: Professional Crime in Modern Britain*. Oxford: Oxford University Press.

Hughes, G. 1998. *Understanding Crime Prevention: Social Control, Risk and Late Modernity*. Buckingham: Open University Press.

Lloyd J. 2000. 'The Left Discovers Adam Smith', *The New Statesman*, 12 June.

Matthews, R. 1999. *Doing Time: an Introduction to the Sociology of Imprisonment*. London: MacMillan.

Muncie, J. 2000. 'Decriminalising criminology'. In Lewis, G., Gewirtz, Clarke, J. (eds) *Rethinking Social Policy*. London: Sage.

Rose, N. 1996. 'The death of the social? Refiguring the territory of government', *Economy and Society*, 25, 2: 327–89.

Rose, N. 2000. 'Government and Control', *British Journal of Criminology*, 40, 2: 321–339.

Rawlinson, P. 1998. 'Russian organised crime: moving beyond ideology'. In Ruggiero, V., South, N. and Taylor, I. (eds). *The New European Criminology: Crime and Social Order in Europe*. London, Routledge.

Sheptycki, J.W.E. 1995. 'Transnational policing and the makings of a postmodern state', *British Journal of Criminology*, 35, 4: 613–635.

Sim, J. 1990. *Medical Power in Prisons: the Prison Medical Services in England 1774–1989*. Milton Keynes: Open University Press.

Stenson, K. 1991. 'Making sense of crime control'. In Stenson, K. and Cowell, D. (eds). *The Politics of Crime Control*. London: Sage.

Stenson, K. 1998. 'Beyond histories of the present'. *Economy and Society*, 29, 4: 117–44.

Stenson, K. 1999. 'Crime control, governmentality and sovereignty'. In Smandych, R. (ed) *Governable Places: Readings in Governmentality and Crime Control*. Aldershot: Dartmouth.

Stenson, K. 2000(a). 'Crime control, social policy and liberalism'. In Lewis, G., Gewirtz and Clarke, J. (eds) *Rethinking Social Policy*. London: Sage.

Stenson, K. 2000(b). 'Someday our prince will come: zero tolerance policing in Britain'. In Hope, T. and Sparks, R. (eds) *Crime, Risk and Insecurity*. Routledge: London.

Stenson, K. and Watt, P. 1999. 'Governmentality and the "Death of the Social"? A discourse analysis of local government texts in south-east England', *Urban Studies*, 36, 1: 189–201.

Van Swaaningen, R. 2000. 'Dutch Crime Prevention Politics and the Possibilities of a Replacement Discourse'. Paper delivered to the symposium on 'Rethinking Crime Prevention and Community Safety', The Open University, Milton Keynes, UK, 29 June.

Taylor, I. 1999. *Crime in Context, a Critical Criminology of Market Societies*. Cambridge: Polity.

Young, J. 1999. *The Exclusive Society*. London: Sage.

The schizophrenic state:
neo-liberal criminal justice

Robert R. Sullivan

For more than three centuries, or since John Locke, liberal states have practised a schizophrenic form of criminal justice.[1] One form of such justice is for the rich, enlightened, and occasionally blessed. Quite another is for the 'noxious' and 'degenerate' underclasses that have declared themselves quit of the principles of human nature.[2] That the traditional Anglo-Saxon liberal state practised a dual system of criminal justice has long been recognised and written about, and not just by Locke, whose words were paraphrased above. More recently others have weighed in against the aforementioned duality in eighteenth-century English criminal justice. Such a claim was integral to Douglas Hay's well-known argument about the uses of the criminal law in respect to property, and a similar claim was also central to E. P. Thompson's presentation of the origins of modern liberal criminal justice in *Whigs and Hunters*.[3] Even at the level of popular opinion in Britain and the United States, there has long been a strong belief that the rich get different treatment from the poor. So there is nothing new in the basic claim of this chapter.

But what of the more recent history of liberalism in the leading Anglo-Saxon democracies, the United Kingdom and the United States? The more recent litany of British and American neo-liberalism contains such terms as *downsizing* the state, its *hollowing out,* even its *reinvention,* as if the state were nothing more than the product of some mad inventor's consciousness. Such neologisms express values and suggest that there will be less governance, not more, and we easily recognise the recurrence of a time-tested Anglo-Saxon liberal value. Operational terms then suggest how such reduced governance will be attained. Some state services will be *privatized;* what remains will be conducted in terms of the ideology of *managerialism;* and citizens will be treated as *customers* buying services (see McLaughlin and Murji, Chapter 6). To the extent that citizens are not prepared for this neo-liberal revolution, they will be *responsibilized* by the downsized state, and thus the neo-liberal state will prove to be socially inclusive rather than marginalizing and socially excluding, as was the old welfare state at its death-watch. The new neo-liberal state also contains its 'experts' by moving toward more *actuarial* control in such matters as criminal justice, collecting information so that better informed customers can make better decisions, that is, their own decisions. On the face of it, the neo-liberal state looks like it will do less, not more, about crime; its citizens take more, not less, responsibility.

The most telling attacks on the welfare-liberal criminal justice presupposed its schizophrenic character as well, and thus implicitly promised that a new liberalism would bring to an end such divisions, which amounted to programmes of social exclusion. Thinkers whose names are now household words mounted such attacks. Goffman, for example, criticised the prison in the welfare state for being a 'total' institution intent on destroying individual character.[4] Michel Foucault's *Discipline and Punish* argued that the essence of liberalism vis-à-vis the lower orders of society was the attainment of docility, hardly a liberal value.[5] Francis A. Allen announced the end of the rehabilitative ideal in the 1970s.[6] Closer to our time, such a theme is at the centre of David Garland's *Punishment and Welfare,* which argued that the early twentieth century British welfare state laundered its true ends by hiding them behind the evangelical crusading of official discourse.[7] Implicit in all these critiques was the notion that a better liberalism, not yet named, was in the offing.

There were numerous kindred thinkers, less well known but no less sound in their argumentation, who chose to attack welfare-liberalism by coming to terms with its vulnerable criminal justice flank, making similar points. Stan Cohen and Laurie Taylor made a devastating critique of English prisons in *Psychological Survival* and so followed Goffman and anticipated Foucault.[8] They made it crystal clear that official discourse had nothing to do with what actually went on in the prison. Jock Young broadened the argument and reiterated the theme of totality by pointing to the 'absolutist' character of welfare-liberalism's conception of social solidarity and thus began the attack on social consciousness which culminated in Jean Baudrillard's well known essay on the 'death of the social'.[9]

More fully than any other thinker of his generation, Stan Cohen spelled out the questionable basis of social solidarity in his best book, *Folk Devils and Moral Panics.* Cohen showed how a society keyed to industrial conformity was increasingly prone to panic at the first sight of deviance. It thus took little for the police, working with the British popular press, to create an 'other' – in this case two 'others', the 'Mods' and the 'Rockers' – against which mainstream society could reaffirm its own solidaristic identity.[10] Cohen thus set the stage for one of the other major texts of the decade, Stuart Hall's *Policing the Crisis.* Hall and his students wrapped Cohen's thinking in a theoretical framework that portrayed the welfare-liberal state as itself creating the consensus that supposedly legitimated its actions. The folk devils in Hall's case were young Afro-Caribbean males, the diabolical practice was 'mugging', and the resultant moral panic firmly moved the white working class toward the support of aggressive policing in the Afro-Caribbean communities. The argument implicit in Cohen was made explicit in Hall: the liberal state, in this case the welfare-liberal state, was thoroughly corrupt.

How is such schizophrenia to be explained? One way is by paying attention to the press, as Cohen and Young did when editing *Manufacturing the News* in the early 1970s, for the press can *amplify* emotional responses to mundane events.[11] As subsequent British thinkers like Sparks and Reiner have recognised, the media is worth studying for the fear of crime it evokes and creates, and fear is worth isolating for its policy potential (see the chapters by Reiner *et al* and Sparks and Green in this volume). Not all hatred is borne of fear, but there are few more creative explanations of the intense passions that support draconian punishments, the building of more prisons (and in liberal America the death penalty) than a deeply rooted fear of society's lower orders. Fear expands to incorporate all its possibilities. Nowhere is this intensification more evident than in the presentation of crime in a gothic style, the essence of which is amplification, not of crime but rather of the emotional response to crime (see Simon, Chapter 7). Better to keep the criminal and crime out of sight, better to show only his shoes or shadow or the sound of his footsteps on the creaking stairs. Better to shroud him in fog or rain or endow him with superhuman powers of insight or strength. The point is to amplify the fear of the unknown by creating the impression of a totalized power relationship between offender and victim, the latter preferably a young and defenceless female or a guileless child. So amplification is the first step in the creation of schizophrenia.

It was Locke who gave this totalized power relationship its classical poetic formulation. His words are inestimably valuable in pinpointing the amplified fear that nurtures the eventual hatred. 'And hence it is, that he who attempts to get another Man into his Absolute Power, does thereby *put himself into a State of War* with him; it being to be understood as a Declaration of a Design upon his Life.'[12] The war Locke refers to, which is the precursor to the modern war on crime or war on drugs, leads to disproportion, or what I have here called amplification. This disproportion, the emotional prolegomenon to a totalized power relationship, is evidenced in the following passage:

> This [fear] makes it Lawful for a Man to *kill a thief,* who has not in the least hurt him, nor declared any design upon his Life... because using force, where he has no right, to get me into his Power, let his pretence be what it will, I have no reason to suppose, that he, who would *take away my liberty,* would not when he had me in his power, take away every thing else. And therefore it is lawful for me... to kill him if I can....[13]

The disproportion described here is rooted in fear, and it all too easily leads Locke himself toward verbal excess, as when he argues that murderers may '...be destroyed as a *Lyon* or a *Tyger,* one of those wild Savage Beasts, with whom Men can have no Society nor Security.' Once again, there is a disproportionate response here, for even though the killing of a murderer is an understandable reaction to an intentional killing, one can feel the more demanding emotions running through Locke's description. The murderer is not just killed in return, he is destroyed in the passion for revenge that Locke elsewhere admits may be carried too far. At his best, Locke soberly argues that the disproportion of a criminogenic vengeance provides reason to have a formal criminal justice institutional arrangement founded on independent judgement and proportionate punishments, but his main message is concerned with the direct response to crime.[14] Crime and punishment make up an explosive stew of emotional juices.

It is evident from Locke's words that the criminal is risking more than he knows when he engages in crime. For one thing, he is risking something more than the criminal wrath of the victim, who may, in hot blood or cool, choose to respond to crime with force. The charged response may even come to infect the system. A shop in Trenton, Georgia, in the United States, carries the warning in its window, 'We don't call 911', and the distinctive aspect of such a sign is its forthrightness. Most shops similarly situated have the same policy but without the warning. In other words, the shooting of a thief in the rural American south is very close to being a premeditated affair, and probably the courts would support such a response. In this manner the American death penalty becomes democratized, but when that happens it is increasingly difficult to draw a line between crime and justice.

Locke's thinking can be and has been explained by Tully as a secularization of Calvinist theological categories and as such it is an expression of rage at those who have parted company with God's revealed order of things.[15] Fortunately, if that is the proper word, we have something close to a re-enchanted Calvinism in the American South, where the contemporary competition between welfare liberalism and neo-liberalism is triangularized by the presence of a resurgent Christian fundamentalism bent on making war on sin. This reenchanted Calvinism presents itself as a moral solidarity intent on identifying deviants as folk devils, making holy war on them and finally banishing them altogether from the society of saints. But at the end of the day the significance of the American south is only its literalness. What is expressed there is elsewhere secularized and represented as a conservative tendency to reaffirm what social solidarity there is by use of the exclusionary tools of the criminal justice system. The widespread support for the building of more prisons in both Britain and the United States is an instance of this passion for social exclusion. But it is the American South that most persistently reminds us of the triangularized character of contemporary liberal politics.

The claim of this chapter is finally filled with its own little devils and ironies. Nothing is new in the schizophrenic character of liberal criminal justice in the two leading Anglo-Saxon democracies, but there are plenty of points where that character bears close watching for developments that are novel to the last two or three decades. These will be developed in a description of the prevailing schizophrenic sense of self in criminal justice within the United States and the United Kingdom.

*   *   *   *   *   *

The society that has fitfully come into existence since the elections of Margaret Thatcher and Ronald Reagan has been called, with some reason, the risk society.[16] The term is too broad to say much that is significant without a good deal of further elaboration, but it nonetheless functions as an umbrella to cover some significant topics. Americans, as the world knows, grow ever more willing to define their lives in market terms, which amounts to risk terms; and so not surprisingly they have been willing to redefine their criminal justice systems in risk terms. Such openness to risk is less widespread in Britain, but the basics of British society have also been restructured. Once Europe's risk-averse industrial centre, Britain has had a makeover into Europe's risk-oriented financial centre, and no group has paid more heed to this profound social change than the new Labour Party. Once a complex society characterized by distinctly collective alternatives to rampant market liberalism, Britain has become more like the United States in becoming risk-oriented from one end of the active political spectrum to the other.

A basic reinforcement of this social change has been the changing character of property. It is not so much that property has been redefined, it is rather that movable personal property has expanded vastly, and with it the sheer volume of risk, in the more prosaic sense of that term. The illustrations are familiar: The family television, once an unstealable piece of collective family property, now shares pride of place with a proliferation of portable and thus easily stealable television sets. The mainframe computer gives way to the personal computer, which in turn is personalized so that each member of the family has his or her own laptop computer. Collective transportation in the form of buses or trains gives way to what the Germans nicely call the PKW, or the *personal* automobile. Family sound systems give way to personal sound systems and eventually to the Walkman, and the family telephone gives way to the personal telephone and eventually the cellphone.

In such a situation, the *risk* of crime appreciates exponentially. Homes have never been more worth burglarizing. There are more of them and they are less guarded than ever before by women. People on the streets, too, have never been more worth robbing. One might get a Walkman, a cellphone, and a notebook computer, not to speak of the traditional watch and wallet. In such fluid conditions, the police are increasingly ineffective. Citizens are therefore encouraged to responsibilize, and discard the welfare mentality that told them to let the police provide for their security; they are now urged to do it themselves. Homes are equipped with anti-burglary systems which, when triggered, inform local police who are trained to make an immediate response. In the United States, more localized policing arrangements have proved to be convenient, because the police are seldom more than five minutes away from any home in any wealthy American suburb. The more centralized British policing arrangements were less suited to quick response and have had to be rethought. This is not to say that the British police have not responded adequately; but having had a more centralized welfare state and a more centralized police, they started at a higher level of organisation.

But the police have done much more than reorganize. They have also responded to a changing situation and a different mood by redefining most everyday activities in terms of risk. Where one goes at night, whom one's children play with, whether the baby is getting enough attention, where the car is parked, all this and much more are defined as risks, and the police, and law-enforcement personnel in general, have participated in this. Such thinking is keyed to the way the middle classes already think, especially when their savings are invested in stock markets, where they have actually bought *shares* of risk. When the police in the British home counties and the high-end American suburbs were not in hot pursuit of the criminal, they were expected to pursue an actuarial approach and make the concept of risk meaningful by providing statistical profiles of crime, neighbourhoods, and the like.[17] Real estate values depended on at least this much diligence. And there are few things that the new moneyed classes are more attentive to in selecting a home than the level of crime in the neighbourhood. The result is that the suburbs, the wealthy ones at least, have become not just secure places with effective policing arrangements but also places with good or bad statistical profiles.

It is hardly surprising that even developmental psychology has been re-keyed to risk calculations. The stages of the child's development are defined in terms of risk and risk avoidance as well as in conventional terms, so much so that children are seen to be *at risk* of not qualifying for their parents' school of choice, of slipping behind the established norm for the appropriate age group, or perhaps even of being victimized by crime. The result of such a shift in emphasis has been to make developmental psychology more inclusive. It has always been that. Middle-class parents have long been intervening with tutors, dietary supplements, or pastoral visits to get their children to conform more closely to the middle-class ideal of a child's career. But now more than ever the emphasis has been to orient developmental psychology to corrections in the criminal justice sense of the term. This has meant changing the social conditions that were seen to produce deviance, even crime, in the lower classes, and even intervening with drugs to produce proper, orderly behaviour so that development can proceed appropriately, and risk of failure is avoided.

Although developmental psychology has never been more inclusive than it is today, social exclusion is still very much a part of the risk society. The middle classes also need an 'other' to sustain their sense of self, their identity. Numerous 'others' are embedded in previous moral litanies of middle-class society, but have been shed in the continuing evolution of middle-class sensibilities, also known as their moral code. It is now scandalous to stigmatize Jews, African-Americans, Asians, Arabs, and sundry other peoples. Indeed, it is sometimes illegal. In the United States, such groups are wrapped in the protective covering offered by Title 7 of the Civil Rights Act of 1964. And the most significant other of recent times, the Communist of the erstwhile evil empire, is no longer available for the role. Thus by default the indistinct figure of the criminal regains the position Locke gave him at the origins of modern Anglo-Saxon liberalism. Here we find the generic other against which the modern middle-class self gains its basic identity. The criminal in Locke's portrayal was never specific and thus remains ever available as a label to be applied. Locke argues that 'Cain was so fully convinced, that everyone had a right to destroy such a Criminal, that after the Murther of his Brother, he cries out, *Every one that findeth me, shall slay me*, so plain was it writ in the hearts of man.'[18] The criminal is the embodiment of an envisioned relationship of absolute power, and from its birth in Locke's *Second Treatise* the modern liberal state has been aimed to reverse this relationship and put absolute power in the hands of the state.[19]

It is instructive to watch continental European societies and note the extent to which they differ in identifying the other with the generic foreigner in Haider's

Austria or Le Pen's France. The Anglo-Saxon democracies frown on this overt and unjustified bias, but insofar as Anglo-Saxon societies have no less of a need for an other as a focus of social frustrations, the generic criminal performs that function. This is nowhere more evident than in Locke's writings, for precisely because they are completely untainted by bias against Jews, foreigners, women, or proletarians, they are that much more keyed to the criminal as the generic other.

With these comments we come quickly to the end of a depiction of the successful, but not completely unproblematic, side of neo-liberal criminal justice, its distinctly middle-class side. Anglo-Saxon citizens have been very nicely responsibilized and the care for their security very much privatized. Law enforcement agencies in middle-class areas have taken on a greater managerial tone, and the actuarial side of policing has been given a much greater emphasis. But this undoubted success has been bought at the price of a certain emerging schizophrenic character to criminal justice, as investments in security have been justified in the minds of middle-class homeowners by the looming, dark figure of crime, portrayed again and again as the absent other on television programs on the operations of law enforcement agencies. The management of this dark figure is not quite the bright portrait that we have above.

*   *   *   *   *   *

As noted at the outset, the contest between welfare liberalism and neo-liberalism in the two leading Anglo-Saxon democracies was triangularized from the outset by the presence of a moral fundamentalism that fashioned its own identity in terms of wedge issues. These divided the world in a Manichean manner and took it as a struggle between good and evil, saints and sinners, law-abiding citizens and criminal elements. The Manichean vision is most obvious in the American South, but in secular and milder form it exists throughout the rest of the United States and the United Kingdom as well. It entails a war on drugs and, more generally, a war on crime itself. The significance of this powerful metaphor of war is that it shifts the emphasis strongly in the direction of social exclusion.

This emphasis on a Manichean war on crime suggests that the triumph of neo-liberalism in Britain and the United States was always something less than perfect. My explanation for this is the continued presence of a residual moralism in both the Conservative and Republican parties. Mrs Thatcher conquered a Conservative party but apparently did not drive out Toryism as much as it looked with her reconstruction of the financial markets in the 'Big Bang' of 1986. Or perhaps she did drive out the gentle Toryism of Harold Macmillan or Ted Heath, but this only opened the way for stronger claims for the need for moral community. From the outset, Ronald Reagan depended on the Southern coalition initiated by Barry Goldwater, and thus compromised his neo-liberal instincts by putting them to bed with a Christian fundamentalism intent on making war on abortionists, homosexuals, secular humanists, and other assorted criminals. However the details worked out, both right-wing parties were beholden to a residual conservative moral influence bent on social exclusion.

The resultant war on crime has entailed a number of distinct features of criminal justice seemingly at odds with the spirit of neo-liberalism. For one, aggressive policing and a related militarization of policing – mainly in the United States, to a lesser extent in the UK – have little to do with the marketization concept that is central to neo-liberalism. But these phenomena are keynotes in the new moral militancy. There is in addition in corrections a renewed emphasis on prisons as the main means of social exclusion. In a related vein, there is an emphasis on aggression in sentencing policy, up to and including the death penalty in the United States. I will start with the matter of aggressive policing in neo-liberal society.

Policing in neo-liberal society

Every political era creates its own catchwords that work to capture and even create the spirit of the times, but few are stranger than zero tolerance. The term announces an inflexible stance designed to replace the presumed permissive tolerance of crime in the old welfare state. In some respects, the term conveys a desirable corrective to a permissiveness that went too far. It also contains within it a radical impatience with state programs that are rehabilitative or redemptive in character, and that is a significant break with a long Anglo-Saxon tradition. But what is most strange about the term is its manifest illiberalism. No term can be more in conflict with the spirit of any liberalism than one that announces itself as intolerant, and zero tolerance does just that.

Not the least interesting aspect of the term zero tolerance is that it originated not in the American south but rather in New York City, a supposed bastion of liberalism. Very quickly thereafter it attained the height of its popularity in Britain. I am here talking about the rhetoric rather than the practice of zero tolerance or aggressive policing. In practice, with the one exception of the Cleveland constabulary, no force in Britain has formally adopted zero tolerance policing, although many forces there have become more aggressive in their policing of the lower classes. But once again, the point has to do with rhetoric rather more than with practice. Zero tolerance is an ideology legitimating a practice: aggressive policing. The latter is not particularly novel, and thus it is the intolerant ideology rather than the commonplace practices associated with it that is interesting. What then do we make of such a state of affairs? An example from one of the most neo-liberal American states is germane.

Without using the term, the New Jersey state police use zero tolerance policing in the form of racial profiling of drug traffickers and related searches on the state's highways. The practice involves racism not because the profiles suggest that African-Americans are most likely to be involved in drug trafficking. It may well be the case that young African-American males are disproportionately involved in drug trafficking, and New Jersey troopers have every right to know that fact; but to act willy-nilly on such knowledge is to confuse a statistical probability with probable cause. At best this is a problem of logic, at worst, racial profiling is a sudden instance of political forgetfulness. The heart and soul of liberalism is the ontological claim that only individuals exist and that collectivities are artificial and consequently questionable. But here is a case of individuals being put under suspicion because of their race, and surely that flies in the face of the most basic liberal tenets.

When polling revealed that the force was very popular among the white citizens of New Jersey, legislators rose to the occasion in defence of the state police, and so the governor – a rising star in American national politics – found herself between a rock and a hard place. New Jersey is a distinctly neo-liberal place, with perhaps the largest concentration of white-collar business people of any state in the United States. But now the white population was showing that it had a side that was not in the least neo-liberal (in the marketization sense of the term) but was rather bent on an exclusionary tactic, racial profiling. The lesson of the story is the simple one that the triumph of neo-liberalism in the Republican Party was never that complete. If the Alabama state police had practised racial profiling and been supported by white voters, there would be no great surprise, but New Jersey was another case altogether.

In Britain the situation is apparently reversed, with the public being in favour of zero tolerance policing but the forces for the most part not practising it in any questionable form. But what would happen if, say, the Essex constabulary began practising a zero tolerance policing aimed at a profiled group of young British males whose appearance and demeanour were said to be criminogenic? Conceivably, the popularity of the Essex constabulary would rise among the otherwise neo-liberal business community, and what politician would then have the stomach to take them on publicly? Obviously the question is rhetorical, but so too is the term zero tolerance, and its abiding popularity in Britain suggests the real possibility of exclusionary practices designed to take advantage of the favourable climate of opinion staked out by the ideology.

Also, in their routine searches on the New Jersey turnpike, the state police were not combating crime but were rather combating the risk of crime, a prospect conveyed to them by a technique invented for the purpose of assessing risk. Their example is not unlike that of the Diallo case in New York, insofar as the police officers who fired forty-one shots at an unarmed man before killing him were reacting to the risk that he might kill them. Although they were equipped with Glock semi-automatic pistols, these still only fired one bullet at a time, and so the officers were denied a physical excuse and forced back on their mental states. In the best case, they were firing and firing rapidly because of the risk that the victim might fire back at them. Such policing is now more problematic than ever before because an ideology of risk and a related ideology of policing sanction it.

Zero tolerance is also related to a certain militarization of policing. The resistance to public policing of any sort in eighteenth century England meant that the army itself had to be used in large public order disturbances such as food riots, and so already in that eighteenth-century there was a certain militarization of liberal criminal justice. The ineffectiveness of the army in such affairs gradually led to the recognition that public policing would have to be created. But instead of being a local affair, the alternative was cast in the form of an *ersatz* military establishment, namely, the Metropolitan police. Under the direction of the Home Secretary, and ultimately the Prime Minister, the Met could be deployed anywhere in England, and in fact was as recently as the 1984–85 miners' strike. But too much attention to the Met distracts attention to other instances of militarization in British policing, for example the 1911 general strike in Liverpool, the use of the 'Black-and-Tans' in Ireland in 1919, and the deployment of the Royal Ulster Constabulary as a virtual military force in Ulster in the 1980s. And lest Britain forget the most sensational instance of militarized policing not working, there were the events in Boston leading up to the outbreak of open hostilities with the colonies in 1775, at Lexington and Concord. Arguably the American Revolution could have been avoided if the English had had a well-trained police force in Massachusetts at the time.

Still, militarization remains more a question of potential than reality in most contemporary British forces. That is not the case in the neo-liberal United States, where there has been a widespread militarization of policing, most noticeably through the creation of such overt military operations features as SWAT (Special Weapons and Tactics) units.[20] Such policing has a long historical pedigree in the United States, mainly in the western states, but in the empty spaces of the Wild West there was always good reason to invest heavily in types of equipment that increased mobility, such as the horse, later the motorcycle, most recently the helicopter.[21] There was nothing particularly liberal or illiberal about such militarization. But this additive to policing has proved irresistible throughout the rest of the United States, where it is less justified by spatial considerations. Now most big city police departments in the United States have the helicopters and the highly mobile SWAT teams that were first deployed in Los Angeles. Clearly, there is not a great deal of resistance to militarization.

But such a description is benign and does not confer the reality of what is happening in the present United States. Historically in both the United Kingdom and the United States, large standing armies have been dissolved immediately after military conflicts. Retired or released military personnel have often been taken care of by being given positions in the criminal justice systems. The 'Black-and-Tans' in Ireland in 1919 were veterans of the Somme just three years earlier, most prison wardens throughout the nineteenth century were retired army officers, parole departments in both the United Kingdom and the United States have usually been staffed by retired army officers rather than social workers, and one of the recent American 'drug czars' was a retired army general, indeed, one with a questionable military record in the Gulf War.[22] The militarization of criminal justice is a constant possibility in countries that dismantle armies after Napoleonic-scale conflicts.

Predictably, such militarization of policing has become a pressing problem since the end of the Cold War.[23] The downsizing of the American military promised a 'peace dividend', but what in fact resulted was a surplus of military equipment that was made available to American police departments. Innumerable police departments took such equipment to enhance their existing SWAT teams, but the result was also something of a change in policy, as the new equipment enabled the existing SWAT teams to think in terms of becoming more offensive. The result was similar to the introduction of the tank into modern armies in the interwar period: that one weapon facilitated a shift from the defensive machine-gun mentalities of World War I to the offensive *Blitzkrieg* mentalities of World War II.[24]

To sum up at midpoint, changes in policing in the neo-liberal governments that have existed since 1980 have indicated the advent of a more aggressive attitude toward the purported sources of crime in society. Actuarial thinking has enabled authorities to profile likely offenders, thus substituting statistical probability for probable cause. This shift in causal thinking has been coupled with the advent of a condoning zero tolerance ideology, and the result has been the advent of a socially divisive aggressiveness in policing. Compounding this state of affairs has been the militarization of policing since the end of the Cold War. Hence, and not without a certain measure of irony, the instincts of a residual conservatism to restore moral solidarity by excluding the offenders of society's purported moral code has been strengthened. All that is needed now is an advocate for the building of still more prisons.

*   *   *   *   *   *

In an ideal neo-liberal state, corrections would prefer to see itself and be seen in terms of a commercial relationship in which the customers get what they deserve, a matter of just deserts rather than rehabilitation, and these deserts are served up by outsourcing companies running private prisons. The concept of just deserts is obviously a legal concept, an attractive one in that it promises something of a contractual relationship between the prospective criminal and the state. Commit this crime and incur the risk of being caught and it will cost you the following, and we promise truth-in-advertising, no discounts for bargaining, and no reductions in cost after the fact of conviction. Such wording, give or take a little, became official discourse in neo-liberal corrections in the late 1970s and, increasingly, in the 1980s.

But it seems clear that the immediate 'customers' of the corrections system were (again increasingly) getting more than they deserved in the risk society. New prisons were being built at record rates, in the United States and in Britain as well during the tenure of Michael Howard at the Home Office; and notoriously, the proclivity of judges to rise to the bait and fill all available prison cells remains a probability into the indefinite future. Legislators were reducing discretion in sentencing, giving judges still less choice in the matter, and even the semblance of rehabilitation was being eliminated for recidivists. At first glance this was precisely what just deserts meant. But the argument entailed or implicit in Goffman's *Asylums* is still applicable forty years later, and perhaps more so. Prison was much worse than official discourse made it out to be, and in the neo-liberal state, more persons were spending more time there.

The American example was more dramatic than the British because prisons in the United States were more likely to be used for minor drug offences, and so the American prison population doubled from its record one million inmates in the mid-1980s to more than two million inmates in the late 1990s.[25] When felonies added up, as in the American 'three strikes' sentencing policy, the book was thrown at the perpetrator, a practice dictating that sentencing policy pay attention to a pattern of crime rather than to the specific crime (see Hudson this volume).[26] Solitary confinement, which might be taken as an added cost, was increasingly used, and the question of the inmate's psychological survival was every bit as pressing in the neo-liberal state as it had been for Stan Cohen and Laurie Taylor in the welfare-liberal state. Nevertheless, the mantra of the right, whether neo-liberal or conservative, became the refrain 'Prison Works!' and in a certain irrefutable sense there was truth in that claim. When social exclusion becomes absolute, as it does with the policy of incapacitation, it is bound to reduce rather than incite crime.

The American example is not without its instructive political ironies. In the 1970s, New York Republicans put into place the so-called Rockefeller drug laws, the gist of which was that small drug retailers would be punished with a harshness hitherto reserved for drug wholesalers. The motive was moral outrage at a situation seemingly out of control, but the result was a vast expansion of the New York State prison system. This proved to be a politically desirable result in that it provided employment for upstate Republican voters, even though it meant building prisons more than one hundred miles from the families of most of the prisoners in New York City. The Democrats were constantly critical of this aspect of New York criminal justice, and over drinks in the legislators' taverns in Albany the Republicans were sometimes heard to admit that the Democrats had a point. But public criticism by the Democrats only earned for them the Republican retort that they were 'soft on crime', and so the Republicans knew they had a good thing going.

But neo-liberal Republicans are different, and so eventually, in 1999, the Republican leaders George Pataki and Joseph Bruno publicly proposed reforming the Rockefeller drug laws. An age of enlightenment had apparently arrived. But when the Republican leaders made their proposal, the leaders of the Democrats, no doubt sensing a trap, refused to agree, and suddenly the tables were turned. Now it was the Republicans who were soft on crime, the Democrats apparently tougher. The point is that crime in the generic sense is now one of the five leading issues in any election, and politicians across the political spectrum are duty-bound to say that they will do something about crime. But crime has become a generic category, not one that is at all specific, and on those rare occasions that it does become specific, as for example with the murder of Megan Kanka, after whom Megan's Law was named, politicians are still likely to respond by saying that if elected, they will do something about it.[27] There is now no politician who is 'soft on crime'.

Change some of the details and this ironic twist of political events has its counterpart in Britain. Old Labour had no crime policy to speak of and consequently was easily made to appear 'soft on crime'. New Labour found its political origins when the shadow Home Secretary Tony Blair reversed Old Labour's crime policy, or lack thereof, and announced that he and New Labour would be 'tough on crime, tough on the causes of crime'. The formula was deceptive in practice, because only half of the dual crusade was zealously pursued. Old Labour had always implicitly promised to be tough on the causes of crime, meaning the unequal system of distributive justice that prevailed in capitalist Britain. Old Labour's problem was that it never promised to be tough on crime itself, seeing it as an outcome of social injustice. Insofar as Blair accepted the Thatcherite social revolution, it is fair to surmise that he never intended to be tough on the causes of crime; he would be tough only on crime itself. When Jack Straw inherited Blair's position as shadow Home Secretary and thence became Home Secretary in the Blair government, he demonstrated the truth of the above claim by being without doubt tough on crime but far less tough on the causes of crime. New Labour is new mainly because it is no longer vulnerable to the electoral charge of being 'soft on crime'.

In this survey of political ironies, it might pay to pause and look in some detail at that ultimate act of social exclusion, the death penalty, for if anything makes no sense at all from a neo-liberal perspective, it is this (see Simon, Chapter 7, in this volume).[28] For one thing the death penalty costs too much of the taxpayer's money, and if there is one issue close to the hearts of every neo-liberal, it is the burden of taxation. But like zero tolerance in policing and three strikes in sentencing policy, the death penalty is expressive more of public mood than of anything else, and social conservatives (as opposed to neo-liberals) are willing to pay for their passions.

As long as New York state did not have the death penalty, debate about it was abstract and nicely 'academic'. It was a matter of claiming that we should or should not have the death penalty, and no sharp emotions were evoked. Thus it was a blunt instrument of governance. Even if you were in favour of the death penalty, you somehow just knew (or believed) we would never have it. It was something that *they* had down South. But then as soon as New York actually adopted the death penalty, the character of public debate changed. Now the question was whether to use it or not in this or that specific case and thus it became a practical political tool for dividing upstate from downstate, the suburbs from the city, and the governor from specific district attorneys such as Robert Johnson and Robert Morgenthau. State (district) attorneys are normally elected in populist American democracy, and even when they are appointed, as federal attorneys are, many of them see the office as a stepping-stone to higher office, hence making them susceptible to the charms or curses of the death penalty. Not for nothing had the then Governor Clinton of Arkansas boasted that he had agonized over many a death penalty decision, and then of course signed the order on his desk. He understood the necessity to be tough on crime just as well as Tony Blair did. The death penalty thus joins zero tolerance, three strikes, and SWAT as a very powerful tool of governance; but what should be clear is that the death penalty is mainly a matter of moral expression.

The death penalty is also a sanction that can be radically democratized, and with surprising ease. The second amendment to the United States Constitution prohibits the government from infringing on the right of American citizens to bear arms. Originally, that amendment was one of a package of civil liberties written into the Bill of Rights. As with freedom of speech, press, assembly, religious worship, and the freedom from having the army quartered on the people, the guiding idea of the framers was an expansive vision of citizenship. The ideal citizen was well-informed, had opinions, expressed them, if need be projected them over distances in a free press, assembled with his fellow citizens, and, finally, carried arms to remind the state that the restrictions to power enshrined in the Bill of Rights were to be taken seriously. It is not an exaggeration to say that the second amendment right to bear arms is the crown jewel of the United States Constitution. It sublimates the vision of the Minutemen rising up at Lexington and Concord to take on their British cousins. More than free speech or any other first amendment right, bearing arms is a literal embodiment of the autonomous citizen.

But things have not worked out exactly as the framers intended. Today the United States is covered with arms producers who manufacture sophisticated hardware and ammunition and market it to various clients, some of whom might actually want the arms to enhance their sense of citizenship and guarantee their civil liberties. But willy-nilly, over this or that state line, the criminal community is supplied with a steady stream of ever more potent arms. And yet there is nothing vague about this criminogenic corner of American life. Fifty per cent of crime guns recovered by the ATF, the federal gun regulator, come from three per cent of the retail gun outlets in the United States, but only a tiny fraction of those questionable gun outlets have been prosecuted. One gun dealer in southern California has made thousands of 'straw' sales, or sales to persons who are funded by a convicted criminal, and some of these have been exported to Canada and Australia, but prosecutions amount to a slap on the wrist, and the dealer (B&E Guns) is still open for business.[29] In such a manner is the 'death penalty' democratized.

Matters related to the darker side of criminal justice do not end here. Few things are more revealing of changing society than funding and staffing of law enforcement agencies. In 1973, the Drug Enforcement Agency (DEA) employed 1,622 agents but currently has 4,261. That is an increase of about 150 per cent. Since 1973, Alcohol, Tobacco, and Firearms have grown from 1,622 employees to 1,631, a growth of only nine agents, or 0.005 per cent. Drug arrests and convictions have grown proportionately. Or rather, they have grown disproportionately, because of the way the drug laws are written. Gun convictions have declined in proportion to the size of the agency, and this change too is attributable to the way the gun laws are written. For example, the law prohibits ATF agents from posing as felons, requiring the agency to use actually convicted felons to make illegal purchases. But then when this is done, the agency is impugned in court for consorting with felons and entrapping honest gun dealers.[30] Such cases are then often dismissed.

My original claim is that the death penalty can be radically democratized, and that thought brings me back to the Trenton, Georgia, and the shop with the sign, 'We don't call 911'. In fairness to the citizens of the southern states, most such talk is male bravado, but in keeping with a sense of distinction between *mentalité* and practice, such signs and the collections of guns in every household (no one has just one gun), bespeak a state of mind that is socially significant. The latter point – its social significance – is that virtually everyone, but above all African-Americans, has to watch where they are going, what they are doing, and how their actions are interpreted. A society of social exclusion is ultimately a society in which everyone, and this includes white southerners as well, is isolated and excluded from easy social relations with neighbours and even with folks down at the country store, who are probably the ones declaring their unwillingness to phone 911. The predominant mindset of the American South is deeply atomizing.

*   *   *   *   *   *

In this chapter, I have argued within the temporal confines of the neo-liberal states introduced by Margaret Thatcher and Ronald Reagan and attempted to arrange the argument by splitting criminal justice into halves. The first half is a happy story about the self-policing of the new middle classes, the other half a somewhat more complicated tale about the governing and governance of the lower classes by means of new, or at least newly named, techniques of policing and corrections. The happier half of the story actually provides some of the language of official discourse, and so talk about new actuarial techniques of policing, about managerialism, privatization, customer satisfaction, responsibilization, and the like are not misplaced. It is entirely possible to use this vocabulary alone to describe criminal justice in neo-liberal Britain and America, but the resultant picture would be less than complete.

The other half of the story is more interesting and has an *official discourse* of its own. Words and phrases like zero tolerance, SWAT, prison works!, militarization, tough on crime, three strikes, the death penalty, and the like describe this other world of aggressive policing and corrections. I have tried to show not so much how these terms describe government operations, which they to some extent always do, but how they work as elements of governance in neo-liberal society. Thus a term like zero tolerance was defined first as a governmental operation and then eventually as an aspect of governance. The death penalty was attractive because, although describing a governmental operation, it obviously finds the overwhelming gravity of its meaning as a term of governance.

In a now well known publication, David Garland argued in 1996[31] that the sovereignty of the modern state was contingent on its provision of security and that recently this condition had come under severe challenge from rising crime. For the most part, Garland was talking about Britain and the United States, and his point was that politicians wanted to back off from ambitious claims about the provision of domestic security but were aware of the disastrous political costs such a move was likely to have. What then emerged was a volatile and ambivalent period of policy development. For Garland, the volatility was not entirely without its order, for it involved a split between what he called a 'criminology of the self' and a 'criminology of the other'. The state that Garland was describing as jumpy and ambivalent could also be described as schizophrenic.

But Garland's dualistic and schizophrenic state was very different from the one described in this chapter. It was a state uncertain of itself in the face of a problem that was threatening to its very *raison d'etre*. It thus ran hot and cold, running at the problem with much bravado and still running away from it by engaging in denial, privatization of programs, and responsibilization of the citizenry. Garland's paper thus posed a question that he could not answer, that is, where were the limits of modern sovereignty, and would the contemporary state ever be able to find them and return itself to stability? The schizophrenia described in this chapter has been very different, often with reference to the same materials Garland used, and I would suggest that the difference is due to the problematic but still highly confident presence of a residual moralististic conservatism in the neo-liberalism analyzed here but absent in Garland's more narrowly focused argument.

Absent this moral conservatism, neo-liberalism is not terribly well equipped to handle crime, and this is because it tends to be socially inclusive. The criminal is treated as a normal and rational actor, and programs of situational crime prevention are tailored to induce the criminal to engage in condoned activities of profit taking rather than in proscribed activities that involve the use of force to take profits. If such a neo-liberalism had a monopoly on the playing field, then there can be little doubt that its criminal justice would be unsure of itself and volatile. It would run hot and cold, toward and away from the criminality in its neighbourhoods. Its particular brand of criminal justice is practised in the high-end suburbs, where it is sure of itself and very successful because for the most part unchallenged, but it does not transport very well into the inner cities.

The real challenge is elsewhere, and the criminal justice that takes it on originates in a residual conservatism's instinct to engage in social exclusion for the sake of recreating the society that Mrs Thatcher denied existed. Social exclusion of criminals through exile, transportation, prisons, ghettoization, hanging in Tyburn, or electrocution in Georgia or Texas has always been a more efficient way of asserting the sovereignty of the state in the face of severe challenge. The ambivalence that Garland sees is actually that of the two faces of the main political alliances of the two largest Anglo-Saxon states, and thus in a fashion such apparent volatility and instability is only apparent and not in the least volatile or unstable.

If there is ambivalence, it is elsewhere, in civil society rather than in the state. The more crime-ridden a section of New York or Fresno in the United States or Middlesbrough in England, the more favourable is opinion toward zero tolerance, profiling, SWAT, the death penalty, and three-strikes sentencing policies, and this favourability extends to minority communities as well. For example, Orlando Patterson has argued that African-Americans in Boston make a distinction between aggressive and racist policing, favouring the former but abhorring the latter. Similarly remarkable findings were evident in New Jersey in respect to the state police when they practised racial profiling. A recent survey indicated that 37 per cent of African-Americans living in New Jersey admired or otherwise had a favourable attitude toward the New Jersey State police.[32] Such statistics indicate that the sovereign authority of the United States has been strengthened by policies of social inclusion and not in the least threatened by volatility in criminal justice policy. I would assume the same is the case in Britain. The fact that Afro-Caribbean communities abhor the policing demonstrated in the Lawrence inquiry does not mean that they do not want aggressive policing of their communities.

I argued at the outset that the figure of the criminal was the generic form of the other because it sketched out an absolute relationship of power. The terror of being alone with a murderer who has his knife to your throat and has no reason not to cut it is absolute. The deepest goal of criminal justice is to do a chiasmatic reversal of this relationship and have the overwhelming power of the state brought to bear on the same criminal. This vision of crime describes what Locke called a state of war. I suggested that more familiar others – the traditional figure of the Jew, the Arab, African-Americans, the Hun and the like – are all specifications of the generic category of criminal. Thus in practising governance through crime control, the neo-liberal states discussed in this paper are getting back to basics. They are identifying the criminal as such as the appropriate other. The danger, of course, is that law enforcement authorities will confuse one group with the criminal as such, and thus revert to traditional stigmatizing, and in fact much of this is done. But the sovereignty of the United States is on much more solid ground when the other is not the traditional African-American (or the Jamaican living in Bristol) but is rather the generic criminal.

Much of what the residual conservatives provide – intolerance (or rather zero tolerance), militarization, the death penalty, draconian punishments, more prisons – is hard to swallow, but there is no question about such measures working. Yet we must understand what it is to say that such measures work. When Martinson argued that nothing works, he meant to refer to the policies of social inclusion of the welfare state. Rehabilitation did not work. It was after all a long shot from the outset. When I hazard the guess that everything works in the contemporary neo-liberal state, I mean to say programs of social exclusion are bound to have success. They are frankly infinitely easier to carry out successfully than programs of social inclusion.

So finally, and in sharp distinction to David Garland's argument, it is possible to come to the ironic conclusion that the sovereignty of the United States and even the United Kingdom has seldom been on more solid ground. Nothing succeeds in politics like talking out of both sides of your mouth, and nothing succeeds more in criminal justice than a little schizophrenia.

Notes

1   The term *schizophrenic* is of course a metaphor and thus is not bound to its medical meaning. Such schizophrenia is ultimately a function of class society and is probably reducible to a single coherent system. But to do so is a costly mistake, for the system is better looked at as two warring halves.
2   See Locke (1988, II, 10, p. 273).
3   Hay (1975), Thompson (1975). Thompson addresses the welfare state in the section on rule of law, pp. 258–269.
4   Goffman (1961).
5   Foucault (1978).
6   Allen (1981).
7   Garland (1985).

8   Cohen and Taylor (1972).
9   Baudrillard (1983).
10 Cohen (1972).
11 Cohen and Young (1973).
12 Locke, op. cit., III, 17, p. 279.
13 Locke, op. cit., III, 18, pp. 279–280.
14 Locke, op. cit., II, 12, pp. 274–275.
15 Tully (1993), esp. ch. 6.
16 The term originated in Ulrich Beck's *Risk Society* (1992). See also Giddens (1990).
17 See Ericson and Haggerty (1997).
18 *ibid.*, chap II, para. 11.
19 Here then is what might (but won't) be a theme of this paper. Locke as the founder of modern Anglo-Saxon liberalism provides it with a social formula for sustaining itself. It is not enough for middle-class selves to live for the pursuit of property, they must also sustain their sense of selfhood by putting themselves in an absolute relationship of war with an other which is also in pursuit of property, although illicitly. Locke might have created a relative and hence milder social relationship between property-owners and thieves, but he chose to absolutize the relationship (the thief becomes a murderer) for the advantages such a harsh portrayal offered.
20 *New York Times,* March 1, 1999, p. 1.
21 Historically, the United States is characterized by three traditions of policing – the eastern, southern, and the western. The latter tradition has been keyed to covering large expanses of territory and thus has always been oriented to sophisticated technology and equipment, initially horses but eventually the first police cars, police radios, motorcycles and eventually helicopters.
22 The general is Barry McCaffrey. See Seymore M. Hersh, 'Overwhelming Force', *The New Yorker,* May 22, 2000.
23 Peter B. Kraska, 'Questioning the Militarization of U. S. Policing: Critical vs. Advocacy Scholarship', *Policing and Society,* 9, 2, 1999.
24 P. A. J. Waddington has argued that Peter B. Kraska, an American criminologist, is mistaken in his reading or these recent events, but Waddington was evidently thinking more of British than American experience. See P. A. J. Waddington, 'Swatting Police Paramilitarism: A Comment on Kraska and Paulsen', *Policing and Society,* 9, 2, 1999.
25 The model for this pattern was provided in New York state with the so-called Rockefeller drug laws, which imposed draconian sentences on small drug dealers (retailers). They continue in effect to this day.
26 Sentencing has always paid attention to the pattern of crime and not just the individual crime, but traditionally the imposition of harsher sentences was a matter of judicial discretion and not legislative will.
27 *Megan's Law* was first of all a New Jersey statute that said that sex offenders being released from prison had to register with the police and prospective neighbors had to be forewarned that a sex offender was moving into their neighborhood. It raised the question of enhanced punishment for the released offender.
28 The United States Constitution neither requires nor prohibits the death penalty. It says in the fifth and fourteenth amendments that life may not be taken away without due process, meaning that it may be taken away with due process. Such language also puts the death penalty in that curious in-between condition of being *not unconstitutional,* a double-negative that is similar to the everyday claim that the coffee in such-and-such a restaurant is *not bad.* States may choose to have the death penalty or make do without

it, and the same may be said for the federal government. In this respect the death penalty resembles slavery, which was also not unconstitutional, meaning that some states had slavery and others did not. Such a condition, which is one of the prices paid for the federal arrangements of the United States, gave rise to the abolitionist movement of the 1840s, and it is no accident that the death penalty has given rise to a similarly named 'abolitionist' movement in the contemporary United States.

29   *New York Times,* July 22, 1999, p. 1.
30   *ibid.*
31   Garland (1996).
32   *New York Times,* July 20, 1999, p. B1.

References

Allen, Francis A. *The Decline of the Rehabilitative Ideal* (New Haven: Yale Univ. Press, 1981).

Beck, Ulrich *Risk Society*, transl. by Mark Ritter (London: Sage, 1992).

Baudrillard, Jean *In the Shadow of Silent Majorities or, The End of the Social and Other Essays,* transl. Paul Foss, John Johnston, and Paul Patton (New York: Semiotext(e) Foreign Agents Series, 1983).

Cohen, Stan *Folk Devils and Moral Panics* (London: MacGibbon & Kee, 1972).

Cohen, Stan & Laurie Taylor, *Psychological Survival* (Harmondworth: Penguin, 1972).

Cohen, Stan & Jock Young, *Manufacturing the News* (London: Constable, 1973).

Ericson, Richard and Kevin Haggerty, *Policing the Risk Society* (Oxford: Oxford Univ. Press, 1997).

Foucault, Michel *Discipline and Punish, the Birth of the Prison*, transl. Alan Sheridan (New York: Vintage Books, 1978).

Goffman, Erving *Asylums* (New York: Doubleday-Anchor, 1961).

Garland, David *Punishment and Welfare* (Aldershot: Gower, 1985).

Garland, David 'The limits of the sovereign state: strategies of crime control in contemporary society', *The British Journal of Criminology*, 36: 445–71 (1996).

Giddens, Anthony *The Consequences of Modernity* (Cambridge: Polity Press, 1990).

Hay, Douglas 'Property and the Criminal Law', in Hay, D. Linebaugh, P. and Thompson, E. P., *Albion's Fatal Tree* (London: Allan Lane, 1975).

Kraska, Peter B. 'Questioning the Militarization of US Policing: Critical *vs.* Advocacy Scholarship', *Policing and Society*, 9, 2, 1999.

Locke, John *Second Treatise* in *Two Treatises of Government* (Cambridge: Cambridge Univ. Press, 1988).

Thompson, Edward P. *Whigs and Hunters* (London: Penguin, 1975).

Tully, James *An Approach to Political Philosophy: Locke in Contexts* (Cambridge: Cambridge Univ. Press, 1993), esp. ch. 6.

Waddington, P. A. J. 'Swatting Police Paramilitarism: A Comment on Kraska and Paulsen', *Policing and Society*, 9, 2, 1999.

2

Community initiatives and risk

3

Risk and correctional practice

Todd R. Clear and Eric Cadora

Introduction

Risk and its artifacts may be found in just about every aspect of the correctional apparatus. The prison wall is a response to the risk that a confined person may prefer not to stay inside; the razor wire atop a cyclone fence is meant to affect the calculation of the costs of freedom for those behind the fence. The probation officer's recommendation to the court is a venture into probable futures and an assessment of their likelihood. Wherever one looks in the world of what Garland (1990) has called 'penality', the traces of risk are found.

This chapter has two aims. The first is to provide an essay on 'risk' as it concerns penology. We will define the elements of risk in penal operations and describe the domain of risk in penal life in a way that, we hope, will further specify the significance, the essentiality, of risk for penal institutions. The purpose of this first objective of the paper is to hone the contemporary critical analysis of the 'new penology' with an understanding of risk which, while accounting for the restrictions its new significance may impose on emerging penal practices, also suggests opportunities that it creates within whatever changes may be afoot in penal thought.

The second aim of this chapter is to hold up this sharpened understanding of risk against the 'community justice movement', and to examine the ways in which the inescapable reality of risk might be purposefully manifested in particular strategies of community justice. Here, we will rely on a particular version of the community justice 'ideal' (Clear and Karp 1999), and we will try to draw out from that ideal some of the risk implications.

The 'new penology'

In their influential critique of the 'managerial' ethic in correctional work, Feeley and Simon (1992) describe what they see as the recently emerging importance of formal consideration of risk in penology, and they represent it as a fundamental shift in correctional ethics. They describe a migration away from traditional concerns for offender reform and humanitarian programs – due in great part to the abandonment of external social goals of normalization through workforce integration – toward a 'warehousing' ethic, in which bodies are sorted according to formalized assessments of their risk, and their time and movement under penal authority managed according to rationalized images of 'control' and 'desert'. Their analysis has stimulated an important debate about the wisdom and value of these recent shifts in penal thought, but also is housed within a critical assessment of broader social shifts in the political economy of the body. Simon and Feeley critique the 'new penology' as humanistically unsatisfactory and politically destructive of human identity.

Their analysis makes an undeniably important contribution to our understanding of contemporary penological activity. By situating the progress of penal reform within a broader concern of generalized social control inside and outside the confines of penal institutions, they broaden and update the observations of Stanley Cohen (1985, 1988) regarding the monotonic growth of formal control in all social sectors, both in mechanisms and through ideology. By unweaving the assumptions that they propose as the foundations of new penology, they continue the tradition of looking critically at the claims of the agencies of social control to uncover 'hidden' meanings (or in this case, not so hidden meanings) to the advances of the techniques. Without disputing their insights, we want to add a few cautions and some complicating data, to the model they have provided. Their work treats risk as a strategy increasingly devoted to the control of offenders as an end in itself rather than simply as a means to achieving broader social reintegration purposes. We want to argue that risk is deeply and necessarily embedded in the penal idea in ways that reach beyond narrow interests in control. To make this case, we begin with a clarification of the phenomenon of risk in penal action.

Elements of risk in corrections

'Risk' is defined as the probability that some undesirable event will occur. Four aspects of correctional action come together to produce risk as an inescapable aspect of the penal world. They are: uncertainty, non-randomness, stakes, and hierarchy. While each is a separable element of penal risk, taken together they place risk in the center of the penal mission.

Uncertainty

It is not possible to predict the outcomes of correctional decisions with certainty. Said in another way, there is no certainty about the best ways to employ strategies of penal intervention. The vicissitudes of human behaviour and behaviour are such that there are people who are wise in these ways and people who are foolish, but there are no true experts. Long-term professionals know that their strongest impressions may eventually prove wrong. The effect of uncertainty is to enforce a powerful conservatism in decision-making. The inability to prevent erroneous outcomes to decisions is the dominant aspect of everyday life at the line level for corrections professionals. Most penal decisions flow at least in part from a calculation of potential errors and their likely consequences.

Non-randomness

Although penal uncertainty means that error cannot be prevented, it can be reduced, because error in correctional work is not random. This is the essential meaning of risk as a variable, that certain 'risk factors' are taken to indicate greater or lesser vulnerability to error and to the consequences of uncertainty. Non-randomness means that although risk cannot be overcome, paying attention to the correlates of undesirable outcomes can reduce it. In recent years, these correlates have become well known: prior record, age, and lifestyle indicators (drug use, unemployment, gang membership, etc.), among others (Andrews, *et al.*, 1990). These 'risk factors' are understandably taken into account as decisions are made under conditions of uncertainty. It is hard to imagine a correctional worker making decisions without weighing anticipated risks.

Stakes

All errors are not equal; this is an important point made some time ago by Don Gottfredson (1987). Some errors cost more than others, and different errors produce different cost profiles. Gottfredson points out that most people would feel comfortable betting $1 on a 10 per cent chance of winning $10, but far fewer would bet $100 on the 10 per cent chance of winning $1000: the odds (risks) are the same, but the stakes are different. The nature of penal error is such that conservatism about stakes inevitably runs against the offender: to keep an offender under control, who could otherwise do well, imposes a largely invisible (and extremely localized) cost in liberty, while failing to provide control over an offender whose new crime makes the mistake obvious and imposes new costs on the victims of the crime and potentially enormous costs on the credibility of the penal system. The stakes in the first type of error, called a false positive, are typically thought far less than the second type, the false negative. This existence of these stakes tends to skew the type of conservatism resulting from inevitable errors toward greater control on offenders rather than reduced control on offenders.

Hierarchy

Correctional activities occur in a volatile force-field of accountability. Those who administer correctional practices answer to political interests. These interests enforce a subservient caution to the fluctuations in events that may affect the accountability force-field. In California, a paroled recidivist murders a young girl in her bedroom; in New Jersey, a released sex offender rapes and butchers a child, and within months these impossibly irrational events are translated into dozens of new laws prohibiting release of recidivists and requiring the neighbour notification of the presence of former sex offenders, laws that affect practices in places far removed from their originating events. In a similar vein, penal innovation in one locality is soon transported elsewhere. In a (historically futile) search for a penal panacea, policy makers keep looking for new programs undertaken in other locations that seem to solve old problems in their own, and they are inclined to easily believe the claims of the program's inventors. The aphorism that 'all politics are local' seems to apply in reverse to penal policy – no penal entity can be fully insulated from events and practices occurring elsewhere.

These four aspects of correctional decisions – uncertainty, non-randomness, stakes, and hierarchy – combine to guarantee an interest in risk. As correctional dynamics, they are not new; however as penal ends they gain increasing significance under the 'new penality', a point to which we shall return later.

Risk technologies

The elements of penal risk come together to pose a specific type of vulnerability to penal leadership, which is particularly aggravated when assessing risk loses its contingent and instrumental primacy. The problem of uncertainty means that errors are inevitable. The problem of non-randomness means that commonly known correlates of errors will call observers' attention to factual bases for questioning the wisdom of the original decision, after it has failed to work out (the sharpness of hindsight is always 20:20). The combined effect of stakes and hierarchy is to provide an incentive for a cold conservatism in risk taking of particular types.

Historically, to allow this structure of risk to play itself out in conservative everyday practice was an untenable option, for two reasons. First, the image of a penal system unwilling to take any chances with offenders, no matter how small, was constrained by dominant penal practices structured around normalization through labour force regimentation and the opportunities afforded by working-class reintegration. Subsumed within these purposes and practices, the risk associated with several hundred thousand offenders being released from confinement every year without having served their entire sentences did not entail the stakes that contemporary formulations of risk engender. Secondly, line correctional employees who had direct, everyday contact with offenders found it unpalatable to do the job without ever being able to take the risks their experience told them are wise. However, as extant purposes became less available as a rationalization of risk-taking, these constraints are weakened and the previously fiscally and socially unthinkable has given way in contemporary America to the incarceration of over two million individuals at any one time.

Thus, the human workers in the penal system find themselves caught in the jaws of a vice. On the one hand, they face the certain prospect of vulnerability as a consequence of any errors that result from their everyday risky decisions. On the other hand, they are permanently in situations where their only function is to take calculated risks. Thus, they turn to their experience for protection and solution.

In the face of the impact of ubiquitous penal risk, contemporary penal policy makers use two strategies to manage their vulnerability to error: Bayesian risk models and program-process strategies of risk.

Bayesian models of risk

We are used to thinking of risk in a deterministic manner, either present or not. Bayesian approaches treat risk as continually present, to a lesser or greater degree. This model of risk fits well to the circumstances of the new penality, in which risk can be perpetually addressed as an end in itself. To assess risk then is to be always assessing the degree of risk (and the stakes of an error). Under contemporary correctional practices, the most common way to calculate risk is by a mathematical model built around its correlates. Because these correlates are now well known (Gendreau *et al*, 1996), the practice has developed to list them in a single risk assessment instrument, and 'add them up' into a scored index of risk. Typically, these indices are used to group offenders into levels of risk, and correctional processes are designed to reflect risk interests suggested by the index. It is proper to think of these approaches as 'prior experience' strategies designed to systematize the impact of proven risk indicators on risk-related decisions.

Risk indices have been subjected to considerable criticism. In our view, some of this criticism is misplaced. There is little question that index-aided risk decisions are more accurate (and less conservative) than unaided judgments (Gottfredson and Gottfredson, 1986), a fact that supports use of indices whenever risk is a consideration. In instances where risk instruments are now used, they clarify, standardize, and objectify the criteria for judgements previously made on the basis of the rater's own opinions and skills, not taking into account prior experience. These instruments do not force a risk lens onto decisions that were previously made without appeal to considerations of risk; instead they provide a standard and tested risk criterion for decision-makers to employ under conditions of uncertainty.

Program-process strategies of risk

The most common use of these risk assessment-aided decisions is to inform the offender's assignment to penal programs. This has different implications depending upon the setting for those programs. In confinement, the level of risk may determine the degree of security. In community settings, risk typically helps in establishing the level of supervision and nature of treatment interventions. Offenders are then moved from greater to lesser control (or the reverse) as their behaviour in the program warrants.

It is, perhaps, this idea that the formalized interest in risk links to the degree of control that most concerns the critics of the 'new penology'. We believe that upon closer inspection, it is apparent that the 'risk' idea does not trouble the mind as much as the 'control' idea. The ascendance of risk instruments does not necessarily raise control to a new level of importance in penality (below we will discuss this issue in more detail), rather it shifts the context within which the techniques of control are rationalized from one of the labor structure to one of a risk structure. Applying the structures of reason to the instruments of control does more to highlight the inadequacies of the aims of control than it does to question the value of reason when applied to decision problems.

*   *   *   *   *   *

The concern about the 'new penology' is not primarily a result of the emergence of risk-based correctional management systems in recent years. Risk and its management have been a central concern in the business of penality for quite a long time. What is new is a honing, a sharpening of the instruments of risk, and in the close connection between the strategies of risk assessment and the closer linking of risk assessments to regimes of control. These recent developments are perhaps troubling, but they cannot be described as 'new' in substance. Rather they are new in illustration of a broader underlying essence of penality under the democratic state, one that has been accompanied by an ever-greater reach of control.

Risk and rationality

There are good reasons why one might wish to reorganize the direction of correctional thought since the advent of democracy. But within these longstanding themes, risk-indexing tools must be seen as rationally useful devices. That is, a person may fairly object to the entire enterprise engendered by the 'new penology' in which risk and control are penal objectives rather than instruments of other penal purposes. There are plenty of problems with the risk-control model that might persuade a concerned citizen to look for an alternative. Typically, this search would end up replacing risk and control, we suppose, with a system designed simply to sanction (von Hirsch, 1985).

But this way out of the problems of risk-control is not without its own discomforts (see Clear 1988; Hudson, 1987). One would, we think, want to sanction in a way that affirms moral rules of the social order. Leaving aside the legitimacy of the social order itself, this means that one is forced to search for appropriate sanctions that morally educate. And as long as the target of the education is the morally ambivalent citizen, then the duty is to size up the capacity of this or that sanction alternative to convincingly persuade. But once one accepts that it might be nice to select a sanction that is also persuasive of the extant rule violator, then there is a need to be concerned with most of the same classification issues that arise with the problem of risk. In the end, even the opponent of risk-control will be forced to employ the most advanced risk assessment techniques available to think about risk even for purposes of moral persuasion. This is true because under conditions of uncertainty, making a penal decision aided by structure is a demonstrably superior method. Four established ways in which structured decision approaches are superior to unstructured approaches bear this out.

1 Structured assessments promise broader and often more accurate coverage of issues in assessing risk

Human decision-makers tend to consider a very limited (and often somewhat idiosyncratic) range of information in making a decision. Any risk assessment boils down to a matter of using experience to make predictions about the future. In the worst case scenario, a human decision-maker might make decisions about risk using irregular information that arose in an unusual case that has distorted the decision-maker's understanding of risk, since the case stands out as unusual in some regard or another. The use of an index ensures that certain index variables, known to be correlated with risk, will be assessed in every case; and others, generally unrelated to risk, will be given a secondary importance (Clear, 1988).

2 Structured assessments promise greater consistency in the assessment process

Many ills follow from idiosyncratic risk calculations, and the most obvious of them is inconsistency. Inconsistency is undesirable for two different reasons. First, unpredictability of offender treatment dilutes the effectiveness of penal programs. It results in inappropriate assignments to correctional programs, and research shows that poor program assignments can result in negative outcomes, not just neutral outcomes (Andrews, Bonta and Hoge, 1990). Second, unpredictability raises the possibility of injustices, as offenders' treatment becomes more closely linked to the vagaries of the decision-maker than the characteristics of the offender.

3 Structured assessments allow for statistical programming out of racial bias in ways that purely discretionary decisions cannot promise

The most troubling problem of contemporary justice processing is racial bias. When decisions are left unstructured by 'relevant' factors, the possibility exists that racial factors will influence decisions of individual decision-makers. There are statistical techniques that can cleanse risk models of racial biases (see Farrington and Tarling, 1985) and this holds the promise of reducing the effect of racial characteristics on decisions.

4 Treatments work better on higher risks, but treatment programs (without structure of risk assessments) tend to prefer lower risks

The irony and opportunity of correctional programming is that the lower the offender's risk, the less likely the treatment program will be effective (Andrews *et al.*, 1990). This structural fact fits uneasily with the problem of 'stakes': placing high risk cases in the correctional programs that maximize their chances of succeeding also maximize the chances that a high-profile failure will damage the credibility of the program. Thus the natural pressure is to select 'safe' cases for cherished correctional programs, to avoid the 'stakes' problem; but as a consequence, the programs often fail to reduce recidivism because the clientele are too 'safe' to begin with. Structured risk assessment can be used as an eligibility criterion to make program assignments more consistent with risk data.

These are four standard arguments in favor of structured risk regimes in penal practice. They point out how, in incremental ways, risk models can be layered onto current correctional decisions to improve their accuracy and predictability. The incremental nature of risk management developments is the underlying justification. It is not the intent of these practices to shift penal policy from one agenda to another, but to hone penal strategies within an already established agenda, regardless of that agenda.

Risk and the 'new penology'

To think that the advent of risk technologies has led to a soft paradigm shift in penal thought is a bit like thinking that the advent of the computer led to a paradigm shift in the banking industry. Perhaps, but not necessarily. It may be more accurate to accept that technical advances have sharpened pre-existing emphases, rather than created new ones. Once the state found it useful to invent systems for dealing with offenders – treatment systems and control systems – risk became a factor in the strategies of the systems. Since then, attention has shifted toward the best way to grasp the risk problem, and new risk approaches are innovations in that line of reasoning.

It is perhaps true that *stakes* have increased under current realities, and the costs that flow from certain types of errors provoke more severe consequences in the chain of hierarchy than they once did. The media cover crime issues with, perhaps, greater intensity than before (Beckett, 1997), and recent public politics have been decidedly one-track in the evaluations of the consequences of confinement decision errors. But that is quite a different matter than risks, which remain largely the same, though marginally affected by the growth of risk technologies.

The issue is less whether risk matters in penal practice, but how it matters. In recent penal reforms in the United States, for example, even small evidence of risk seems to generate an overwhelming response. In California and other states, any risk at all of a fourth felony crime results in a life sentence without possibility of release. This intolerance for certain levels of risk is a recent manifestation, as is the use of legislative means to eliminate certain risks (Tonry, 1997).

Risk and its strategies

We have argued above that the 'new penology' fails to distinguish the functions of risk calculation from the strategies of risk control. They are, of course, closely associated both in practice and in most peoples' conceptualization. But they are distinct ideas. Even without the external framework of labour force regimentation, risk is not an independent concern. One calculates risk for some purpose in action. Our point is that control may seem uniquely associated with risk as its only purpose in the absence of pre-existing social reintegration goals, but it is in fact only one of the purposes served by calculations of risk – in many ways, its most extreme and also most problematic. Here we want to distinguish the three main purposes to which a calculation of risks may be directed.

Risk control

This strategy attempts to exert external controls on the risk in order to prevent the recurrence of a new crime. These methods are defined by the relationship between the external agent and the target of control; the former uses penal methods to eliminate choices of the latter. Thus, risk control methods have an incapacitative aim, typically taking two forms: restriction of movement (such as incarceration or electronic monitoring) and psychotropic mechanisms, such as behaviour control drugs. Because these methods involve involuntary restrictions of offenders' choices, risk control strategies raise ethical issues regarding coercion, and they pose practical problems in the limits of control devices (see Clear, 1988; Zimring and Hawkins, 1995). Risk control strategies have as their purpose to take power over situations of risk in an offender's life such that the offender may not engage in crimes. Their primary intent is thus containment, not change; errors are almost always false positives, in which controls are applied that are unnecessary.

Risk management

The use of managerial techniques to deal with risk recognizes the uncertainty associated with risk situations. The intent is not to eliminate risk, but to manage error by marginal improvements in program assignment. Thus, higher-risk offenders receive closer monitoring or custody; lower-risk offenders receive less restriction. The recognition is that even among lower risk offenders, there will be failures, but risk management approaches recognize the costs of false positives as well as false negatives, and offender assignments are made in order to minimize the joint costs of these errors. Unlike risk control, risk management approaches accept the inevitability of error, and this is dealt with by an attempt to shift errors into more acceptable settings and toward marginally reduced levels.

Risk reduction

A final way to deal with risk is to try to reduce it. The most common way is through intervention programs that seek to change offenders' behavior so that risk wanes or disappears. Traditionally, risk reduction programs have come under the banner of 'rehabilitation'. There is a vast literature on this type of approach, and any attempt to summarize it briefly will necessarily be simplistic. For our purposes, it is sufficient to identify these techniques as having a high degree of technical uncertainty, and as employing risk in a counterintuitive way: the best applications of risk reduction come when the risks are highest, not lowest.

Based on these descriptions, we might accept that each strategy has a different attraction and raises a different set of issues. Risk control is the only strategy that makes promises to a worried consumer: it offers the chance that a risk can be completely eliminated from possibility. Neither risk management nor risk reduction makes such an offer. But as it turns out, the promise of risk control is greater than its delivery. Overprediction results in numerous false positives, and the financial costs of over-control are evident in contemporary policy. The limits of risk management and risk reduction, as strategies, are more immediately apparent. In making much less aggressive claims, they leave the strategist still vulnerable to the costs of risk errors, albeit a bit less vulnerable than under a strategy that ignores risk altogether.

In the competition among these three strategies, the weak guarantees of the latter two undermine their value and attractiveness. Risk management is a technical strategy of the system, operated by professional penal workers, while risk reduction is preferred by human service workers, toiling at the line level of the penal enterprise. Risk control, then, is embraced by more visible penal elites, especially elected officials, who feel a certain comfort in the broadness of its promises and who are more directly vulnerable to failure. Faced with a choice among the three approaches, higher level policy interests will tend to prefer control, as it is easier to grasp, leaves less to the imagination, and provides assurances of desirable outcomes. Those who have been immersed in the realities of penal effort and risk problems will tend to prefer the other two options, as they map more completely upon experience.

From the perspective of liberal critique, there seems a more straightforward assessment. Risk control invites a somewhat greater intrusion into autonomy than the other two strategies, and so it is to be de-emphasized as a first-choice option. Risk reduction also poses the familiar problems of paternalism and coercion (von Hirsch, 1985) and is therefore suspect. Perhaps, then, only management of risk is easily compatible with liberal ideas, since it is both rational and its rules are linked to endogenous criteria. It is ironic that risk management is the technique of preference, given the criticisms that have been placed on the model, mostly by those who see all risk models as challenging to liberty interests.

Risk and community justice

In this last section of the paper, we want to explore some of the ways the idea of risk might take unusual forms under the concept of community justice. We begin with a brief description of community justice.

What is community justice?

Community justice can be thought of as at once a philosophy of justice, a strategy of justice, and a series of justice programs. As a philosophy, community justice is based on its pursuit of a vision of justice recognizing that crime and the problems that result from crime are a central impediment to community quality of life. Thus the community justice approach seeks not only to respond to criminal events, but also set as a goal the improvement of quality of community life, especially for communities afflicted by high levels of crime. Strategically, the community justice approach combines three contemporary justice innovations: community policing, environmental crime prevention, and restorative justice. Programs of community justice include a varied package of methods, from crime-mapping to identify where the problem of crime is most concentrated to citizen partnerships between justice agencies and citizen groups to improve the legitimacy of justice programs and to help justice officials tailor their strategies to make them. (For a more extended description of community justice as an ideal, see Clear and Karp, 1999.)

Throughout all its elements, community justice is concerned with taking seriously the problems faced by people who live amidst high levels of crime, some of whom are themselves involved in crime. It differs from traditional criminal justice – and traditional penology – in three important ways: it is based on the neighbourhood rather than on the jurisdiction; it is problem-solving rather than adversarial; it is restorative rather than retributive. Traditional criminal justice is concerned almost exclusively with offenders, and ends this concern once the offender's punishment has been concluded; community justice extends its sights to include the problems faced by offenders, victims, and others, and seeks to overcome those problems.

One of the criticisms of community justice is that its logic applies only to low-risk offenders. Community justice advocates do not agree. In this section of the paper, we want to show how community justice might take risk into account, as it extends its reach to more serious offenders. In this discussion, we will assume a basic understanding of community-oriented policing (Stenson, 1993), environmental crime prevention (Taylor and Harrell, 1996) and restorative justice (Van Ness and Strong, 1995). My discussion of risk is meant to address community justice within these strategic ideas.

The most prominent role of risk in community justice has to do with what has been called, in another context, the 'tasks of the offender' under a community justice model (Clear and Karp, 1999). The offender's misconduct represents a moral and social offence against the community. The behaviour raises questions about the offender's willingness to live within the community according to its prescribed conduct rules and the symbolic claim that one citizen may use others in the community unfairly. Both stand as a challenge to continuing community life and place the offender at odds with the community. The criminal incident in effect suspends the offender's status in the community until a just response to the crime is achieved. This connotes three main tasks of offenders who wish to overcome the community's just concern about the offender as a member:

- The offender must take responsibility for the offense.
- The offender must take responsibility for undoing the effects of the offense on the victim and on the community.
- The offender must restore the community's confidence that he/she will, in the future, live as a law-abiding citizen.

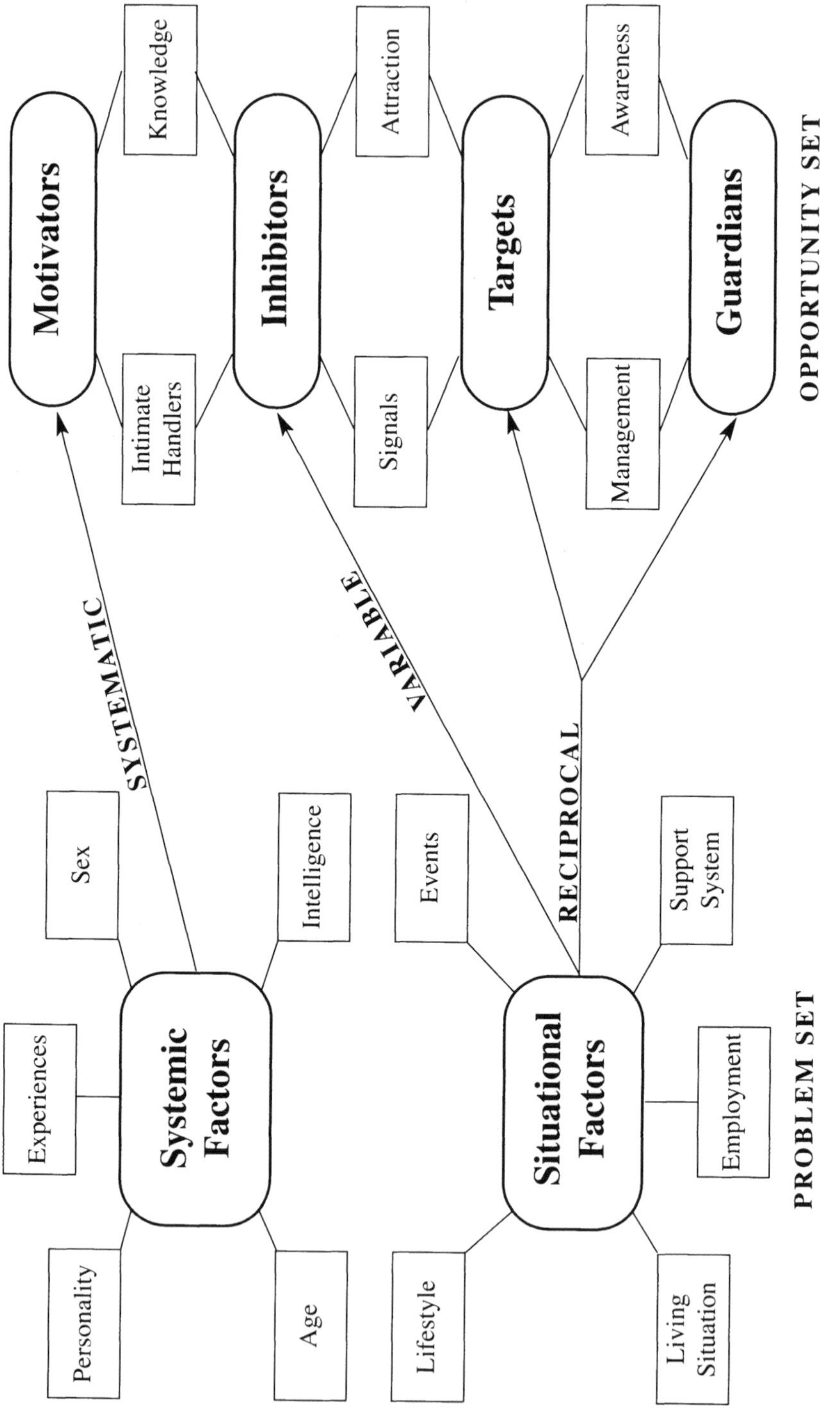

Figure 3.1

This last point relates to the offender's risk. For it is understandable that the community has lost confidence in the offender's behavior, and has little reason to think the offender may be relied upon to be a citizen of fair living. Thus, the offender's task is one of assurance through affirmative acts that give the community a reason to have confidence in the claim that crimes will not again occur. The aim in this assurance process is both symbolic and practical. It symbolizes the joint recognition of the break between citizen and community that occurs in a crime, and it symbolizes the tasks needed to re-establish connection and membership. In Braithwaite's (1989) terms, this is a process of reintegrative shaming for it addresses directly both offenders' suspended status in the community and their reintegration into the moral order and social milieu. At a practical level, the dual legal functions of sanctioning and risk management are enhanced by offenders' actions of remorse, repair, and reform.

Risk as a community justice program

Every time an offender is convicted, the community is asked to take a risk. A prison term risks the eventual return of an offender ill-equipped to comply with the law. A community penalty risks a similar outcome, only sooner. Even an extreme penalty such as capital punishment risks loss of a potential asset and damage to community values. No community can develop a risk-free crime policy. In the end, when it comes to crime, communities are forced to choose from among given risk situations.

A community justice ideal does not ask the community to embrace any risk, no matter how problematic. The concern for risk assessment and intervention puts precisely into context the community's risk paradox. If a reasonable risk management plan can be established, then the community is free to chose it. Should no reasonable risk management plan emerge, the community may be wise to postpone its risk until after a prison sentence has been served. In rare cases, even that risk may prove too extreme for a community to tolerate.

Risk-related programs in community justice express the community's desire for public safety, but within the context of an equivalent desire for restoration of the community to more just conditions. If perfect public safety is out of reach, as is almost always the case, then an imperfect community justice may be a preferable choice. A risk-free community is not attainable, but a rational approach to risk is possible. Such a system, once in place, will provide the community with more than a reasonable risk management regime, it will enable the community to become involved in deciding on its own risks, something not possible when the offender is removed and sent to prison.

Figure 3.1 displays a schematic for a community justice risk program. The model here proposes two general arenas of risk assessment, the Problem Set and the Opportunity Set. The Problem Set involves those factors that the offender brings to the day-to-day world, and which have an impact on probability of offending. The Opportunity Set is based on implications drawn from the rapidly developing field of situational crime prevention (Clarke, 1993). Including the

Opportunity Set in risk assessment and intervention planning formally incorporates the community as a partner in risk management.

Most risk assessment begins and ends with 'systematic factors' within the offender's problem-set. That is, we know that age, sex, personal competencies (intelligence, education, etc.) and personal variables (thrill-seeking desires, prior experiences as a victim, with other victims and with the justice system) all combine to predict new offending (Andrews and Bonta, 1994). These risk factors are 'historical' in nature, and generally are not subject to change.

It is less typical (though not unknown) for risk assessments to take into account 'situational' factors that may vary over time: employment, living situation, lifestyle, and support system (as well as occasional 'events' that may create or reduce risk-related stressors in life). These changeable aspects of the offender's situation have well known, broad relationships to risk, and so targeting them to reduce risk may also be an appropriate strategy – for example, helping an offender obtain good employment or providing support for coping with marital stress, or parenting a newborn child; each may alter the life course of criminality (Laub and Sampson, 1993).

The Opportunity Set includes situational components of risk, and borrows from 'routine activities theory' (Cohen and Felson, 1979), which states that crimes occur when four components correspond in space and time: the presence of a motivated offender and a suitable target is combined with the absence of an effective guardian (a person who provides surveillance or supervision in a criminogenic situation) or an intimate handler (a loved one who reinforces crime-free living). Each of these elements may be a target of an intervention program. For example, the offender's motivation level may be reduced by developing techniques for controlling temptation (anger management or relaxation methods). The presence of intimate handlers may also act on motivation levels by strengthening inhibitors. Targets may be 'hardened' in traditional ways by locks or street lights, but when targets are individual community members, they may be hardened by informing them of 'signals' of reoffending (Pithers, 1987) or providing potential guardians more access to knowledge of the offender and possible targets (Felson, 1996).

The Opportunity Set shows just how important the community is to crime prevention, even when crime prevention focuses on the offender. Moreover, it opens up a new array of potential crime prevention activities designed as risk management interventions, run by justice system officials, working with offenders and the people with whom they live.

Under the model, systematic factors such as age and personality have a reliable, patterned impact on an offender's motivation for criminality. Situational factors have a variable impact on motivation and inhibitors – as criminogenic situations occur, motivation increases or inhibitors decrease. Most importantly, situational factors have a reciprocal relationship with targets and guardians. The latter can be strengthened by the former, but the former may also be augmented by planned changes in the latter. This suggests that community member participation in crime prevention with offenders being 'recovered' to the community can be a central contribution to overall community safety.

This model highlights the range of intervention programs different communities might develop, under guidance of crime prevention specialists. There might be target hardening programs for families of offenders which improve their capacities as 'intimate handlers' and 'capable guardians'. There could be jobs programs to alter situational factors, and individual treatment programs targeting 'motivators' and 'inhibitors'. There could also be a wide range of community-based crime prevention strategies focused on 'targets' and 'guardians'.

This model also shows that under a community justice ideal, a concern for risk does not lead, automatically, to a suggestion of risk control as a strategy. To the contrary, risk concerns under community justice models lead toward risk reduction initiatives as a first choice, and then risk management strategies as a preferred approach when risk reduction is not suggested. This occurs because of the emphasis placed by community justice on restoration of offenders and victims as a consequence of the response to criminal events, and it also follows from the way community justice views the offender within a broader problem-solving context rather than a narrow public safety context.

Summary

This chapter has addressed two issues. First, it has discussed the 'new penology' paradigm, most effectively described by Feeley and Simon (1992), by drawing a distinction between risk as a penal focal concern and risk control as the object of that focal concern. Our argument has been that the emergence of risk as a systematic concern in today's penal practice reflects more upon the development of technologies (and systems) generally than the discovery of risk in particular. Second, we have argued that the concerns some critics raise about the 'new penology' apply more effectively to the problem of risk strategies – in particular, the preference for risk control over other alternative risk strategies – rather than to risk itself.

We then turned our attention to community justice as an emerging movement in penology. Here we showed how a systematic concern for risk can have a particular expression in community justice programming. Such programming need not be centrally concerned with risk control, but can give a much higher emphasis to risk reduction and risk management.

References

Andrews, Don, James Bonta, and Robert D. Hoge. 1990. 'Classification for effective rehabilitation', *Criminal Justice and Behavior*, 17(1): 19–52.

Andrews, Don, Ivan Zinger, Robert D. Hoge, James Bonta, Paul Gendreau and Francis T. Cullen. 1990. 'Does treatment work? A clinically relevant and psychologically informed meta-analysis', *Criminology*, 28: 369–404.

Andrews, Don A. and James Bonta. 1994. *The Psychology of Criminal Conduct*. Cincinnati: Anderson.

Augustus, John. 1852. *A Report of the Labors of John Augustus, for the Last Ten Years, in Aid of the Unfortunate*. Boston: Wright and Hasty, republished as John Augustus: *First Probation Officer*. 1939, New York: Probation Association.

Braithwaite, John. 1989. *Crime, Shame and Reintegration*. NY: Cambridge University Press.

Beckett, K. 1997. 'Political preoccupation with crime leads, not follows public opinion'. *Overcrowded Times*, 8 (5, Oct): 1, 8–11.

Clarke, Ronald V., ed. 1993. *Situational Crime Prevention: Successful Case Studies*. NY: Harrow and Heston.

Clear, Todd. 1988. 'Statistical prediction in corrections', *Research in Corrections*. National Institute of Corrections, Washington, D.C.

Clear, Todd R. and David R. Karp. 1999. *The Community Justice Ideal: Preventing Crime and Achieving Justice*. Chicago: Westview Press.

Cohen, Lawrence E. and Marcus Felson. 1979. 'Social change and crime rate trends: a routine activities approach', *American Sociological Review*, 44: 588–608.

Cohen, Stanley. 1988. *Against Criminology*, New Brunswick, NJ: Transaction Books.

Cohen, Stanley. 1985. *Visions of Social Control*. Cambridge, UK: Polity Press.

Farrington, David and Richard Tarling, eds. 1985. *Prediction in Criminology*. NY: State University of New York Press.

Feeley, Malcolm, and Jonathon Simon. 1992. 'The new penology: notes on the emerging strategy of corrections and its implications', *Criminology* 30(4): 449–471.

Felson, Marcus. 1987. 'Routine activities and crime prevention in the developing metropolis', *Criminology*, 25(4): 911–931.

Felson, Marcus. 1996. 'Those Who Discourage Crime', in John E. Eck and David Weisburd, eds, *Crime and Place: Crime Prevention Studies, vol. 4*. Albany, NY: Harrow and Heston, 53–66.

Foucault, Michel. 1977. *Discipline and Punish: the Birth of the Prison*. NY: Pantheon.

Gendreau, Paul, Tracey Little, and Claire Goggin. 1996. 'A meta-analysis of the predictors of adult offender recidivism: what work!' *Criminology,* 34(4): 575–608.

Gottfredson, Stephen D. and Don M. Gottfredson. 1986. 'Accuracy of Prediction Models' in Alfred Blumstein, Jacqueline Cohen, Jeffrey A. Roth and Christy Visher, eds, *Criminal Careers and 'Career Criminals'*. Washington, D.C.: National Academy Press.

Gottfredson, Don M. 1987. 'Prediction and classification in criminal justice decision-making', in Don M. Gottfredson and Michael Tonry eds, *Prediction and Classification*. Chicago: University of Chicago Press.

Hudson, Barbara. 1987. *Justice Through Punishment: a Critique of the 'Justice' Model of Corrections*. New York: St. Martins Press.

Laub, John H. and Robert J. Sampson. 1993. 'Turning points in the life course: why change matters to the study of crime', *Criminology*, 31(3): 301–325.

McCleary, Richard. 1993. *Dangerous Men: the Sociology of Parole*. Albany, NY: Harrow and Heston.

Pithers, William D. 1987. *Relapse Prevention of Sexual Aggression*. South Burlington, VT: Vermont Department of Corrections.

Stenson, Kevin. 1993. 'Community policing as a Governmental technology', *Economy and Society*. 22(3): 373–389.

Studt, Elliot. 1973. *Surveillance and Service in Parole Supervision*. Washington, DC: U.S. Government Printing Office.

Taylor, Ralph B. and Adele V. Harrell. 1996. *Physical Environment and Crime*. A Final Summary Report Presented to the National Institute of Justice. Washington, DC: U.S. Department of Justice.

Tonry, Michael. 1997. *Sentencing Matters*. New York: Oxford University Press.

Van Ness, Daniel and Karen Strong. 1995. *Real Justice: Restorative Justice Theory, Principles, and Practice*. Cincinnati: Anderson Publishing Co.

von Hirsch, Andrew. 1985. *Past and Future Crimes: Deservedness and Dangerousness in the Sentencing of Criminals*. New Brunswick, NJ Rutgers University Press.

Zimring, Franklin and Gordon Hawkins. 1995. *Incapacitation: Penal Confinement and the Restraint of Crime*. New York: Oxford University Press.

4

Rethinking crime control in advanced liberal government:
the 'third way' and the return to the local

Kevin Stenson and *Adam Edwards*

Introduction

Crime control has steadily ascended the political agendas of the advanced liberal democracies. This focus has been maintained by the centre left, 'third way' administrations that have replaced the neo-liberal administrations of the 1980s. However, in deploying varying combinations of the repertoire of crime control technologies, there is a renewed focus on the need to foster an inclusive social solidarity at local levels while not losing the support of the fearful, fiscally conservative middle classes – a core meta-dilemma of 'third way' governance. The 'regulation' and 'governmentality' schools have helped explain the constraints and enabling conditions within which crime control politics operate, yet are inadequate in explaining the role of political agency in interpreting and managing the links between meta-dilemmas and local strategic dilemmas of crime control, such as the tension between the principles of cooperation and competition.

This chapter aims to remedy these deficits by outlining a framework of concepts to enable us to investigate the uneven developments and dilemmas of the local politics of crime control, as they involve both official and unofficial political actors. This is illustrated by reference to recent research into local crime prevention partnerships in two English cities. These examples demonstrate the tensions and costs involved in trying to conceptualize and manage the development of local crime control policies in troubled areas, where there are shifting alliances and local residents may have their own visions and agendas of crime control.

Criminology and the political turn

Criminology has experienced in recent years a 'political turn'. By this we mean that a range of theorists and commentators, within criminology but also in other social sciences which have contributed to debates about crime, have highlighted *inter alia*: the increasing salience of crime control on the political agendas of the advanced, liberal democracies; the fact that academic theory and research on crime and justice issues have played central roles in the conduct of political debate over crime and the formation and implementation of policy; and that new strategies of crime prevention and reduction have provided opportunities for the development of new forms of public governance – especially at local levels – tailored to varying social contexts (for example, O'Malley, 1992; Garland, 1996; Crawford, 1998; Benyon and Edwards, 1997; Downes and Morgan, 1997; Hughes, 1998; Simon, 1998; Stenson, 1991, 1998, 1999, 2000a and b; Stenson and Watt, 1999b; Pawson and Tilley, 1997; Taylor, 1998).

Claims about the significance of criminology and other social sciences in the governmental process may seem hyperbolic from the perspective of criminologists of the liberal and hard left. They are still deeply critical of state policies. From these perspectives, academic criminology may appear, as an influence on policy, to be a weak competitor with corporate interests, the vengeful, punitive tabloid press and populist politicians keen to garner votes with 'get tough' policies and expansion of the prisons (Garland, 1996). Nevertheless, we should recognize that criminological ideas and broader social science theories, to which they are related, cover the broad political spectrum and have contributed to the discourses through which debate is conducted, problems conceptualized and solutions proposed. In this sense criminology and related social science theories and concepts can, at every spatial level, become elements in governmental *savoirs*, the intellectual instruments of, in this case, the newly emerging modes of liberal government in the broadest sense of that term (Stenson, 1991, 1998, 1999; Ekblom, 1998).

This intellectual movement is particularly important in the formation of the new political discourses of the 'third way', or as 'progressive governance' as it is now more frequently referred to by intellectuals and politicians of the centre left. Despite local differences, there are common themes linking the projects of centre left administrations in the US and across the EU and in particular, the UK and Germany, of Clinton's New Democrats, Blair's New Labour and Schroeder's *Neue Mitte*, and Jospin's revamped French Socialist party (Blair, 1998; Giddens, 1998; Rinaldi, 1999, Lloyd, 2000). In his articulation of the need for a 'third way', Giddens (1998) identifies five basic dilemmas that render the two meta-narratives of advanced liberal government, 'classical social democracy' and 'neo-liberalism', obsolete. These dilemmas establish the challenges for the renewal of social democracy:

- the impact of globalisation on the governing capacity of liberal democratic authorities;
- the rise of individualism and its threat to social cohesion;
- the failure of modern conceptions of politics, in particular the left-right dichotomy, to capture the complexity of advanced liberal polities;
- the failure of representative democratic institutions to give 'voice' to this complexity;
- and the ecological challenge to indefinite economic growth.

These dilemmas are seen as acutely present, particularly, in the challenges presented by crime and disorder. In an effort to forge syntheses of the old Keynesian political rationalities and policies of the social democratic left and the neo-liberal and neo-conservative rationalities and policies of the right, crime control and the appropriate use of its attendant bodies of professional expertise, have moved from the political margins to the centre. This is especially so as they operate through new modes of governance at local levels.

It is argued that the risks associated with crime are part of the burgeoning agenda of the grave risks, the 'bads' of civilization, that citizens expect modern state governments to manage, contain or redistribute (Ericson and Haggerty, 1997). This is so, in part, because of the acceptance by 'third way' intellectuals that the crimogenic risks, inequalities and social dislocation associated with globalization and the economic and social policies of the right are now a constant feature of the political landscape. However, it is argued that they must be managed in ways that attempt to incorporate the marginalized and disaffected populations but in ways that will retain the electoral loyalties of the tax averse, fiscally conservative, and anxious suburban middle classes. These people are increasingly removed spatially and emotionally from the lives of the poor and the alienated (Galbraith, 1992). In these conditions, the promises of the left shift from an emphasis on the need for economic redistribution and high cost public services towards a greater emphasis on the need for a moral renewal based on communitarian and Christian social principles. These would be orchestrated by the state and include the fostering of the work ethic among the young; better, more authoritative parenting; and the promotion of morally driven informal social control and care in local 'communities', buttressed by law and seedcorn funding (Hughes, 1998).

Hence, the principal meta-dilemma confronting the 'third way' is how to include the 'truly disadvantaged' minority without alienating the contented majority who constitute the political base of support for parties of the 'radical centre'. In securing this electoral coalition New Labour, New Democrats and the *Neue Mitte* of the German Social Democratic Party have all had to accept the neo-liberal economic agenda of public expenditure retrenchment and a taboo on noticeable increases in personal income taxation. The acceptance of this macro-economic framework places severe limitations on the capacity of these administrations to invest in the re-integration of those designated as socially excluded. It is in this context that universal welfare has been subordinated to highly targeted social investment policies (Downes, 1998).

This is not to claim that 'third way' politics is simply 'second way', or neo-liberal politics, in disguise. The other horn of the 'third way' dilemma is that, within a neo-liberal macro-economic framework, 'radical centre' administrations still are, and have to be, committed to the re-integration of those deemed to be socially excluded. The dislocation of these populations has become so great that they present a serious challenge to the legitimacy of advanced liberal societies. This challenge is exemplified in the increasing disenchantment of these people with the representative democratic process (Lazare, 1998) and the concomitant search for other forms of political articulation. These range from the proliferation of 'sub-political' single-issue movements (Beck, 1992) through to more sinister vigilante and armed militia groups (Johnston, 1996).

This disenchantment with the representative democratic process has driven, and been driven by, processes of socio-cultural, as well as economic and political, fragmentation. The old, simpler urban divisions of social class and black/white racial divisions, evident in the 1960s riots, are now overlaid by divisions rooted in much more complex religious/ethnic and other cultural identities – within the white as well as non-white populations. The tide of 'asylum seekers' seeking refuge from war, famine and poverty in the cities of the west has created a new urban demography, echoing the human cauldrons of Chicago and Berlin in the 1920s (Castles and Miller, 1993). These groups add to the liberal mosaic by spawning multiple sites of formal and informal governance as people struggle to survive in the cities. In liberal societies these centrifugal forces have always been met by centripetal strategies to create the ground rules underpinning liberal diversity. These usually operate through nation-building and the struggle to renew sovereign law (Stenson, 1998, 2000b).

This dilemma both clarifies the meaning behind the experiments in holistic, but highly targeted, government and suggests other related dilemmas that are specific to the alignment of crime control strategies. Hence, the turn to the local via the rise of community/restorative justice, problem-solving policing and community safety partnerships, can be understood as part of this pervasive struggle to revitalize liberal democracy and its sovereign authority.

The shift of focus away from the provision of universal welfare benefits and services towards the targeted provision of resources and services to those 'high risk' neighbourhoods and populations is moderated to a degree by the centre left's revival, within a framework of targeting, of holistic, social, policy agendas, the goals of which are the fostering of social solidarity and the growth of trust and social capital in problematic populations and areas (Stenson and Watt, 1999). The plethora of internationally transferable models of community development place special significance on prevention and reduction of crime as preconditions for local economic and social development (Hope, 1996; Kelling and Coles, 1996).

However, it should be recognized that though these policy tendencies have been intensified under centre-left administrations, the green shoots of these tendencies were already apparent in the later periods of Conservative administration. In Britain, for example, the introduction of the state's City Challenge in 1991 and the Single Regeneration Budget in 1994, highlighted the need for integrated partnerships in developing holistic, targeted, urban development strategies. This created a managerialist performance culture among participants rooted in the logic of competitive bidding, partnership and localism (Stenson and Watt, 1999a: 191; Stenson, 2000b; see McLaughlin and Murji, Chapter 6 in this volume). Related to these initiatives, the Morgan Report into community safety in 1991, while not given state endorsement, stimulated Labour local authorities to experiment with such holistic initiatives with a specific social crime prevention brief. These provided pilots for the development of New Labour policies after 1997 (Edwards and Benyon, 2000).

While current developments are complex and uneven, it is possible to discern some generic, emerging emphases in the 'third way' politics of crime control. It should be remembered that these policies and practices represent tendencies at work against the backcloth of the everyday operations of the complex field of institutions of policing, crime prevention and criminal justice. In the liberal democracies these differentiated institutions of crime control are usually described very optimistically as (by implication functionally interdependent) 'systems' of policing and criminal justice (Davies *et al*, 1995), and their mandated tasks involve the management of those who may be likely to, or who have, transgressed the criminal codes. Yet, given the awesome density, complexity of, and multiple functions performed by, these institutions in most modern societies, they resist crude, caricatured descriptions and it would be misleading to imagine that particular governments can easily effect change in a simple mechanistic, top down fashion.

Technologies of crime control

Remembering this caveat, it is, nevertheless, possible to distinguish three focal clusters of technologies of crime control that have crystallized in recent years (Stenson, 2000a). These include: punitive sovereignty, that attempt to regain control of public places from perceivably disorderly groups (Grimshaw and Jefferson, 1987; Kelling and Coles, 1996; see the chapters by Simon and Hudson in this volume); target hardening, linked with actuarial justice, that try to reduce the opportunities for crime and apply the logic of risk assessment and management to crime and criminals (Clarke, 1997; Feeley and Simon, 1994); and community security technologies that try to link crime control to efforts to defend affluent neighbourhoods and regenerate decaying and disorderly localities. The latter interventions have become linked with other 'local' and 'community'-oriented initiatives, including the internationally fashionable emphasis on problem solving, community policing and community/restorative justice (Hope, 1996; Hughes, 1998; Brazemore, 1998; Clear, 1998 and see Clear and Cadora Chapter 3 in this volume). They are also linked with the rehabilitation and reformulation of liberal, therapeutic interventions that crystallized during the high period of the welfare states. This is manifested, for example, in the 'harm reduction' approaches to the management of illegal drug use, aiming to work with offenders within the 'community' rather than resorting to wholesale incarceration (O'Malley, 1999 and Chapter 5 in this volume).

However, they operate, often in considerable tension, in a variety of hybrid forms at local levels. Moreover, despite the consensualist rhetoric about combating social exclusion that usually accompanies the legitimation of these policies and practices, managing the tensions between these elements is likely to pose enormous challenges for those mandated to manage the local tensions and dilemmas of 'third way' crime control politics. In the UK, for example, the Crime and Disorder Act 1998 and complementary, holistic, 'joined-up' policy initiatives, crystallizing in local community safety strategies to prevent and control crime, embody a wide range of initiatives from support to parents at risk, to zero tolerance policing, that aim to cleanse public spaces of those perceived to be a threat to order and civility (Goldblatt and Lewis, 1998).

Mindful of the way that our theories can become drawn into service as governmental *savoirs* (intellectual tools of governance), let us return to an older role for theory: how it may help us grasp these developments in policies of crime control. However, we would argue that a normative, and therefore governmental, underpinning to theory is inescapable. In our case, the overall value that underpins our analysis is a commitment to renew liberal democracy in ways that expose the obstacles to, and enhance the prospects of, inclusion of the poor and the alienated into government at every level. Within the broader field of theories that attempt to make sense of new modes of governance we draw particularly on parallel theoretical narratives in the Marxist regulation school of political economy and the Foucaultian governmentality school (Barry *et al,* 1996; Burrows and Loader, 1994; Jessop, 1993; Lea, 1997; O'Malley, 1992; Rose 1996; Stenson, 1998, 1999, 2000a).

Regulation

Amongst the regulation school's main objects of concern are the interrelationships between state forms at the centre of new social modes of economic regulation and the evolution of regimes of capitalist accumulation. The trajectory of change in contemporary political economy has been conceived in terms of an ideal-typical contrast between the crisis of Keynesian welfare states in 'Atlantic Fordist' accumulation regimes and their replacement by 'Schumpeterian workfare states' in emerging 'post-Fordist' economies (Jessop, 1993). The distinctive policy objectives of Keynesian welfare states were the promotion of full employment in relatively closed national, 'autocentric', economies through demand-side management and the provision of redistributive welfare rights enabling new forms of mass and collective consumption. Conversely, the objectives of Schumpterian workfare states are to strengthen the structural competitiveness of national economies, through the promotion of (organizational, product, labour process and market) innovation in relatively open, 'globalized', economies, and to subordinate social policy to the needs of flexible labour markets and/or the constraints of international competition (Jessop, 1993).

Commentary on the implications of this trajectory of change for crime control suggest that 'post-Fordist' economies and their 'Schumpeterian' regulation produce severe social-economic polarization between and within the regions and localities of advanced capitalist nation states as multi-skilled professionals are increasingly segregated from peripheral, casualized, low- or no-income communities. In turn this polarization drives the growth of 'informal' economies amongst the 'peripheral', especially the illicit drugs trade, and the reconfiguration of crime control away from welfare and reintegration towards the punitive and actuarial goals of incapacitation, risk assessment and the militarization of public space (Davis, 1990; Lea, 1997).

Governmentality

The second approach focuses on the *political*. Its main objects of concern are the shifting forms of rule traversing older boundaries between statutory, voluntary and commercial institutions in liberal polities and the new ways in which populations are rendered thinkable, measurable, differentiated and sorted into hierarchies for the purposes of government (Rose, 1996, 2000; Stenson 1998, 2000a). In this perspective, domains like the economy, the state, the social and the sphere of policing and criminal justice are seen as politically constituted and differentiated. With the decline of social modes of government characteristic of the welfare state, which aimed to promote social solidarity and the broadest sharing of life's risks, and the rise of targeted, partnership-based strategies of crime control and community regeneration, the boundaries between crime control and older policy fields defined as 'social policy' and 'economic policy' are blurring. Moreover, it should be remembered that a central, connecting theme in liberal modes of government, sadly neglected within much governmentality work, is the struggle for sovereign control by agencies of the law and state over geographical territory and perceivably disorderly populations at local levels (Stenson, 1998, 1999).

Local politics of crime control: fields of struggle

However, despite the respective virtues of these schools, there is a danger of general abstract theories congealing into enclosed, self-referential systems of ideas. While we wish to contribute to the theorizing of new modes of liberal governance, we also wish to develop, in a grounded way, concepts at meso- and micro-levels of analysis (Bourdieu, 1990). These should enable us, in empirical research, to focus on the unevenness and spatial variation in patterns of government in local, economic, cultural and social contexts. The two theoretical schools in question present general, abstract narratives of change which, while insightful about the new political and economic constraints and possibilities for social practice, are less helpful in providing tools to investigate the oral discourses and situated social practice by human agents. Nor do they recognise sufficiently the important role of emotion in experiences of crime and victimization, and the formation and implementation of policies (Garland, 1996, 1997; Peck and Tickell, 1995; Stenson and Watt, 1999a and b).

Local political struggles over policies and practices of crime control involve a very complex and varying combination of elements that cannot be uncovered by the perusal of policy documents alone. General political strategies are filtered through the prism of, for example, local sensibilities of place (see Sparks, Chapter

10 in this volume; Loader *et al*, 1998; Watt and Stenson, 1998). These embody shared, often taken for granted, conceptions of local human and spatial identity and cognitive maps of safe and dangerous people and places, of fear, danger and risk. These create forms of 'habitus', cultural and emotional repertoires and dispositions for cognition and action (Bourdieu, 1984, 1990). As we shall see this applies to both lay citizens and professional networks. However, while sensibilities can be largely habitual, it is important to recognize the scope for local political actors to employ instrumental, goal-oriented sensibilities in the local fields in which people struggle for recognition, position, material advantage and legitimate authority. These fields are often arenas that bring together a range of individuals and groups distinguished, in part, in terms of their 'habitus'.

Hence we wish to avoid according theoretical privilege to approaches that highlight, on the one hand, either emotion and habituated action, or on the other hand an exaggerated emphasis on conscious, rational decision-making processes. Where there are fierce struggles over local, perceived social problems like prostitution, youth crime, incivilities and so on, we need tools to focus on the means by which political actors, both formal and informal, play out these struggles. These involve, firstly, attempts to interest others in adopting preferred ways to conceptualize problems and the appropriate ways to respond to them. Secondly, they involve means through which support and coalitions are enrolled and formed around these modes of problematization. Thirdly, they involve exploring the unfolding dynamics of political association and the interaction between informal and more formal, legally sanctioned agents of governance. In these terms, the challenge of explaining contemporary crime control strategies involves an account of the uneven way in which they are configured in different localities by coalitions of actors. In short, what is needed is a theory of the local politics of crime control (Callon, 1986; Latour, 1986).

In employing this repertoire of concepts, in particular, we focus on how we may understand the strategic dilemmas confronting both formally accredited and informal political actors engaged in governance through crime control at local levels and the ways that varying, hybrid combinations of strategies and technologies of crime control are deployed (Stenson and Watt, 1999a and b; Edwards and Benyon, 2000).

Crime control and the strategic dilemmas of the 'third way' of 'progressive governance'

The claims by Giddens, outlined in the introduction, about the dilemmas faced by advanced liberal government, provide an arbitrarily asserted checklist of issues rather than an analytical statement of the dilemmas that shape policy change. Conversely, Jessop (1997: n18) defines a strategic dilemma as a situation in which 'agents are faced with choices such that any action undermines key conditions of their existence and/or their capacities to realize some overall interest'. From this starting-point it is possible to clarify the challenges confronting 'third way' liberal government and, crucially, the interpretation of problems of government by certain political actors.

This conception of a strategic dilemma provides a method of linking explanations of how the struggle to reintegrate the truly disadvantaged within the structural context of a neo-liberal economic strategy is played out in the diverse 'fields' of the differentiated liberal democratic polity. This differentiation sets the limits to universal sovereign authority, enables local actors to interpret the constraints and opportunities of the structured context they inhabit, and thereby generate the uneven development of liberal government.

Strategic dilemmas and the local polity

The idea of strategic dilemmas is useful in that it clarifies the 'field' of forces confronting local actors engaged in crime control. It is possible to view the 'meta-dilemma' of reintegrating the socially excluded through neo-liberal economic strategies as a core dynamic in the 'social space' of the 'third way'. Central to the constitution of this social space is the attempt to forge governing strategies that transcend the perceived failings of bureaucracy and the market and produce a new synthesis capable of adapting to the perceived imperatives of structural competitiveness in open economies. It is this objective which accounts for the ubiquitous emphasis on public–private partnerships now found in all areas, or 'fields', of public policy in advanced liberal democracies, an instance of what Jessop calls 'heterarchic governance' (1997).

Within heterarchic governance it is possible to identify second-order dilemmas such as that of cooperation versus competition (Jessop, 1997). We concentrate on this specific dilemma given its particular importance in the current politics of local crime control. A core attribute of public-private partnerships for crime prevention and 'community safety' is trust amongst the network of actors involved. Whilst, however, networks provide an opportunity for exchange relationships based on trust, they simultaneously create opportunities for short-term, self-interested, competitive behaviour. Partners are always, therefore, confronted with the dilemma of maintaining inter-organizational trust in the face of incentives for self-interested competition. A comparison of case studies into the practice of crime control partnerships in England confirms the diverse interpretations placed upon this dilemma and, therefore, in effect, the centrality of political agency (Coleman and Sim, 1998; Crawford, 1998; Edwards and Benyon, 2000; Hughes, 1997).

Political agency in local crime control

The incentives to competition have been particularly prevalent within local crime prevention and community safety partnerships in England given the dependence on grant-aid and the application of agency-specific performance criteria to the statutory partners. It would be possible to examine this agency in terms of the 'rational choices' made by these partnerships and the actors that constituted them.[1] Notwithstanding the conscious, instrumental behaviour of political actors, however, the reduction of political agency to 'rational choice' precludes an understanding of the habitual, culturally-shaped, emotion and sub-conscious elements of this agency. The importance of local *political culture* and the habitus of actors in local partnerships for crime prevention was revealed in research undertaken by one of the authors comparing the political action undertaken by partnerships on outer estates in Nottingham and Leicester.[2] Despite variations and dissenting voices, in each setting it is possible to discern dominant, taken for granted tendencies in the emotional and cognitive dispositions operating in networks of politicians, local government officers and those routinely involved in partner agencies.

In both cities there has been a long-standing majority Labour Party control of the local authority, both share a common economic base in the textile industry, and both are subject to the same regional governing structures.[3] The principal difference in the political climate of the two cities was, however, over their orientation towards the local communities targeted by the partnerships. The culture of political authorities in Nottingham emphasized the active participation of local citizens in deciding the priorities and objectives of policy, such as crime prevention, and tailoring interventions to the varied needs of local communities.[4] To this extent, the Nottingham case reflected the progressive community development and empowerment role envisaged for crime prevention partnerships by Hughes (1998). Our focus here, however, is on the culture of political authorities in Leicester, in which charismatic leadership and relations of patronage were salient. In this setting, local citizens' interests were subordinated to those of big business and the focus was on the role of the local authority in creating a business-friendly environment and levering in external investment. This orientation toward external, business interests had a critical impact on the interpretation placed on the dilemma between cooperation and competition by the statutory partners in Leicester's crime control partnerships. This impact is best demonstrated by reference to the central struggles over the acquisition and use of grant-aid and in terms of the negotiation of controversial 'acid-tests', of partnership such as the issues of youth crime prevention and street prostitution.

Grant-aid and the logic of competition

The proliferation of local crime prevention partnerships, especially in the wake of the Morgan Report into Safer Communities (Home Office, 1991), was premised on the competition for national government grant-aid, in particular the Single Regeneration Budget. The absence, during this period, of a statutory basis for local crime prevention partnerships rendered local actors dependent on non-local sources of funding. A principal form of competition has, therefore, been between the priorities of the communities targeted for the investment of scarce resources and those of the non-local funding agencies. In particular, a key priority of non-local funding agencies has been for quantifiable, output-oriented, indicators of performance. The paradox of this 'new managerialist' (Clarke and Newman, 1997) priority is, however, the extent to which it undermines the other core priority of using partnerships to re-connect those excluded communities selected for targeted intervention.

Field of outer-estate partnership

This paradox was exemplified in the Leicester outer-estate partnership. A youth worker involved in the Leicester estate partnership identified this problem as a key reason for the difficulties encountered by the partnership in addressing the priorities of local residents. At the outset of the partnership, the City Council commissioned a survey of local people to ascertain the principal crime problems and suggestions about what should be done. One of the most favoured suggestions, confirmed at a number of public meetings, was to establish a motor project to work with youths who were involved in car crime and 'joyriding' them round the estate. In the final draft of the partnership's 'action plan' however, this proposal was excluded on the basis that its 'crime-reductive' outputs were insufficiently clear. As a result the elaborate exercise of consulting with local residents on the estate, as a means of enrolling them as active participants and supporters of the partnership's work, was fatally discredited. This aroused the expression of considerable local negative opinion and cynicism about the dashed expectations raised by authorities. The outcome of this was to further exclude the local citizenry.

The logic of competition for limited resources inscribed in the ethos of grant-aid also created conflict amongst distinct coalitions within the partnership. Whereas youth workers wanted to prioritize investment in 'outreach' work with young people on the estate, representatives of the resident's association and the housing officers called for a focus on security measures to reduce burglary. These represented alternative visions of the nature of local problems and their amelioration. The former approach involved those community security crime control technologies that included attempts to draw young people, deemed to be at risk, into programmes of self and community improvement. These aimed to enhance the scope for creative self-governance and the channelling of potentially destructive emotions and energies into more socially acceptable avenues. This is a local manifestation of one of the key motifs of 'third way', moral governmental ambitions for young people.

Yet, ultimately, burglary reduction, and its associated risk management technologies of target-hardening, were prioritized as they were perceived to be more amenable to output measurement. This perspective was based on a bleak acceptance that there was more potential in containment, dealing with the effects of local crime, than with trying to attack its possible causes. Crucially, however, in both these instances of competition it was the role of the local authority leaders of the partnership which determined the choice of priorities, and this in turn was a feature of their orientation toward the interests of non-local agencies. It was not simply a function of the workings of a deeper structural governmental logic, or diktat from a remote state ministry.

Acid tests of partnership

A local manifestation of 'third-way' targeting is competition amongst different neighbourhood partnerships within a district. This is, arguably, the most virulent challenge to the reproduction of partnerships as a governing technique. There is a clear incentive for statutory, voluntary and private organizations with an interest in a particular neighbourhood to amplify the presentation of problems of crime and disorder to secure scarce resources. This leads to the erosion of trust amongst neighbourhood-specific representatives asked to cooperate at the district-wide level.

Preliminary findings from ongoing research into the conduct of the local crime and disorder strategies legislated for in the Crime and Disorder Act 1998,[5] suggest that the new statutory duty for the formulation and implementation of these strategies at the district level has exacerbated the erosion of trust. According to the Morgan Report, the provision of a statutory duty would remove tendencies toward internecine competition within and between local crime prevention partnerships, as it would reduce dependence on competition for non-local grant aid. However, without new resources for this statutory duty, competition intensified within the fields of interaction created by the new governmental regime. Specifically, this operated amongst district partnerships, for the limited funds provided by the eclectic pots of resources made available by non-local programmes,[6] and struggles emerged between neighbourhood partnerships falling within the same district crime and disorder strategies. Those neighbourhoods deselected as targets for these strategies lost out doubly: by not receiving inward investment and by losing resources redirected from the mainstream budgets of the statutory agencies into the selected neighbourhoods as a means of ensuring the statutory duty is met.

In the case of the district-wide Leicester partnership, the local authority co-ordinator of the crime and disorder 'action teams' fostered vigorous competition amongst the district partnership's action teams for project funding. This was also replicated at the sub-neighbourhood level. So tight was the focus of targeting in crime and disorder partnerships that the selected 'high-risk' areas were defined at the level of enumeration units, that is, sub-ward level (in terms of local authority jurisdiction) and sub-beat level (in terms of the constabulary's administrative units).

Struggle over prostitution

In one of the action team areas this produced a situation in which residents falling outside of the remit protested about the lack of support for managing their perceived problems of crime and disorder, and the potential for the displacement of problems from the selected areas into their part of the neighbourhood. One issue in particular demonstrates the divisive effect of this targeting. The area concerned has, for many years, been the focus of street prostitution which has routinely been displaced from one part of the neighbourhood to another after police crackdowns. This poor area had a complex and volatile demographic mix, including poor white households, gentrifying white incomers, Afro-Caribbeans and Bengali and Pakistani Muslims. These groups had had few opportunities to forge democratic dialogue over local issues and the potential for conflict was considerable. Furthermore, in the past, under the cloak of British traditions of constabulary independence, the police maintained an emotional distance and had avoided direct, official dialogue with local fora. This was perhaps understandable given that local meetings and demonstrations about these issues could be cauldrons of powerfully expressed emotions. Such meetings in poor and volatile neighbourhoods can be bruising, stressful encounters for police and local authority managers (Stenson and Watt, 1999b).

However, the introduction of new local action teams for crime prevention and reduction created a new field with officially accredited links to the democratic polity. These created arenas in which struggles over how to conceptualize issues, express shared emotions and form new alliances and coalitions between groups with different interests and forms of 'habitus', were able to crystallize in new ways. New coalitions of resident groups, spearheaded by Muslim groups in alliance with a representative of sections of the gentrifying newcomers, petitioned the action team to prioritize, in effect, the deployment of what we have characterized as tough, punitive sovereign technologies. The goal of these techniques was to cleanse the streets of prostitutes, pimps and customers and drug dealers. In particular, the group coalitions demanded the use of the Anti-Social Behaviour Orders provided by the UK Crime and Disorder Act 1998 against the deviant 'others' in their midst.

In the struggle to define issues in terms of public order, the moral agenda of Muslims to protect their children and womenfolk from what they saw as the pollution of vice found common cause with middle-class and other white residents concerned about the dangers of criminal attack and the detritus of used condoms and dirty needles associated with the sex trade. These pressures competed strongly with other ways of problematizing the area, favoured by police managers and welfare professionals. These included, for example, outreach work with street gangs, educative, therapeutic interventions with prostitutes and the need to avoid displacement effects. These more liberal versions of community security technologies aimed to avoid the social stigmatization and exclusion of 'deviants' favoured by embryonic anti-sex trade alliances (Young, 1999). This 'official' liberal/welfare approach created an angry reaction by those demanding a punitive response, some of whom threatened to withhold their council taxes in protest against the failure to deliver an adequate service of security.

However, it would be naïve to view the favouring of 'inclusive', community security technologies by the police simply as expressions of a liberal-progressive political rationality. More deeply, this community security strategy could be seen as operating in hybrid relation with a broader actuarial risk management strategy in the city of long provenance. It had long been convenient to contain the sex trade and related illegal economies in such poor neighbourhoods. To deliver the New Labour promise contained in the Crime and Disorder Act by reclaiming sovereign control over such poor areas from criminal networks would risk destabilizing illegal markets and displacing the problem to surrounding middle-class, white areas with very effective political representation. The political costs to the police and other authorities in developing that strategy would be potentially enormous.

Conclusion

Notwithstanding the need to develop further a conception of political agency, the essential point of these examples of 'heterarchic governance' in action remains. The idea of strategic dilemmas within the framework of this developing local governance theory, enables the conduct of concrete research and analysis into the nuances of the local politics of crime control. At the same time this facilitates the connection of this analysis back to macro-theoretical theses on the changing structural context or social space of advanced liberal government. In so doing it enables the anticipation of the effects which this restructured context could have on the stability and cohesion of advanced liberal democracies. The logic of competition and targeting, however innovative, clearly tends toward the institutionalization of parochial, internecine, interests. These are likely to be exacerbated by the shift, in 'third way' governmentality, away from the universal provision of welfare and enforcement of law toward a highly specific neighbourhood targeting of interventions. It is possible that as this competitive process unfolds, enmity will increase both between different neighbourhoods and groups within them and the governing authorities.

In such a scenario, authorities, committed to the reassertion of sovereign authority in 'anti-social', excluded neighbourhoods may have greater recourse to punitive sovereign and target-hardening crime control technologies. And it is important to recognise that these pressures to enact sovereign technologies of rule do not always come directly from the central or local state. In the complex, volatile mosaic of the modern city, our examples indicate that there are sites of governance beyond the state. The sophisticated, media-driven flow of political communication ensures that versions of official governmental *savoirs*, including elements of criminological theory like the underpinnings of zero-tolerance crime control, can be taken up and incorporated in local, oral discourses and agendas of governance. The populist flavour of 'third way' rhetoric about crime control enhances the likelihood of this and despite the best of intentions, this process may further fragment an already unstable and differentiated polity.

Notes

1   For an example of the application of rational choice theory to the study of public-private partnerships, see Dowding *et al* (1995) and John and Cole (1997).

2   This project, entitled 'Local Strategies for Crime Prevention: Co-ordination and Accountability', formed part of the Economic and Social Research Council's Local Governance Programme. Adam Edwards acknowledges the support of the ESRC for its completion (reference number: L311253035).
3   Of particular importance for our purposes is the role of the Government Office of the East Midlands and the East Midlands Regional Development Agency which manage the Single Regeneration Budget. The SRB has been a principal source of grant-aid for local crime prevention and community safety partnerships.
4   A significant difference in the approach to crime control adopted by the Nottingham partnership was its focus on crime control as one, not necessarily primary, element in the regeneration of the outer-estates. In Leicester, the partnership was defined in terms of crime control. Economic and social policy interventions featured only insofar as they were seen to reduce crime and disorder.
5   This project, entitled 'The Strategic Dilemmas of Crime and Disorder Partnerships' is an ethnography of the local action teams in the Leicester Crime and Disorder Partnership undertaken by Adam Edwards.
6   For example the Single Regeneration Budget, New Deal for Communities, Crime Reduction Programme, Sure Start, Estates Renewal Programme, etc (see Audit Commission, 1999: 12).

References and further reading

Audit Commission (1999) *Safety in Numbers: promoting community safety*. London: Audit Commission.
Bailleau, F. (1998) 'A crisis of youth or of juridical response?', in V. Ruggiero, N. South and I. Taylor (eds) *The New European Criminology: crime and social order in Europe*. London: Routledge.
Barry, A. *et al* (eds.) (1996) *Foucault and Political Reason*. London: UCL Press.
Beck, U. (1992) *Risk Society: toward a new modernity*. London: Sage.
Benyon, J. and Edwards, A. (1997) 'Crime and Public Order', in P. Dunleavy *et al* (eds) *Developments in British Politics 5*. London: Macmillan.
Benyon, J. and Edwards, A. (1999) 'Community governance of crime control', in G. Stoker (ed.) *The New Management of British Local Governance*. London: Macmillan.
Blair, T. (1998) *The Third Way, new politics for the new century*. Fabian Pamphlet 588. London: Fabian Society.
Bourdieu, P. (1984) *Distinction: a social critique of the judgement of taste*. Cambridge, MA: Harvard University Press.
Bourdieu, P. (1990) *The Logic of Practice*. Cambridge: Cambridge University Press.
Bowling, B. (1998) *Violent Racism, Victimisation, Policing and Social context*. Oxford: Clarendon Press.
Brantingham, P.J. and Brantingham, P.L. (1981) *Environmental Criminology*. Beverly Hills, CA: Sage.
Brazemore (1998) 'Assessing the citizen role in community sanctioning: restorative and community justice dimensions'. Paper delivered to the Conference of the American Society of Criminology, Washington DC, November 11–14.
Bright, J. (1998) 'Preventing youth crime', *Criminal Justice Matters, 33:* 15–17.
Bureau of Justice Assistance (1997) *Revitalizing Communities: innovative state and local programmes*. Washington, DC: US Department of Justice.

Burns, D. *et al* (1994) *The Politics of Decentralisation: revitalising local democracy*. London: Macmillan.

Burrows, R. and Loader, I. (eds) (1994) *Towards a Post-Fordist Welfare State*. London: Routledge.

Callon, M. (1986) 'Some elements of a sociology of translation: domestication of the scallops and the fishermen of St Brieuc Bay', in J. Law (ed.) *Power, Action and Belief.* London: Routledge and Kegan Paul.

Castles, S. and Miller, M. (1993) *The Age of Migration: international population movements in the modern world*. London: Macmillan.

Clarke, J. and Newman, J. (1997) *The Managerial State*. London: Sage.

Clarke, R. (1997) (ed.) *Situational Crime Prevention: successful case studies (second edition)* . Albany, NY: Harrow and Heston Publishers.

Clear, T. (1998) 'Community justice and public safety'. Paper delivered to the conference of the American Society of Criminology, Washington DC, November 11–14.

Cohen, L.E. and Felson, M. (1979) 'Social change and crime rate trends: a routine activity approach', *American Sociological Review*, 44: 588–608.

Cohen, S. (1985) *Visions of Social Control*. Cambridge: Polity.

Coleman, R. and Sim, J. (1998) 'From the dockyards to the Disney store: surveillance, risk and security in Liverpool City Centre', *International Review of Law, Computers and Technology*, 12(1): 27–45.

Cornish, and Clarke, R. (1986) (eds.) *The Reasoning Criminal: rational choice perspectives on offending*. New York: Springer-Verlag.

Crawford, A. (1998) *Crime Prevention and Community Safety: politics, policies and practices*. London: Longman.

Cruikshank, B. (1998) 'Moral disentitlement: personal autonomy and political reproduction, in S. Hanninen (ed.) *Displacement of Social Policies*. Jyvaskyla: SoPhi Publications.

Davis, M. (1992) *City of Quartz*. London: Vintage.

Dear, M. and Wolch J. (1987) *Landscapes of Despair: from deinstitutionalisation to homelessness*. Cambridge: Polity.

Dench, (1986) *Minorities in the Open Society: prisoners of ambivalence*. London: Routledge and Kegan Paul.

Dowding, K. *et al* (1995) *Rational Choice and Community Power*. Oxford: Blackwell.

Edwards, A. and Benyon, J. (2000) 'Community Governance, Crime and Local Diversity', in *Crime Prevention and Community Society: an International journal*, 2/3: 35–54.

Ekblom, P. (1998) *Community Safety and the Reduction and Prevention of Crime: a conceptual framework for training and the development of a professional discipline*. London: Home Office.

Ericson, R. and Heggarty, K.D. (1997) *Policing the Risk Society*. Oxford: Clarendon Press.

Etzioni, A. (1995) *The Spirit of Community*. London: Fontana.

European Forum for Urban Security (1994) *Security and Democracy*. Paris: European Forum for Urban Security.

Feely, M. and Simon, J. (1994) 'Actuarial Justice: the emerging new criminal law', in D. Nelken (ed.) *The Futures of Criminology*. London: Sage.

Felson, M. (1998) *Crime and Everyday Life (second edition)*. Thousand Oaks, CA: Pine Forge.

Ferrell J. (1996) *Crimes of Style, Urban Graffiti and the Politics of Criminality*. Boston: Northeastern University Press.

Foucault, M. (1977) *Discipline and Punish*. Harmondsworth: Penguin.

Foucault, M. (1991/1979) 'Governmentality', in G. Burchell, C. Gordon and P. Miller (eds)

The Foucault Effect: studies in governmentality. Hemel Hempstead: Harvester Wheatsheaf.

Galbraith, J. K. (1992) *The Culture of Contentment*. London: Sinclair-Stevenson.

Garland, D. (1996) 'The limits of the sovereign state: strategies of crime control in contemporary society', *The British Journal of Criminology*, 36(4): 445–71.

Garland, D. (1997) '"Governmentality" and the problem of crime: Foucault, criminology, sociology', *Theoretical Criminology*, 1(2): 173–214.

Giddens, A. (1979) *Central Problems in Social Theory*. London: Macmillan.

Giddens, A. (1990) *The Consequences of Modernity*. Cambridge: Polity.

Giddens, A. (1998) *The Third Way: the renewal of social democracy*. Cambridge: Polity.

Goldblatt, D. and Lewis, P. (ed.) (1998) *Reducing Offending*. London: Home Office RSD.

Gordon, C. (1991) 'Governmental rationality: an introduction', in G. Burchell, C. Gordon and P. Miller (eds) *The Foucault Effect: studies in governmentality*. Hemel Hempstead: Harvester Wheatsheaf.

Grimshaw, R. and Jefferson, T. (1987) *Interpreting Policework*. London: Allen and Unwin.

Home Office. (1991) *Safer Communities: the local delivery of crime prevention through the partnership approach,* The Morgan Report. London: Home Office.

Hope, T. (1996) 'Community Crime Prevention', in M. Tonry and D. Farrington (eds) *Building a Safer Society, strategic approaches to crime prevention.*

Hughes, G. (1997) 'Policing Late Modernity: changing strategies of crime management in contemporary Britain', in N. Jewson and S. MacGregor (eds) *Transforming Cities*. London: Routledge.

Hughes, G. (1998) *Understanding Crime Prevention*. Buckingham: Open University Press.

Jessop, B. (1993) 'Towards a Schumpeterian Workfare State? Preliminary remarks on post-Fordist political economy', *Studies in Political Economy*, 40: 7–39.

Jessop, B. (1995) 'The regulation approach and governance theory: alternative perspectives on economic and political change?', *Economy and Society*, 24(3): 307–333.

Jessop, B. (1997) 'The governance of complexity and the complexity of governance: preliminary remarks on some problems and limits of economic guidance', in A. Amin and J. Hausner (eds) *Beyond Market and Hierarchy*. Aldershot: Edward Elgar.

John, P. and Cole, A. (1997) 'Economic policy-making networks in Leeds and Lille: emerging regimes or public-sector alliances?', in D. Marsh (ed) *Policy Networks: theory and method*. Buckingham: Open University Press.

Johnston, L. (1996) 'What is Vigilantism?', *British Journal of Criminology*, 36(2): 220–36.

Kelling, G. and Coles, C. (1996) *Fixing Broken Windows*. New York: The Free Press.

Kooiman, J. (1993) 'Governance and Governability: using complexity, dynamics and diversity' in J. Kooiman (ed.) *Modern Governance: new government–society Interactions*, London: Sage.

Lacey, N. and Zedner, L. (1995) 'Discourse of community in criminal justice', *Journal of Law and Society*, 22(3): 301–325.

Latour, B. (1986) 'The Powers of Association', in J. Law (ed.) *Power, Action and Belief*. London: Routledge and Kegan Paul.

Lazare, D. (1998) 'America the Undemocratic', *New Left Review*, 232: 3–40.

Lea, J. (1997) 'Post-Fordism and Criminality', in N. Jewson and S. MacGregor (eds.) *Transforming Cities: contested governance and new spatial divisions*. London: Routledge.

Lloyd, J. (2000) 'The Left discovers Adam Smith', *The New Statesman*, 12 June.

Loader, I., Girling, E. and Sparks, R. (1998) 'Narratives of Decline: youth, dis/order and community in an English "Middletown"', *The British Journal of Criminology*, 38(3): 388–403.

McLaughlin, E. and Murji, K. (1995) 'The End of Public Policing? Police reform and the "New Managerialism"', in L. Noakes, M. Levi and M. Maguire (eds) *Contemporary Issues in Criminology*. Cardiff: University of Wales Press.

Mawby, R. (1990) *Comparative Policing Issues*. London: Unwin Hyman.

Morgan, R. and Newburn, T. (1997) *The Future of Policing*. Oxford: Clarendon Press.

Newman, O. (1972) *Defensible Space: crime prevention through urban design*. New York: Macmillan.

Offe, C. (1996) *Modernity and the State: East, West*. Cambridge: Polity.

O'Malley, P. (1992) 'Risk, Power and Crime Prevention', *Economy and Society*, 21(3): 252 –75.

O'Malley, P. (1999) 'Consuming Risks: harm minimisation and the government of drug users', in R. Smandych (ed). *Governable Places: readings in governmentality and crime control*. Aldershot: Dartmouth.

Osborne, D. and Gaebler, T. (1993) *Reinventing Government: how the entrepreneurial spirit is transforming the public sector*. Massachusetts: Addison-Wesley.

Pawson, R. and Tilley, N. (1997) *Realistic Evaluation*. London: Sage.

Peck, J. and Tickell, A. (1995) 'The social regulation of uneven development: "regulatory deficit", England's south-east and the collapse of Thatcherism', *Environment and Planning A*, 27: 15–40.

Reiner, R. (1985) *The Politics of the Police*. Brighton: Harvester Wheatsheaf.

Rhodes, R.A.W. (1997) *Understanding Governance*. Buckingham: Open University Press.

Rinaldi, A. (1999) 'No Turks, please, we're German'. *The New Statesman*, 1 January: 23–24.

Rose, N. (1989) *Governing the Soul, the shaping of the private self*. London: Routledge.

Rose, N. (1996) 'The Death of the Social? Refiguring the territory of government, *Economy and Society*, 22(2): 283–299.

Rose, N. 2000. 'Government and Control', *British Journal of Criminology*, 40(2): 321–339.

Simon, J. (1996) 'Criminology and the Recidivist', in D. Shichor and D.K. Sechrest (eds) *Three Strikes and You're Out, vengeance as public policy*. Thousand Oaks: Sage.

Simon, J. (1998) 'Managing the Monstrous. Sex Offenders and the New Penology', *Psychology, Public Policy and Law*. Vol. 4(1): 1–16.

Skolnick, J. and Bayley, D. (1988) *Community Policing: issues and practices around the world*. Washington: National Institute of Justice.

Stenson, K. (1991) 'Making Sense of Crime Control' in K. Stenson and D. Cowell (eds) *The Politics of Crime Control*. London: Sage.

Stenson, K. (1993) 'Community policing as a governmental technology', *Economy and Society*, Vol 22(3): 373–389.

Stenson, K. (1996) 'Communal Security as Government – the British experience, in W. Hammerschick, I. Karazman-Morawetz, and W. Stangl (eds) *Jahrbuch Für Rechts und Kriminalsoziologie*. Baden-Baden: Nomos.

Stenson, K. (1998) 'Beyond Histories of the Present', *Economy and Society*. 29(4): 333–352.

Stenson, K. (1999) 'Crime Control, Governmentality and Sovereignty', in R. Smandych (ed.) *Governable Places: readings in governmentality and crime control*. Aldershot: Dartmouth.

Stenson, K (2000a) 'Crime Control, Social Policy and Liberalism', in Lewis, G., Gerwitz, S., and Clarke, J. (eds) *Rethinking Social Policy*. London: Sage

Stenson, K (2000b) 'Someday Our Prince Will Come: zero-tolerance policing and liberal government', in T. Hope and R. Sparks (eds) *Crime, Risk and Insecurity*. London: Routledge.

Stenson, K. and Watt, (1999a) 'Governmentality and "the Death of the Social'? A discourse analysis of local government texts in south-east England', *Urban Studies*, 36(1): 189–201.

Stenson, K. and Watt, P. (1999b) 'Crime, risk and governance in a southern English village', in G. Dingwall and S. Moody (eds) *Crime and Conflict in the Countryside*. Cardiff: University of Wales Press.

van Swaaningen, R. (1998) *Critical Criminology: visions from Europe*. London: Sage.

Taylor, I. (1998) 'Crime, market liberalism and the European idea', in V. Ruggiero, N. South and I. Taylor (eds) *The New European Criminology, crime and social order in Europe*. London: Routledge.

Watt, P. and Stenson, K. (1998) 'The Street: "It's a Bit Dodgy Around There": safety, danger, ethnicity and young people's use of public space', in T. Skelton and G. Valentine (eds) *Cool Places, Geographies of Youth Cultures*. London: Routledge.

Weatheritt, M. (1993) 'Measuring Police Performance: accounting or accountability?', in R. Reiner and S. Spencer (eds) *Accountable Policing: Effectiveness, Empowerment and Equity*. London: Institute of Public Policy Research.

Wilson, D. *et al* (1994) *Local Government in the United Kingdom*. London: Macmillan.

Wilson, W. J. (1987) *The Truly Disadvantaged*. Chicago: Chicago University Press.

Young, J. (1999) *The Exclusive Society*. London: Sage.

3

Policing and the risk society

5

Risk, crime and prudentialism revisited

Pat O'Malley

Introduction

In 1990 I wrote a paper eventually published under the title 'Risk, Power and Crime Prevention' (O'Malley, 1992). It mapped out a model of risk-based regimes of government as the product of two related changes that had occurred since the 1970s: the erosion of the welfare state's 'social actuarialism' (epitomized in the model of social insurance); and its displacement by an individually-based risk management or 'prudentialism'. The paper suggested that risk itself was not a new category in government, but appeared to be novel because of the radical change in its configuration from social to individualized forms. It further suggested that we could not understand this shift unless we paid close attention to its nexus with the ascendancy of neo-liberalism. Using the example of crime prevention, it proposed certain elective affinities between themes in neo-liberal rationalities and risk-linked trends in crime control policy and practice:

- Particularly in the field of administrative criminology, predictive, risk-oriented rational choice models are displacing socially oriented and explanatory criminology. These are consistent with neo-liberalism's distaste for social causation and models of social justice, and with its emphasis on the individual responsibility of offenders;
- In their turn, these elements are highly compatible with the promotion of tariff-based 'truth in sentencing' models of punishment and deterrence over more indeterminate and rehabilitative 'welfare sanctions';
- Neo-liberal agendas of individual responsibility and 'activity' foster devolution of crime prevention to the citizenry and promote risk-based models for governing crime in the community;
- Rationalities of cost effectiveness and protecting the consumer reinforce these themes to promote risk-based, preventative interventions.

Revisiting this thesis ten years on, it seems substantially to have been supported by subsequent developments (see, e.g., Hughes,1998). Still more recent developments such as 'sexual offender orders' and 'anti-social behaviour orders' introduced by the English Crime and Disorder Act 1998 (Piper, 1999) and related provisions under 'Megan's Laws' in the USA (Simon, 1998) suggest that the regime of individual responsibility linked with risk-based and punitive interventions shows few signs of losing its momentum.

Nevertheless, like many such models, the thesis is probably overstated. It largely ignores the development of other agendas in crime and punishment and their possible impact – perhaps most importantly the diverse array of restorative, re-integrative, disciplinary and purely punitive innovations that have assumed a high profile of late (Garland, 1996; O'Malley 1999a; and see chapters by Simon, Hudson, and Stenson and Edwards in this volume). Few of these have risk as a central focus, and some are linked to agendas that valorize a notion of the social, albeit not always one that can be referred to as 'the welfare-social' (Stenson and Watt 1999; Pratt, 1998). As well, the thesis may represent neo-liberalism as too coherent and unchallenged, leaving little space for political intervention, for recognition of resistance, or for understanding the hybridity that characterizes policies in practice (Hannah-Moffat, 1999; Stenson, 1999).

In this chapter I wish to examine the extent to which diverse agendas of 'the social' remain contested issues in political or governmental contention, and to suggest how these in their turn may affect the way we think of risk in contemporary governance of crime. In the process I wish to stress that the nature and politics of risk and the social are not fixed, nor is the march of neo-liberalism inexorable (see McLaughlin and Murji, Chapter 6, this volume). They remain unstable, unfinished, multivalent and always available to change. Such considerations are raised here, in part, to encourage a movement of critical analysis away from the sense of political pessimism and inevitability that sometimes dogs the risk literature and work on neo-liberalism (O'Malley *et al.* 1997; O'Malley, 1998). In the first part of this chapter I wish to examine the nature and impact of conservative agendas of the social that are built into the 'New Right' alliance through which neo-liberalism has achieved and attempts to sustain its ascendancy. While distinct from the notion of the 'welfare social', the 'conservative social' can create certain tensions with individualism, especially in the market forms preferred by neo-liberals. In later sections, I will explore other tensions in the 'translation' of welfare-social practices and arrangements into the tools of neo-liberal governance. Further, I want to suggest that at least some of the innovations that we ascribe to neo-liberalism are not evidence of its successful imperialism, but perhaps signal defensive responses against such tensions and the failures of government that might arise from them. In sum, these sorts of considerations warn against imagining neo-liberalism as a finished project, or one that is being fully realized in every governmental innovation that seems to bear its mark.

The 'conservative social': risk and exclusion

Most of the early neo-liberal regimes (notably Thatcher and Reagan) emerged in the context of alliances between neo-liberals and conservatives, in formations known as the 'New Right'. While these overlapped on such common ground as anti-welfarism and advocacy of markets, there have also been key areas and issues where they do not align so neatly – creating tensions within the alliance. Many of these tensions arise around the value and importance to conservatism of a common and overarching morality, and an organic notion of the social that is quite distinct from the welfare social that has been the focus of much recent analysis (see generally, Hayes 1994; Scruton 1984; Hoover and Plant, 1989; Thorne, 1990; Berman, 1994). Three closely interlinked matters are of particular relevance:

1. Tensions about the 'death of the social'

Doubtlessly, conservatives helped to bring about the major erosion of welfare rationalities that Rose (1996b) refers to as the 'death of the social'. Yet for conservatives, the social represents a source of obligations and duties rather than a source of claims – and Thatcher's own comments on there being 'no such thing as society' on closer examination reveal allegiance to a much more traditional concept of the social than the welfare-social category invented at the end of the nineteenth century (Thatcher, 1993). Properly 'social' order to such conservatives is not about entrepreneurial individualism alone, but equally is about obedience to a shared and superordinate morality, and to the organic social cohesion to which this corresponds. In this sense, rather than the 'death' of the social, it may be that the past few years have witnessed the ascendancy of one organic conception of the social (a source of obligation and authority) over another (a source of rights and welfare).

2. Tensions about the primacy of the market, and the focus on consumer led lifestyle

While the market may appear as the testing-ground of the fit, and may be valued both by conservatives and neo-liberals as a field of freedom and individual effort, for conservatives it is not to be regarded as a universal technique for governance. Rather, there are grave reservations about the ethos of consumption-led markets (the sovereign consumer) where this leads to threats to social cohesion and morality. Rose's (1990) depiction of a world in which the consumer 'assembles a lifestyle' from commodities, creates particular tensions with conservative concerns about a decline in moral authority, and associated excesses of hedonism, irrationality and rampant individualism (e.g., Bell, 1976).

3. Tensions focused on a minimal state linked with internationalist or global economies versus an interventionist state with strong powers and intense national responsibilities

While the neo-liberal motto has been 'markets where possible and states where necessary', the perceived erosion of traditional unities such as the national interest, God, the family and the rule of law has been the source of politics that reflect a rather different perception of the activity of states. The state is not merely the necessary means of governance that should give ground where the global economy (or lesser entities such as the EC) requires, but also is a source of respect and power associated with potent nationalist symbols and moral agendas. Associated with this, the state retains an obligation to interfere in any area of life, including the market and the family, in order to ensure the nation's interest, morality and cohesion (e.g., Thorne, 1990).

Of course, in practice it is not always easy to pull apart conservative and neo-liberal strands in particular instances. There is very substantial agreement and identity on many issues, and there are many shades between the two poles. Nevertheless the nature of this alliance between neo-liberalism and the conservatives helps explain what David Garland (1996) regards as evidence of the 'limits of the sovereign state' – a volatile and contradictory politics of crime that has characterized penal policy for over a decade (O'Malley, 1999a). This politics appears as a struggle between two extremes. On the one hand a policy that regards crime as normal, performed by rational choice actors 'like ourselves'. This is to be dealt with primarily in civil society, by 'partnerships in crime control', situational crime prevention, restrained classical penality and so on. It is precisely this vision that corresponds to the kinds of risk-based approaches to crime prevention that are mapped out above as symptomatic of neo-liberal risk government. On the other hand there is a conservative response that emphasizes the duty of the state to act strongly in a sovereign capacity to uphold the rule of law, to intervene purposefully and to punish and exclude transgressors (see chapters by Stenson, and Stenson and Edwards in this volume). It is a response aligned with a criminology of the Other, in its extreme forms focused on what Jonathan Simon (1998) has referred to as 'managing the monstrous'. This sense of an unstable political alliance between neo-liberalism and conservatism may apply to our understanding of how government through risk may be limited and/or shaped by the impact of conservative agendas of the social. I will briefly examine two examples.

Illicit drug control

With respect to the governance of illicit drugs, almost the quintessential neo-liberal parallel to the model of situational crime prevention is government through Harm Minimisation. While this term covers some diversity of governmental techniques, its primary characteristic – which it shares with situational crime prevention – is an emphasis on liberal utilitarianism: the minimum harm to the maximum number. In most harm minimization regimes, we can discern the following characteristics which can be aligned with this sense of neo-liberal government of individualized risk (O'Malley, 1999b):

- A 'rational choice' model of the user who is provided with information in order to make 'informed choices' about risk minimization in drug consumption, in which process the state takes up the role of public education on drug risks;

- Pragmatic emphasis on minimizing risk. In pursuit of this, law enforcement often becomes subordinate and issues of the rule of law sidelined. Instructions to police to avoid policing in the vicinity of needle exchanges, or even requiring police to assist users in finding such facilities – even where drug consumption is specifically prohibited by law – provide clear instances;
- An 'amoral' image of the drug user as a 'normal' consumer, for example, by stressing that legitimate drugs cause more harm than the illicit drugs, or that stigmatization of users increases risk;
- Promotion of programmes such as methadone maintenance that are concerned primarily with restoring the individual to the status of an economically functioning, low-risk consumer (low crime risks, low health risks, etc.) rather than with eliminating drug dependence *per se*;
- An emphasis that, as a result of this strategy, the users take responsibility for the government of their actions and for their consequences.

Clearly such programmes are risk-focused, with an emphasis on a radical market-like model of individuals as consumers, and with the role of government being to 'empower' such individuals in the process of making informed choices. Yet while some federal and state regimes in Australia, Canada and New Zealand, for example, have pursued such programmes in varying degrees it would be absurd to regard harm minimization as necessarily spreading with the rise of neo-liberalism. In particular, state and federal governments in the USA are almost universally and virulently opposed to harm minimization (Broadhead, 1991). The war on drugs reflects precisely opposite features – characteristically conservative features – to those exhibited by our example of neo-liberal governance through risk. Perhaps primary here is the categorical refusal to accept illicit drug use as a problem of 'harm' and its minimization, a refusal driven by a vigorous identification of drug consumption with immorality, and as willed participation in crime. This is linked more or less directly with a focus on illicit drug use as threatening such core values as the family, religion, rationality, sobriety, independence, respect for law and authority and so on. These are not regarded by conservatives as optional 'lifestyle choices', but as crucial features of American identity and propriety. Such moral elements, in turn, are integrated with the identification of core sources of drug-related problems as based outside the national and communal boundaries – South American and other Third World drug-producing nations, Hispanic drug runners, Black traffickers. This is readily linked to a criminology of the Other and the location of crime as a national threat to be met with punitive sanctions and social exclusion. Where appropriate – as in the 'Border War Against Drugs' – this is to be dealt with by military strategies, material and personnel, and orchestrated via metaphors of warfare (Wardlaw, 1990). The sovereign and highly punitive, deterrent and retributive criminal justice responses dovetail almost seamlessly with this warfare imagery.

Here, neo-liberal governance through harm minimization is rejected as a strategic model, precisely because of the 'amorality' and 'tolerance' projected by this particular form of risk-based response. However, this is not to suggest that risk-based techniques be eschewed. The war on drugs has been a major stimulus for research and development in this respect – for example in profiling drug traffickers, or in identifying drug users through random drug testing (O'Malley and Mugford, 1992). Conservatism is not categorically opposed to risk, but shapes and deploys it in characteristic ways reflecting its own assumptions about the social and 'society'. Rather than risk being linked with models of informed choice and public health, and with techniques such as information brochures, needle exchanges and bleach sachets, by and large it is given shape and direction as a weapon to be wielded by the police and military in the nationalist war on drugs (Wardlaw 1994, Broadhead 1991).

Excluding the underclass

The conservative project has focused not only on the war on drugs, but also on the 'war on crime', leading to the identification and exclusion of an 'underclass' – primarily, and predictably, African and Hispanic Americans. More recently this discourse of the 'underclass' has spread to Britain and beyond (Hughes, 1998; see Hudson, Chapter 8 in this volume). Although genetic and other 'positivist' accounts impinge on the racial politics of risk, the response primarily is to regard the underclass as the 'new dangerous classes' (Simon, 1995). This imagery is significant, in part because in contrast to most neo-liberal governance, conflict, race and class are valorized. The resulting criminology of the Other consigns such outsiders not to punishment *per se*, but to incapacitating exclusion, often linked with mandatory actuarial sentencing (Feeley and Simon, 1994). But contemporary judicial discourses of exclusionary sentencing and punishment pay equal attention not just to risk but also to the unfitness of these subjects to be 'in society'. It is in many respects not simply a strategy of incapacitation, but a reversion to traditional visions of the social as unified, consensual and authoritative, and to traditional sovereign state strategies for reinforcing them. This is not to suggest that analysts such as Feeley and Simon mistakenly have identified exclusionary responses as risk-based strategies. It is more that they have focused on risk characteristics and have eclipsed the equally salient conservative agenda of the social with which it is melded. Much the same point has been raised recently by Jonathan Simon himself, with respect to Megan's Laws – laws requiring that relevant communities be informed of the residence of former sex offenders:

> The development of modern institutions, particularly the prison, was aimed at displacing popular emotions from the centre of punishment by extending the control of state-based professionals. From a spectacle of solidarity between state and the people against their common enemies, punishment became a vehicle for inculcating habits of order suitable to a democratic society. Megan's law is a shift away from this process of modernization. Starting with its name, and with the central role given to local prosecutors in applying the risk classification, Megan's law advertises itself as a new hybrid of public and private vengeance. (Simon 1998: 464)

In such ways risk has been shaped and channelled by conservative agendas of the social. It would be possible to extend such analyses considerably – for it may be argued that it is conservatism that primarily is identified with the return of strict discipline, 'boot camps' and probation, the humiliation of chain gangs, the return of the death penalty and a host of other punitive responses that reflect moral agendas as values in their own right – whatever the risk-based implications.

Yet if all this suggests that risk is a politically contested space in which divergent agendas of the social are still salient, it projects a rather grim image in which there is still little space for a 'progressive' politics. Elsewhere, there may be more promising signs. But in order to look for these, it is necessary first to locate the ways in which welfare-social knowledges and practices were not universally marginalised by neo-liberals but selectively reconstructed to form a more individually focused governance of rehabilitation and therapeutics.

Neo-liberalism: containing and reconstructing the welfare-social

A significant blind-spot in earlier accounts of the transition to neo-liberal risk governance was the overemphasis on understanding the welfare state as constituted by 'social actuarialism' – in the form of social insurance, social engineering and the social wage, etc. (e.g. O'Malley, 1992). However, this identifies only one aspect of welfare government. Other key characteristics were associated with the triumph of positivism and of its deployment in the government of individuals. As Pratt (1998) and others (Garland, 1981; O'Malley, 2000), point out, the early intellectuals of the welfare state succeeded in disaggregating the dangerous classes into dangerous and pathological individuals. Such individuals became the target of the disciplinary social and human sciences, most particularly criminology, sociology, psychiatry and psychology. Yet, this achievement was nowhere complete. As David Garland (1981) has stressed with respect to the emergence of the welfare sanction, positivist science had to concede considerable ground to traditionalists on the point of individual responsibility for crime. The resultant sanction was an unstable hybrid, as the criminal became the subject of a scientific and therapeutic criminology, and at the same time remained subject to a moral discourse of free will, guilt and punishment. In view of arguments to be made shortly concerning the hybridity of neo-liberal and welfare sanctions, it is vital to note that in criminal justice, punitive regimes and practices remained influential throughout the welfare era.

Despite this compromise, and the corresponding struggles, the incoming New Right regarded the welfare sanction, and the associated human sciences, as having abolished punishment and individual responsibility:

> We had the prisons crowded with counsellors, social workers, teachers and various representatives from a multitude of organisations, all intent on bringing a sudden and irreversible change in those who were considered to be unfortunate, disadvantaged, inadequate and who were in need of care, guidance and understanding. They would baulk at the 'just deserts' model of punishment and have us adopt a 'rehabilitative' model ... 'Wrong' is the cry of the substantial

majority of the community. 'Wrong' is the cry of the elected representatives of the community.
(Micheal Yabsley, NSW Corrective Services Minister, quoted by Brown, 1992)

For conservatives, perhaps even more than neo-liberals, there had to be a turn toward punishment and just deserts. Yet the therapeutic interventions of the social sciences did not dissolve with the 'death of the social'. Rather the response of neo-liberalism to the apparatus and knowledges of the welfare-social state has been to reformulate them in the service of a neo-liberal agenda (Dean, 1995). This has occurred through two principal processes or techniques, each of which, however, may create governmental instabilities related to the welfare-social.

First is the subjection of welfare practitioners of the arcane and disputatious human sciences to the 'transparent' calculative regimes of accounting and management (Rose, 1996a). This rendered the disputing disciplines and professions governable and accountable in terms of market-like efficiency – especially cost benefit analyses and related forms of evaluation. Such techniques of accountability were not likely to support wide-ranging and long-term social interventions of the sort favoured by social sciences – especially sociology – under the welfare state. (O'Malley, 1992). In quite a large measure this has remained the case. However what this did permit was the continued operation and development of other kinds of disciplinary intervention that had been characteristic of welfarism. For example, both psychiatry and developmental psychology, which had been key disciplinary players in the welfare forms of social work and clinical interventions, continued to thrive. It is even possible that some – for example developmental psychology – have expanded into spaces left by retreating programmes focused on broader sociological and discredited social justice agendas. In short, what appears to have occurred was not the erasure of the human sciences, but a selection among them that favoured those that could be positively evaluated in terms of short-range quantitative technologies. In terms of sustaining the neo-liberal project then, the 'firewall' of evaluation plays a key role.

The second of the containing and reconstructive techniques has been subordination of the welfare-social disciplines to the task of creating enterprising individuals and active subjects. As Dean (1995) has suggested, in this way much of the apparatus of the welfare state was transformed into new forms. In the field of unemployment, for example, the model of the labour exchange and unemployment entitlements was replaced by a contractual arrangement in which the unemployed became 'job-seekers', earning their income in exchange for learning and practising skills in marketing themselves. In the criminal justice system, Garland (1996) and Morgan (1999) have pointed to developments in which prisoners and others in custody are governed by regimes that render them 'enterprising prisoners', that 'require the active participation of the offender, are skills oriented and employment focused and so on' (Morgan, 1999: 111). Such changes have led at least one commentator to believe that, in the wake of Audit Commission approval of rehabilitation programs, it is not the 'death of the social' that we are now witnessing, but the 'death of deterrence' (Maguire,

1995:25, quoted by Hughes, 1998: 54). In all probability the latter obituary is as misleading as the former. Nevertheless, by sustaining or reintroducing elements of rehabilitative and therapeutic agendas, this strategy for reconstructing the welfare-social also creates potential instabilities or slippage in neo-liberal governance.

Failures in transformation?

While these illustrate key techniques for reconstructing the 'welfare social' into neo-liberal practices, as noted in each case the process of transformation is vulnerable – for example where those charged with the implementation of policy turn it into something unintended by the planners. If the transition to neo-liberal risk models is thought of in such relational terms, then instead of a gradual and rather automatic process whereby neo-liberalism 'spreads', there is a more labile image in which government must be constantly vigilant against the breakdown or subversion of these techniques. We would do well, in other words, to focus on Hunt and Wickham's (1994) argument that government is a congenitally failing enterprise, and to examine it more systematically in this light.

To pursue this in more detail, let us take the example of developmental psychology. The characteristic approaches of this discipline in the era of social welfare were modelled primarily in terms of pathologies requiring authoritative expert intervention that took over responsibility for the problem. (O'Malley and Palmer, 1996). In current formulations, however, governmental emphasis is on the danger of such interventions producing powerlessness, apathy and passivity in interactions with welfare agency personnel. Instead, the emphasis is to be on 'accessibility', 'assistance', 'help', 'support' and 'empowering'. Thus, with respect to the 'crime risk factor' of abuse, it is stressed that 'the professional focus on the medical model popularized in the 60s' has changed. Now, 'the notion of community and neighbourhood services to *assist* vulnerable families with child rearing in order to diminish abuse is gathering momentum ... The thrust of our work has been maximizing the empowerment of families.' (Tolley and Tregeagle, 1998: 6–8). Despite these rhetorical shifts, the 'empowering' practices of this born-again discipline bear a very strong family resemblance to the interventions of the welfare era – involving 'family support, early intervention, and home visiting programs' (NCP, 1999a: 17). Likewise, developmental psychology's list of crime-risk factors – 'family isolation', 'inadequate parenting', 'single parents', 'attachment difficulties', 'low self-esteem', 'poor social skills', 'poor cognitive skills' and so on, is seemingly identical with the lists of causes of crime with which it worked under the welfare state. The preventative and rehabilitative agendas of the former era are thus reintroduced, ironically, among much fanfare welcoming them as a 'new' approach to crime prevention (e.g. Homel, 1998).

In addition, much developmental crime prevention of late has begun explicitly to identify as risk factors the kinds of 'social conditions' identified under welfare programs, or social justice and social criminologies. Consider the following:

> Children experience different levels and combinations of risk. Social and
> economic disadvantage, however, bring a host of associated risk factors for
> children and families. Conditions of poverty contribute to poor health and
> nutrition and increased levels of family stress. Children born into poverty are also
> at greater risk of experiencing discrimination and victimization … While there is
> much that children· and families can accomplish by working together, additional
> financial resources and supports from governments and communities are
> necessary to reduce poverty and create environments that promote safety, gender
> equality and freedom from discrimination. (National Crime Prevention of Canada,
> 1997: 10)

The report goes on to recommend that a comprehensive crime prevention
strategy provides 'educational, social and health services', and urges that it 'is
essential that this strategy address child poverty' (1997: 11) Perhaps this example
is unusual in that it specifically discounts self-help and community governance, but
the general tenor of its argument is not at all uncommon. Thus, the Australian
National Crime Prevention (1999b: 13) lists 'socio-economic disadvantage',
'population density and housing conditions', 'lack of support services' and 'social
or cultural discrimination' among its crime-related 'cultural and community
factors'. The agenda, although situated within a risk discourse gives expression
to the welfare-social rationalities, and in so doing begins to hint at social
justice and certainly at the kinds of socially – rather than individually –
ameliorative programmes that were associated with the welfare state (Stenson and
Watt, 1999).

Emphasis on cost-benefit analysis operates as a 'firewall' here. Almost without
exception the programmes reviewed, whether from public or private sector bodies,
proposed strict evaluation, and as noted above this is a technique that strongly
restricts the scope of socially-oriented projects. But even this, too, begins to break
down over time. Proposals begin to emerge that advocate the formation of long-
term and large-scale programmes addressing social conditions, by proposing that
each step can be evaluated as part of a long-term chain. Others emphasize that as
developmental programmes deal with children from birth (or before), then the term
of evaluation has to cover a minimum period of ten years, and frequently longer.
(e.g. Everingham, 1998; Rand Corporation, 1998). Driven by the risk discourses
and agendas generated by the born-again welfare disciplines, long-term, large-
scale and long-range projects reappear. Equally important is the fact that
evaluations – which are by no means always either cost benefit nor even
quantitative in practice – will often be carried out by bearers of the same welfare
knowledges. They may, in any case, support the development of rehabilitative
strategies of preventing recidivism, and thus further open the door for the return of
socially oriented rehabilitative or redistributive programs.

In sum, the terrain is a good deal less stable than would be supposed by a strict
reading of the model of prudentialism. Each of the developments can be thought of
as a point of struggle; they are points of possible translation in which seemingly
discarded elements are brought back by persistent disciplines and agendas to

re-socialize risk. Nevertheless, things do not stand still in the face of 'adverse' change. In this respect, consider the emergence of the 'protective factor'.

The invention of the 'protective factor'

Alongside the transformation of causes of crime into risk factors has come the invention of (positive) 'protective factors' – indeed, the category has become almost the partner of risk in recent work in the crime prevention field (e.g., Farrington, 1994; Crime Prevention Council of Canada, 1997; Homel, 1998; National Crime Prevention, 1999a).

If risk factors 'refer to the conditions that predict adverse outcomes', protective factors 'reduce the risk of harm' (National Crime Prevention of Canada, 1997: 4). Thus a current Australian analysis suggests that:

> The significance of protective factors is underlined by the fact that predictions from risk factors are statements of probability. Although factors such as early troublesome behaviour are highly predictive of later offending, more that 50 per cent of at risk individuals may not progress to such outcomes. It is especially important then to identify protective factors and mechanisms that are likely to inhibit the development of antisocial behaviour. Preventative action cannot be solely directed toward risk, especially when risk factors are difficult to modify'. (NCP, 1999a: 11–120)

The last sentence of this passage is something of a give-away. In the Australian example noted earlier, socio-economic disadvantage appears as a risk factor while protective factors emerge as 'access to support services', 'community networking', 'participation in church or other community group' and so on. The emergence of the 'protective factor', in such instances, appears to be part of a process of risk sequencing that defines precise strategies for governing risk in ways that do not address the prime risk factor itself. Where this is the case, and it very often is, two kinds of explanation are given.

The first, seen already above, points out that certain risk factors are recognized, but that they are not amenable to minimization, at least in practical and foreseeable terms. The second argument suggests that such risk factors somehow are inadequate predictors and may thus be, in some fashion, discounted as targets for intervention. Thus with respect to abuse prevention,

> Poverty alone does not differentiate high- from low-risk families, as within poor neighbourhoods, families differ in their incidence of abuse...[However] a high degree of social support is a prime protective factor. Such factors as interaction between families and social institutions, the presence of parents in the home on the return of children from school, cohesiveness within the family and community pride and involvement, differentiate high and low abuse neighbourhoods. (Tolley and Tregeagle, 1998: 3)

Such arguments are familiar New Right responses to claims that 'poverty causes crime' (Thatcher, 1993). The appearance of such claims in this context indicates that even where welfare disciplines recover, they may generate further responses aimed at reshaping them. This is not to suggest that the purveyors of 'protective factors' are in league with the New Right, although of course some are. Rather it is to suggest that disciplines are politically polyvalent and pragmatic: some developmental psychologists may (as with the Canadian example) demand attention to poverty factors, others (as with the Australian example) may not.

Conclusion

To assume that government is a constantly failing process – as with the career of the welfare social itself – is an important but limited observation. One of the matters that needs to be addressed is the response to failure, for it is comparatively rarely the case that this is met with by abandoning governance. Rather, as Miller and Rose (1990) argue, failure – or the prospect of failure – is a key factor that requires governments to be constantly inventive. In its turn, this reminds us that government is always an unfinished project and therefore is a project without a known final form. Consequently there are strong reasons for critical analysis not to assume that all developments are in some way the steps on the road to the realization of neo-liberalism. Many features of government may be the direct or indirect products of resistance in its many guises, rather than the flawless working through of its political rationalities (e.g., Weir 1996; O'Malley *et al.*, 1997).

If politics is thus thought of as struggles over, as well as mentalities of government, then we need to consider the unstable and defensive nature of many of neo-liberalism's projects, categories and innovations. The 'protective factor' case is merely illustrative of the appropriation or design of new categories that may have come about, in part at least, in order to govern its own unruly policies, programmes and practitioners. Let me take a concluding example. Recently, Hannah-Moffat and Shaw (1999) have stressed that the emergence of the category of 'criminogenic need' has been coupled with risk into 'risk-need' models. These are said to restrict the forms of intervention that are offered under the rubrics of prevention, tying interventions by social and justice workers to cognitive-behavioural techniques that are directly limited to crime risks. Hannah-Moffat (1999) focuses her analysis of risk-needs on the extent to which this development tends to result in subjects' needs becoming signs of criminal risk and thus points for further or intensified leverage for punitive intervention. Without casting doubt on this observation, the example is not exclusive of another, and less pessimistic, interpretation. That is, government may not simply be seeking to extend its reach, but to defend its techniques of rule against translation in an area (of servicing 'needs') where welfare practices and knowledge remain highly influential. Hence, as Raynor (1999) has suggested, risk-needs analysis and practices fit with the 'rediscovery of social factors contributing to crime'. If so, then we might rethink our certainties about neo-liberalism and risk. Without being too naïve, but recalling the 'fate' of punitive rationalities in the era of the welfare sanction, let us perhaps say: 'The social is dead. Long live the social'.

References

Beck, Ulrich (1992) *Risk Society*. New York: Sage.

Bell, Daniel (1976) *The Cultural Contradictions of Capitalism*. London: Heinemann.

Berman, William (1994) *America's Right Turn. From Nixon to Bush*. Baltimore: Johns Hopkins University Press.

Broadhead, Richard (1991) 'Social constructions of bleach in combating AIDS among injection drug users', *The Journal of Drug Issues* 21: 713–737.

Brown, David (1992) 'Crime and punishment in the corporation: putting the value back in punishment', *Legal Service Bulletin* 15: 239–47.

Crime Prevention Council of Canada (1997) *Preventing Crime by Investing in Families*. Ottawa: NCPC.

Dean, Mitchell (1995) 'Governing the unemployed self in an active society', *Economy and Society* 24: 559–583.

Everingham, Susan (1998) 'Benefits and costs of early childhood interventions' in Parliament of NSW (ed.) *Crime Prevention Through Social Support*. Sydney: Parliament of NSW Legislative Council.

Farrington, David (1994) 'Early developmental prevention of juvenile delinquency', *Criminal Behaviour and Mental Health* 4: 209–227.

Feeley, Malcolm and Jonathon Simon (1994) 'Actuarial justice: the emerging new criminal law' in Nelken, D. (ed.) *The Futures of Criminology*. London: Sage.

Garland, David (1981) 'The birth of the welfare sanction', *British Journal of Law and Society* 8: 17–35.

Garland, David (1985) *Punishment and Welfare*. Aldershot: Gower.

Garland, David (1996) 'The limits of the sovereign state', *British Journal of Criminology*, 36 (4): 445–471

Hannah-Moffat, Kelly (1999) 'Moral agent or actuarial subject: risk and Canadian women's imprisonment', *Theoretical Criminology* 3: 71–95.

Hannah-Moffat, Kelly and Margaret Shaw (1999) 'Women and Risk: a genealogy of classification'. Paper presented at the British Criminology Conference, Liverpool, July 1999.

Hayes, Martin (1994) *The New Right in Britain*. London: Pluto Press.

Homel, Ross (1998) 'Pathways to Prevention' in Parliament of NSW (ed.) *Crime Prevention Through Social Support*. Sydney: Parliament of NSW Legislative Council.

Hoover, Kenneth and Raymond Plant (1989) *Conservative Capitalism in Britain and the United States*. London: Routledge.

Hughes, Gordon (1998) *Understanding Crime Prevention. Social control, risk and late modernity*. Buckingham: Open University Press.

Hunt, Alan and Gary Wickham (1994) *Foucault and Law*. London: Pluto Press.

Miller, Peter and Nikolas Rose (1990) 'Governing Economic Life', *Economy and Society* 19: 1–27.

Morgan, Rod (1999) 'New Labour "Law and Order" politics and the House of Commons Home Affairs Committee Report on Alternatives to Prison sentences', *Punishment and Society* 1: 109–14.

National Crime Prevention (1999a) *Pathways to Prevention. Developmental and Early Intervention Approaches to Crime in Australia*. Canberra: Commonwealth Attorney-General's Department.

National Crime Prevention (1999b) *Hanging Out. Negotiating Young People's Use of Public Space*. Canberra: Commonwealth Attorney-General's Department.

O'Malley, Pat (1992) 'Risk, power and crime prevention', *Economy and Society* 21:252–75.

O'Malley, Pat (1994) 'Neo-liberal crime control. Political agendas and the future of crime prevention in Australia', in D. Chappell and P. Wilson (eds) *The Australian Criminal Justice System. The mid-1990s.* (4th edition). Sydney: Butterworths.

O'Malley, Pat (1998) 'Genealogy and Rationality in Governmentality Research'. Socio-Legal Politics Conference. Instituto Internacional de Sociologia Juridica, Onati, Spain. September.

O'Malley, Pat (1999a) 'Volatile and Contradictory Punishment', *Theoretical Criminology* 3: 175–196.

O'Malley, Pat (1999b) 'Consuming Risks. Harm Minimisation and the Government of 'Drug Users', in Russell Smandych (ed.) *Governable Places. Readings in Governmentality and Crime Control. Advances in Criminology Series.* Aldershot: Dartmouth.

O'Malley, Pat (2000) 'Risk Societies and the Government of Crime', in M. Brown and J. Pratt (eds) *Dangerousness, Risk and Modern Society.* London: Routledge.

O'Malley, Pat and Stephen Mugford (1992) 'Moral Technology. The Political Agenda of Random Drug Testing' *Social Justice.* 18: 122–146.

O'Malley, Pat and Darren Palmer (1996) 'Post-Keynesian policing', *Economy and Society* 25: 137–155.

O'Malley, Pat, Lorna Weir and Clifford Shearing (1997) 'Governmentality, Criticism, Politics', *Economy and Society* 26: 501–517.

Piper, Christine (1999) 'The Crime and Disorder Act 1998: Child and Community "Safety" ', *The Modern Law Review* 1999: 397–408.

Pratt, John (1998) *Governing the Dangerous.* Sydney: The Federation Press.

Rand Corporation (1998) *Diverting Children from a Life of Crime.* Washington DC: Rand Corporation.

Raynor, Peter (1999) 'Risk, needs and effective practice: the impact and potential of new assessment methods in probation.' Paper presented at the British Criminology Conference, Liverpool, July 1999.

Rose, Nikolas (1990) *Governing the Soul.* London: Routledge.

Rose, Nikolas (1996a) 'Governing "advanced" liberal democracies' in Barry, A., Osborne, T. and Rose, N. (eds) *Foucault and Political Reason.* London: UCL Press.

Rose, Nikolas (1996b) 'The death of the "social"? Refiguring the Territory of Government', *Economy and Society* 26 (4): 327–346.

Rose, Nikolas (1998) 'Living Dangerously. Risk Management in Mental Health Care', *Mental Health Care* 199: 263–66.

Scruton, Roger (1984) *The Meaning of Conservatism.* London: Macmillan.

Simon, Jonathan (1987) 'The emergence of risk society: Insurance, law, and the state', *Socialist Review* 95: 61–89.

Simon, J. (1995) 'They died with their boots on. The boot camp and the limits of modern penality', *Social Justice* 22: 25–48.

Simon, Jonathan (1998) 'Managing the Monstrous. Sex Offenders and the New Penology', *Psychology, Public Policy and Law* 4: 452–467.

Stenson, Kevin (1999) 'Crime Control, Governmentality and Sovereignty'. In Smandych, Russell (ed.) *Governable Places: readings in governmentality and crime control.* Aldershot: Dartmouth.

Stenson, Kevin and Paul Watt (1999) 'Governmentality and "the death of the social"? A discourse analysis of local government texts in south-east England', *Urban Studies* 36: 189–201.

Thatcher, Margaret (1993) *The Downing Street Years*. London: Macmillan.

Thorne, Melvin (1990) *American Conservative Thought since World War II*. New York: Greenwood Press.

Tolley, Sue and Sue Tregeagle (1998) *Children's Family centres: integrated support services to prevent abuse and neglect of children*. Sydney: Bernado's Australia. Monograph 34.

Wardlaw, G (1990) 'The military analogy and drug control' in The Drug Policy Foundation (ed.) *The Great Issues of Drug Policy*. Washington DC: The Drug Policy Foundation.

Weir, Lorna (1996) 'Recent Developments in the Government of Pregnancy', *Economy and Society* 25: 372–92.

6

Lost connections and new directions:
neo-liberalism, new public managerialism and the 'modernization' of the British police

Eugene McLaughlin and *Karim Murji*

> The role of theory today seems to me to be just this: not to formulate the global systematic theory which holds everything in its place, but to analyse the specificity of mechanisms of power, to locate the connections and extensions, to build little by little a strategic knowledge.
>
> (Michel Foucault, 1980)

> I am taking a good firm knot and reducing it to a mess of loose ends.
>
> (Martin Amis, 1998)

One of the fundamental issues in contemporary police studies is the terms in which the relationship between neo-liberalism and new public managerialism – and their function in the reform of the police – are to be understood. In what follows we argue that, to date, the relationship has been conceived in deterministic terms, drawing a one-dimensional, totalizing connection between them. We propose that neo-liberalism is only a partially adequate explanation for the rise and nature of new public managerialism (NPM) and that, in the case of the police and police studies, is certainly not the best way to think through its significance theoretically or politically. This argument is developed through a re-evaluation of the relationship between the Conservative government and police in the UK between 1979 and 1997. The chapter then looks at how the core processes associated with NPM are intensifying and proliferating under New Labour's 'modernization' project.

Making connections: neo-liberalism and new public managerialism (NPM)

There have been many and varied attempts to comprehend and map the relationship between neo-liberalism and policing in the UK and much of it has an apocalyptic tone. For current and heuristic purposes we have organised the crowded interface into two theoretical frameworks.* The first, a predominantly social democratic perspective, tends to view the crucial elements of neo-liberalism – liberalization, deregulation, privatization, globalization – as undermining those core institutions that cemented the social order of the high period of the post-war welfare state. It regards the introduction of market forces into central areas of state, and therefore collective, responsibility as undermining social cohesion and the values and ethos of the public sector. Writers that we associate with this position include Robert Reiner, Neil Walker and Ian Loader, all of whom are extremely sociological in their analysis of current developments in UK policing. More than any other police scholar, Reiner has sketched the key developments in contemporary policing. At the heart of his analysis is the idea that neo-liberal economic re-structuring has intensified the growth of mass and long-term unemployment and the emergence of an 'underclass'.

Post-Fordism, or post-industrialisation and the rise of the 'new economy', are part of a long-term global shift in the 'logic of capital' producing greater marketization and competition. Both contribute to and exacerbate economic and social insecurity. The unleashing of neo-liberalism – including managerialism – has destroyed the preconditions for consensual policing and furthered the likelihood of routine conflict with the ever-growing marginalized sections of society: 'the fashionable languages of managerialism and consumerism overlook the fact that policing is not about the delivery of an uncontentious service like any other' (Reiner, 1992c: 269). Shifts towards a less hierarchical, less deferential culture have weakened traditional sources of social order. For Reiner, neo-liberal ideologies have 'let the genie out of the bottle' because the rise of individualism and consumerism celebrate diversity, choice, difference and fragmentation. This fractures the social order of which the police were once national symbols (Reiner, 1992a; 1992b; 1995; and see Reiner *et al.*, Chapter 9 this volume).

Reiner's neo-Durkheimian emphasis on the intrinsically 'sacred' or 'symbolic' nature of the British police provided an important theoretical pathway for Walker and Loader to follow. Thus, Walker's (1995) main criticism of the Conservative government's attempts to rationalize the core and peripheral activities of the police is that it neglected the 'complex inter-relationship of myriad police functions and outcomes – including symbolic outcomes'. Loader's recent work has developed this theme in a number of ways. First, he has sought to account for the national-popular 'sentiments' and cultural meanings attached to the police in terms of their self-evident value in representing and securing 'the social', that is the solidaristic, collective social ties within the nation state (Loader, 1997a). This suggests to him that policing is indefinable and not susceptible to

---

*In passing it can be pointed out that the two strands we have identified are mirrored in other fields of criminology such as penology, where writers such as Garland (1996) are nearer to the first, broadly Durkheimian, view while those who have identified the emergence of a 'new penology' based on actuarial justice (Feeley and Simon, 1992) are closer to the Foucauldian approach.

rationalization. Second, he argues that the Conservatives' managerial reforms would fast-track consumerization and eventually privatization of core police functions. Demands for policing – reflected in the expansion of private security – are understood as part of a consumer culture that has been promoted by neo-liberal ideologies (Loader, 1997b, 1999). In this reading, NPM is integral to the neo-liberal project of:

- undermining public confidence in the state's commitment to a conception of collective security;
- eroding the legitimacy of the police as guardians of social order;
- demystifying the symbolic role of the public police;
- reducing the overall level of public resources devoted to policing;
- restructuring the internal organisation to make police forces results-oriented;
- and focusing the police on crime-fighting and regulating socially marginal populations.

In the main these writers remain faithful to an Anglo-American sociology of the police that extols the virtues of British police tradition. This forms the basis for rejecting managerialism as a neo-liberal ideology. Instead they advocate the need for reconstructing the normative base of policing as a public good. Given the quasi-transcendental framing of their approach, these writers are, in many respects, arguing for the post-managerial 're-enchantment' of public policing.

The second perspective analyses the ways in which neo-liberalism (or 'advanced liberalism') draws upon and deploys managerial, communitarian and risk discourses in governance. Nikolas Rose has defined 'advanced liberalism' in the following terms:

> Advanced liberal strategies of government operate by acting upon the educated and managed choice of individuals; reinforcing people's desires for self-promotion, self-protection and the best possible quality of life. Rather than seeking to bind experts into centrally administered bureaucratic structures of government, they seek to re-draw the boundaries of the political, and to govern through a range of intermediate, semi-autonomous regulatory bodies, and forms of expertise, imagined according to new logics of competition. Advanced liberal strategies also utilise the devices of consumption and marketing to include individuals within communities of choice, and change the relations between the included and excluded. (Rose, 1996: 6)

The work of writers such as O'Malley (1992, 1997; and see Chapter 5 in volume) and Stenson (1993, 1999 and see this volume) is marked by the attempt to employ a similar, broadly Foucauldian analysis to understand contemporary changes in policing and crime control. They argue that specific neo-liberal applications of market and strategic planning principles to police organisations are part of the construction of a compact but much stronger state that rules 'at a distance' and seeks to autonomize and entrepreneurialize individual citizens. A shift has taken place with the welfare state stepping back and transferring responsibilities onto the private sector and not-for-profit agencies, the community and the citizen. Because of this 'the local' becomes the key site, as well as the determinant, of the nature and content of service delivery.

Both O'Malley and Stenson argue that innovative forms of governance are rooted within the new community policing strategies that have emerged during the last two decades. New highly localized policing relationships are being promoted that emphasize partnership and shared responsibility with local communities. In the process, 'the community' is being responsibilized in ways that heighten awareness of the risks of criminal victimization and the limits of the traditional police role. In describing these developments as 'post-Keynesian policing', O'Malley comes close to the views that we associate with the first perspective (O'Malley and Palmer, 1996). However, it is notable that O'Malley does not draw on the concept of 'the symbolic', and that he argues for the need to examine police reforms carefully in order to identify 'the possibilities for disaggregating neo-liberal strategies and practices, and rendering their often innovative developments available for appropriation and development by a "progressive" post-welfare politics'. When pushed to an explicit stance, O'Malley, in relation to policing, regards NPM as a social technology that is most closely aligned with neo-liberal political rationalities. Managerialist techniques have been introduced in an attempt to transform the police into a modern organization with modernist sensibilities. Police leadership is being re-professionalized through managerialization and the routine activities characteristic of 'low policing' are opened up to rationalist managerial critique (O'Malley and Palmer, 1996; O'Malley, 1997).

The multiple ramifications of these innovative perspectives cannot be examined here. Instead the discussion will be restricted to the assertion or assumption that NPM is a tool or technique of neo-liberalism, or that it is not worth considering in detail. At first sight it is easy to be convinced by the idea that there is a straightforward, obvious connection between neo-liberalism and NPM, especially when it is proposed by some of the most sophisticated theorists working in police studies. However, while these writers have provided significant insights into the present state of policing, we believe that neither perspective is theoretically or politically sufficient for the task of assessing the significance of NPM, and thinking through the distinctions between 'management', 'managerialism' and the process of 'managerialization'. We seek to provide a corrective history of the recent past, first by re-assessing the degree of fit between neo-liberalism and NPM.

Loosening the connections: the multifaceted origins of NPM

Miller and Rose argue that the neo-liberal wing of the incoming Conservative administration in 1979 articulated a powerful critique of the functions and outcomes of the post-war Beveridge-Keynesian corporatist welfare settlement in the UK:

> Against the rationale of government intervention as a way of addressing the ills of social and economic life it [the government's neo-liberalist philosophy] deploys theories of government over-reach and over-load. Against the theme of expertise

at the service of social ends it deploys a critique of a government machine at the mercy of professional interests who ceaselessly work to extract increased resources and grant more powers to sectional groups, whilst utilizing the skills of publicity and lobbying to bounce government into accepting their self-serving agendas. Against the theme of mutual contract of obligations between citizen and state, it articulates a critique of the 'give it to me' society'. ... The welfare state is considered to have morally damaging effect upon citizens as a result of rising expectations fuelled by lavish promises from political parties, constant pressure from bureaucrats to expand their own empires, and the expectation engendered in citizens that it is the role of the state to provide for the individual. (Miller and Rose, 1991: 19)

'Rolling back the state' under neo-liberalism entailed the curbing of state expenditure, privatization of public utilities, the cutting of 'red tape', reducing the power of trade unions, the restoration of 'incentives' and advocating a minimalist public sector. All of this was based on two main beliefs. First, that most decisions were best left to self-reliant individuals, families and private enterprise; and secondly, that the state, as an unproductive burden on individuals and businesses, had to reduce its share of GNP in order for the country to remain globally competitive.

During the life of the Conservative government concerted efforts were made to replace the state's role as a provider of multiple public services with one where it became the purchaser of services from a free market of competing providers. The terms 'the contract state' or the 'entrepreneurial state' have been used to describe the thrust and direction of the Conservative's reform process (Kirkpatrick and Martinez-Lucio, 1995). But, while managerialist elements were present in the government's approach almost from the outset, the key features of a distinct NPM were not immediately 'triggered'. Rather it evolved and developed, as much due to a reaction to political context and a sense of realpolitik, as an incompletely fleshed out political ideology. This 'slow politics' of the early to mid-1980s is rarely accounted for in broad-brush characterizations of the Thatcherite neo-liberal project.

The materialization of a coherent NPM can be placed at the intersection of three developments. First, the neo-liberal think-tanks began to acknowledge that the internal inconsistencies and conflicting political goals embedded within Thatcherism's 'modernization' project meant that the space for outright privatization and deregulation of state activities had closed. The time had come for the post-Thatcherites within the Conservative Party to rethink their assumptions about the future configuration of the public sector (Waldegrave, 1992). Second, as the role of the state changed from provider to regulator and supervisor, a range of public sector auditing and inspection agencies had been established as part of the 'audit explosion' (Power, 1994). The dual effect of these agencies is that they helped to decouple managerial reform from party politics and, to some extent, de-politicized managerial discourses. Third, a distinctive group of transnational NPM advocates from across the political spectrum began to achieve global recognition, successfully claiming a centrality for their analyses, and in the process discrediting some of the domain assumptions of the 'old' public administration (for example, Osborne and Gaebler, 1992). What is crucial, and needs to be acknowledged, is that proponents of a NPM paradigm on both sides of the Atlantic sought to transcend neo-liberalism in a bid to reinvent and revitalize notions of the public sector and public service at the end of the twentieth century. Indeed, it is important to note that their potency and influence was based on the fact that the approach they were promoting challenged the neo-liberal 'there is no alternative' to the privatization of the public sector.

Drawing on the work of writers such as Pollitt (1993) and Clarke and Newman (1998), we would argue that NPM is best understood as a complex, often contradictory set of post-bureaucratic professional knowledges, practices and techniques drawn from a wide variety of sources (reinventing government, new public administration, new wave management, human resource management, postmodern organisational theory). In its cultural projection and discursive meanings this makes NPM a hybrid theoretical and political construction. Its purpose is to fracture and realign relations of power within public sector organisations in order to transform the structures and reorganise the processes for both funding and delivering quality public services. The following NPM mechanisms and techniques have been deemed to be crucial to driving the managerialization of all aspects of the formulation and delivery of public services in an era of the smaller state:

- the creation or appointment of professional managers to be held accountable for using existing resources imaginatively, and extract maximum value from them;
- the setting of clear, measurable standards and targets;
- the explicit costing of all activities, choices and priorities;
- the development of performance indicators to enable the measurement and evaluation of efficiency, and the publication of league tables showing comparative performance against these indicators;
- increased emphasis on outputs and results rather than processes;
- rationalization of the purpose, range and scope of organisations through the identification of core competencies, the externalization of peripheral or illogical activities, and 'market testing' against competitive providers;
- operating in a competitive environment characterised by full or quasi-market relations, service contracts, agency status, the separation of finance from provision, a split between providers and purchasers of services, client-contractor relationships, and customer service;
- the reconfiguration of the recipients and beneficiaries of public services as 'customers' and 'consumers'; and
- the overhauling of the work culture of public sector organisations to improve productivity and accountability.

The most important thing to grasp about this list is the underlying pattern. Taken together, they represent the post-neo-liberal means through which the public sector is to be managerialized so that it becomes performance-oriented. This is why NPM matters and why it is deserving of more analytical attention than conventionally accorded to it by theorizing that links it unproblematically with, and subordinate to, an unfolding neo-liberal agenda.

The Conservatives, NPM and police reform

It is in keeping with the analysis above to record that managerialization processes were felt by degrees within the criminal justice system, and not as a 'big bang' neo-liberal meltdown. Some early signs of the discussion of the emergence of an audit and inspection culture in the criminal justice system are to be found in Jones (1993), Spencer (1993) and McLaughlin and Muncie (1994). Here we want to concentrate on the police. Probably alone among the criminal justice agencies, the police seemed to stand apart from the managerial reform processes initiated in criminal justice. It does not require a conspiracy theory to see this scenario as closely related to the political context and interests of successive Conservative governments. Various commentators have noted that the Thatcherite project necessitated the state to be simultaneously 'rolled back and forward'. A strong state would be needed to manage the convulsions resulting from the attempt to free up the economy and dismantle the post-war settlement. At the core of what Stuart Hall (1979) called the 'coming of iron times' stood the forces of law and order (see Hudson, Chapter 8 this volume). In the 1980s, the front-line role taken by the police in the 'war against crime', outbreaks of serious public disorder and in what were, for the government, 'make or break' industrial disputes, made the police virtually immune from the fiscal restrictions and ideological assault that the rest of the public sector was subjected to at the time. Versions of Hall's 'authoritarian state' thesis are relatively well known and, in broad outline, attract a measure of agreement from a wide variety of commentators.

However, a closer re-examination and re-reading of key policy developments reveals a gradual and complex process of, first, increasing governmental scrutiny of virtually every aspect of public policework and, second, creeping managerialization. Hence, even from the earliest days of the police's 'most favoured' status with the Conservative government, a number of searching questions were being asked about their organizational practices and management capabilities. Traditionally, the 'iron tradition' of operational independence constitutionally accorded to chief police officers had allowed them to ignore critical scrutiny, whether it emanated from the Home Office or elsewhere. But, in a precursor to the auditing processes that would emerge at the end of the 1980s, it proved much harder to deal with the fiscal and budgetary concerns that underlay the government's 'value for money' Financial Management Initiative (FMI). Launched in 1982, the FMI aimed to improve the efficiency, effectiveness and accountability of central government departments (see Jenkins, 1985; Metcalfe and Richards, 1990).

For the Home Office the FMI provided an uncomfortable reality check for a department normally exempted from review and evaluation. This calling to account exposed the Home Office's lack of systematic knowledge about the allocation of police resources, what results or benefits any extra funding delivered, how the performance of different forces compared, and whether public resources were being used efficiently: 'In seeking this information and in taking a direct interest in what the products of policing are, the Home Office has been drawn into a new set of relationships with forces and has signalled very clearly its interest in what forces do and how well they do it: in other words with operational priorities' (Weatheritt, 1986: 104). In its call for more efficient and effective use of existing resources it, crucially, introduced 'a highly specific language of rational management into the process of determining policy priorities' (Weatheritt, 1986: 111). In future, police forces and authorities requesting more personnel would have to demonstrate (i) that existing resources were being used and managed to best advantage; (ii) that they had the means of assessing the extent to which objectives and priorities were being achieved; and (iii) that there was a specified reason for the requested increase (Sinclair and Miller, 1984; Horton and Smith, 1988).

The difficulty that the Home Office had in getting to grips with police performance and evaluation in the 1980s was two-fold. First, in a re-run of one of the problems it had encountered in previous decades, it was necessary to find practical mechanisms to define and measure effectiveness and efficiency. However, the measurement of routine police activities was highly problematic because of the following:

- the doctrine of constabulary independence;
- the multiple points of autonomy resulting from the unusually high degree of legally mandated discretion at the lowest levels of the organization;
- the low visibility of routine policework;
- conflicting and ambiguous tasks of a quasi-military organization;
- the ideological claim that policework is 'different' because it is primarily symbolic and therefore not amenable to instrumentalist evaluation.

The second problem was the political position of the police as the frontier guards of the authoritarian state. In a period of continuing public disorder, questions about the efficiency and effectiveness of the police on 'mundane' crime matters were sidelined, as was the emerging evidence of an escalating crime wave. Any overt fiscal 'assault' upon the police at this time would also have been seen as ideologically giving ground to left-wing critics of the police. The industrial, civil and political disputes of the period can, in retrospect, therefore be seen ironically as the 'saving' or 'making' of the police at this time, without which the emergent FMI agenda might have had greater effect. None the less it is clear that any reverential or sacred view of the police – the idea that they were 'different' and could not be made subject to performance measurement – had already begun to be scrutinized by fiscal and ideological imperatives, and that elements of a managerialist reform programme were being constructed.

Having delivered much for the government, the late 1980s should have heralded a new 'golden age' for the police in their relations with the Conservatives. However, at around this time a revived and re-constituted version of NPM emerged, as outlined earlier. In the case of the police, pressure for radical organizational reform came from a number of sources, both above and below, which connected with new managerialist mechanisms for doing so. First, as we have seen, there was enhanced fiscal scrutiny of the police that would take account of the legally mandated operational autonomy of chief officers. Under the 1964 Police Act, Her Majesty's Inspectorate of Constabulary (HMIC) had a statutory responsibility for examining and improving police efficiency, though it had acquired the reputation of being a sinecure for retired police officers. The HMIC's enhanced role placed it in a pivotal position in the pursuance of Home Office objectives. The resultant 'focused inspections' and various Home Office Circulars furthered the use of technical and rationalist instruments that required police forces to account for their activities, budgets, establishment levels, civilianization, and to produce quantifiable evidence of effectiveness. Because information was now required in nationally agreed functional categories, as opposed to administrative ones, these inspections laid the basis for more comprehensive and comparative information about the activities, costs, resource use and performance of different forces.

Second, the Audit Commission began a series of investigations into the financing and organization of the police. Because of its 'non-political' remit – to evaluate the management of local government activities in terms of economy, efficiency and effectiveness – the Audit Commission proved to be a much more searching scrutinizer of police practices than the more easily dismissable 'politically inspired' left-wing critics of the early and mid-1980s. Since the promotion of 'better management' sounds neutral, it is not something that anyone can easily dispute (Pollitt, 1993). In practice, the Commission provided the government with a means of scrutinizing the police without seeming to trespass on the sensitive issue of operational independence. But in directing its gaze to the management of the police the Audit Commission in fact trampled all over the 'operational independence' of chief police officers, thereby exposing its questionable organizational and political status. The Commission's first report on the police came out in 1988. Successive reports proposed the need to rethink police financing; budget allocation mechanisms; the manner in which police activities were costed, and the organization, rank structure and salary scales of provincial police forces (Audit Commission 1990, 1991). The Commission's avowedly managerialist perspective brought to the fore the need for decentralized, flexible and streamlined organizational structures; clearly stated priorities and objectives, and output-based quantifiable performance indicators covering key operational functions in order to facilitate inter-force comparisons. The language of the market was also introduced as the Commission discussed the needs of 'customers' and methods for delivering a value for money service (Davies, 1992). In later reports the Commission moved 'deeper' into the heart of policing by advocating more effective methods of managing crime investigations and patrolling (Audit Commission 1993; 1996a and b).

A third significant source of pressure 'from above' came from the House of Commons Home Affairs Select Committee. In the late 1980s the committee promulgated the view that while policing was 'big business' in terms of its budget and personnel, police forces were insufficiently 'business-like' in their structure and functioning. The Committee's chairman at the time, Sir John Wheeler, confronted the concerns about the constitutional independence of the police though the argument that the policing needs of the 1990s and beyond, including the advent of the European Union and the emergence of transnational criminal networks and markets, necessitated organisational rationalization, through merger and nationalization. Indeed the latter was something that many senior officers were also advocating and campaigning for at the time. To compensate for what he described as 'glaring deficiencies, incompetent use of resources and blinding incompetence' (*Independent*, 26 July 1990), Wheeler argued that existing forces should be merged, police authorities should be replaced by a small board of appointed directors and a national policing policy committee consisting of regional chief officers and Home Office representatives should be established. Politically there can be no doubt that the Committee's reports reflected increasing government dissatisfaction with police management and performance, as later revealed in a former Home Secretary's memoirs (Baker, 1993).

Changing public opinion of the police also became more evident in the late 1980s and early 1990s. Many newspapers – importantly, including those on the political right – highlighted police inefficiency and malpractice, ranging from rising crime and declining clear-up rates, to general incivility and abrasiveness in their dealings with middle-class people, particularly motorists. Around this time the political fallout from the exposure of serious miscarriages of justice resulted in the establishment of a Royal Commission on Criminal Justice. Critical comments about the state of the police, and demands for reform in both tabloid and broadsheet newspaper editorials, may well have reflected the views of an increasingly critical public. They, in conjunction with a series of opinion polls which suggested diminished public confidence in the police, were certainly read by the Conservative government as indications that its core constituency – 'Middle England' – was not satisfied with the quality of service being delivered by the police, and that further reform would be required.

In 1990 John Major replaced Mrs Thatcher as Prime Minister. In terms of the argument about the correspondence between neo-liberalism and NPM, it is notable that Major was widely thought to have been chosen precisely because he was not a neo-liberal ideologue and more inclined to pragmatic governance. Yet following the re-election of the Conservative in 1992 Major oversaw one of the most volatile periods in the relationship between police and government in post-war British politics. An unprecedented programme of root-and-branch reform was initiated, resulting in the Sheehy inquiry (Sheehy *et al.*, 1993) and the White Paper on Police Reform (Home Office, 1993). The core proposals of both provided distinct NPM-based answers to the questions about what the core tasks of the police should be, and how the organizational and remuneration structure should be changed to deliver measurable ends (McLaughlin and Murji, 1995).

The resulting legislation – the Police and Magistrates' Courts Act 1994 – contained less than the full reform package because of a carefully orchestrated campaign of resistance by the police staff associations (Leishman *et al.*, 1996;

McLaughlin and Murji, 1998). But even the partial reforms introduced under the legislation ruptured the framework in which British policing traditionally operated. It established a statutory framework for the further development of managerialized police forces, making explicit the priorities, objectives, targets and performance indicators for each police force, the available resources and, through the annual report, an assessment of the extent to which the local policing plan has been realized (Weatheritt, 1995; McLaughlin and Murji, 1996; Morgan and Newburn, 1997). The legislation also required senior police officers and more 'business like' police authorities to frame their decision-making with the managerialist discourses of effectiveness, efficiency and economy (see Loveday, 1998). This legislation was the culmination of a long, uneven and incompletely realized managerialization process with many 'false starts' and compromises along the way. While the 'half-way house' position did not please either side, it did at least mark a legislative end-point to battles between the police and the Conservative government.

New directions: New Labour, NPM and the 'modernization' of the police

The central issue for the remainder of this chapter is how the process of managerialization of the police has developed in the changed political conditions following the election of New Labour in 1997. Much effort has been spent on trying to identify the distinctive political configuration of New Labour's self-declared 'third way' politics and policies (Anderson and Mann, 1997; Driver and Martell, 1998; Hall, 1998; Stenson and Edwards, Chapter 4 in this volume). Broadly, these analyses are concerned to establish whether the 'third way' marks a rupture with the past, or whether it is a continuation of quasi-conservative government. Criminologists can be found on both sides of this debate, one view being that New Labour would usher in a period of 'post-managerial' stability, after their predecessor's controversial attempts to impose managerialist reform across the criminal justice system.

The police may have had just cause to anticipate that the new government would halt or reverse the managerial trends of the previous decade. They responded positively to New Labour's pre-election opposition to the Conservatives' NPM reforms, its 'tough on crime' stance, and its enthusiastic support for 'zero tolerance policing'. The police could also have expected that in government New Labour's room for manoeuvre would be limited by the need to 'out-Tory' the Tories on law and order. However, half-way through New Labour's term of office the fogs of spin are lifting and the evolving contours of its strategy for the police have become clearer. The following discussion highlights those elements that form part of a 'joined-up', or connected, approach to the 'modernization' of the police. Looked at as a whole they suggest that NPM is central to the overall framework for enhancing and measuring police performance.

At the heart of New Labour's approach to government and statecraft is the idea of 'modernization'. Despite the absence of programmatic reform along the lines proposed by Anthony Giddens (1994, 1998), New Labour has taken on board his thesis that the capacities of the nation state must be 'modernized' so that it can manage and regulate – rather than being submerged by – the social, cultural and economic changes wrought by the 'new global order'. Significantly, *Modernising Government*, New Labour's long-term programme of renewal and reform of government itself, acknowledges that the managerial reform process of the previous government was a necessary act of modernization to improve productivity and deliver better value for money and to enhance quality of service. *Modernising Government* has initiated a further 'new wave' of NPM to entrench performance management across the public sector. In so doing New Labour is moving towards a managerialized state form first identified by Clarke and Newman (1998).

In the case of criminal justice, 'modernization' involves the:

- establishment of consistent and mutually reinforcing aims and objectives;
- installation of a 'what works'/ 'best practice' culture;
- development of an evidence-based approach to the allocation of resources; and
- institutionalization of performance management to improve productivity.

Thus, New Labour's strategy envisages the intensification and re-invigoration of the managerial disciplines of efficiency, effectiveness and economy that were already working their way, albeit unevenly, through the various parts of this intricate policy environment. Further managerialization is deemed necessary if the contradictions and tensions generated by the Conservatives' uneven public sector reform project are to be 'resolved'. Virtually every Home Office policy document stresses that modernization will be achieved through constant auditing, priority and target setting, monitoring, evaluation and inspection. Criminal justice professionals have been informed that 'the capacity for audit and inspection will be developed to assess the performance of the criminal justice system as a whole; to provide assurance that it is operating economically and efficiently; and is achieving its aims and objectives effectively' (Home Office, 1999: 16).

In office, New Labour's strategy does not regard the police as 'different' from the rest of government; indeed it needs to tackle and reform the police not least because police performance is a key driver in determining demands on the rest of the criminal justice system. Just as significantly, the ability of New Labour to deliver on its electoral promises on law and order is at risk if it fails to modernize the police. Managerialization under New Labour involves enhanced emphasis on performance measurement and service delivery, fiscal controls and the process of localization through financial delegation and partnership arrangements. Together these methods are intended to produce a 'modern crime fighting machine'.

New Labour has sharpened the logics of the Police and Magistrates' Courts Act to ensure that police force and police authority efforts are directed to realizing its crime reduction targets. It has also extended this constitutional framework to the Metropolitan Police, the largest and most resource-intensive police force in the UK. Second, in tandem with the preceding point, it has strengthened the auditing and inspection regime. The Audit Commission, one of the key drivers of NPM under the Conservatives, has been charged with ensuring 'Best Value', a rolling system of audit to ensure that public services are delivering services to clear standards – covering both cost and quality – by the most economic, efficient and effective means available. To demonstrate 'Best Value', public authorities are being required to publish annual performance charts and identify standards, priorities and targets.

Because 'Best Value' is a statutory responsibility under the 1999 Local Government Act, this regime institutionalizes a performance framework that will stress continuous improvement and the application of the '4 Cs' (challenge; comparison; consultation and competition) to all aspects of service delivery. It foregrounds the question of comparison with other similar providers across a range of performance indicators. Underlying this is a clear emphasis on competition as a means of securing efficient and effective service delivery based on performance targets agreed by consultation with stakeholders and sections of the community. In the case of the police, one of the most significant developments is that under the guise of 'joined-up inspection' the HMIC has been given the managerial authority to conduct 'Best Value' inspections that:

- develop the idea of continuous efficiency savings;
- inculcate a culture of continuous improvement;
- develop a diagnostic model based on risk assessment; and,
- conduct local rather than force-wide inspections (see HMIC, 1998, 1999).

In informing the Superintendents Association that the police were to be included within the 'Best Value' framework, Home Secretary Jack Straw said that: 'Best value will also have teeth, it will involve certification, audit and inspection and in those extreme cases where communities are not given the level of service they are entitled to, there will be provision for intervention, ultimately by the Secretary of State' (*The Independent*, 17 September 1998). He also threatened to 'name and shame' poorly performing forces and suggested that 'hit squads' could be sent in to run forces that failed to meet their targets, something that has already happened with schools adjudged to be 'failing' to meet government standards.

For the first time, individual police forces and their constituent Basic Command Units (BCUs) have been given specific crime reduction targets that are intended to narrow the gap between the best-performing forces and those with a substandard track record on fighting crime. From 2001 the targets will be backed up by inspection of the BCUs, rather than just force-wide checks. Thus, it is significant that the 'delivery' of crime reduction targets will rest not on chief constables but on the superintendents who tend to be in charge of local command units. 'A good superintendent', according to Jack Straw, 'is every bit as important to driving up community safety standards as a good headteacher is to educational performance' (*The Times*, 15 February 2000: 6). But as well as 'steering' it is clear that the government also intends to be involved in 'rowing'. Hence the government has also mooted the idea of a powerful regulatory and inspection regime for BCUs which fail to meet set standards. This was dubbed 'Ofcop' in the newspapers, following the naming style of regulatory regimes for the privatized utilities (e.g.

Ofgas, Oftel). Straw spoke of the government's resolution in promoting a 'rigorous performance culture in the police service', and said that increasing officer numbers would only make a difference when the police were operating at 'maximum efficiency' (*The Times*, 14 February 2000).

A further strand is New Labour's promotion of a 'hard evidence' based approach to police work. *Reducing Offending*, a Home Office report published in July 1998 to coincide with the launch of New Labour's crime reduction strategy, stressed that there was no connection between increasing the number of police officers and lower crime rates. The report supported the development of strategic frameworks to deliver locally relevant strategies:

> This calls for local crime audits, good intelligence systems, proper strategic management, monitoring of performance, responsiveness to the constantly changing crime picture and creativity … The current drive to develop better routine performance measures for police also provides an opportunity to distinguish effective working practices more systematically. A package of police performance measures could be used to discriminate police management units at all levels, from force to beat, and relate the outcomes achieved more rigorously to styles and strategies. (Home Office, 1998: 74)

This links into the government's intention to use financial management tools to determine where resources can be deployed more effectively by, (i) dropping initiatives and practices shown to offer poor value for money; (ii) redeploying resources saved to cost-effective activities; and (iii) developing more flexible funding arrangements to transfer funds between criminal justice agencies. Equally significantly, it leaves open the possibility of further rationalization of the functions of the police and the development of intermediate forms of policing.

The final plank of the strategy is to be found in the Crime and Disorder Act 1998. This places new obligations on the police to cooperate in the development and implementation of local crime reduction strategies. This renewed emphasis on partnership aims to instigate significant changes in the working practices of all the criminal justice agencies (see Stenson and Edwards, Chapter 4, this volume). As one of the main players – in terms of their resources as well as functions – the police have been required to develop mutual priorities both with other agencies as well as local communities. This compels them to:

- conduct and publish local crime and disorder audits;
- undertake consultation exercises based on the results of the audit;
- establish and publish objectives and targets for reducing crime and disorder;
- monitor the strategy and its inputs, processes and outputs, and to evaluate its outcomes; and,
- to repeat the process every three years.

Local policing is being increasingly enmeshed in a complex network of relationships and interests. Localization complements and connects with inspection, audit and financial accountability in a network of processes that, taken together, comprise New Labour's aim of creating and institutionalizing a new regulatory framework of performance measurement and review that will hold police forces to account for the resources they use and the outcomes they achieve. Not surprisingly, the discourses and techniques of a modernized NPM are constitutive of the whole process.

Conclusion

This chapter has sought to provide a critique of two of the ways that the relationship between neo-liberalism, NPM and police reform have been conceptualized. It does not claim to have provided a comprehensive review of debates in policing but the two perspectives or approaches that we have looked at seem worth concentrating on because they are, or have the potential to become, the new orthodoxies within police studies. While they represent important contributions to the study of policing we have suggested that these perspectives have under-theorised NPM, and overstated the links to neo-liberalism. We have tried to show that the links are multi-layered and that managerialization as a process is not the simple preserve of neo-liberal ideologies. It is noteworthy for this argument that far from ushering in 'post-managerial criminal justice', New Labour's 'third way' programme of governance is dominated by themes of efficiency, effectiveness and economy. For some or many observers this is taken to mean that it is ideologically indistinguishable from previous Conservative administrations, and that it has taken neo-liberalism to its heart. This is, however, debatable since it is apparent that New Labour has a very different conception of the role and capabilities of the state and of public services. The 'third way' project cannot be treated as synonymous with neo-liberalism. Nor, even more narrowly, can its criminal justice modernization programme be treated as being indistinguishable from the policies of the last Conservative government.

Because of political contingencies, staff association resistance, and a never ending 'backward and forward' reform dynamic, a disorganized picture of policing has emerged over the past decade. The messy and sometimes contradictory provenance of NPM and its hybrid character and sources has produced new fissures and fault lines within policing in the UK. Externally the relationship between police, police authorities and the Home Office has been changed; internally there is observable strain as the rhetoric of efficiency, effectiveness and economy increasingly pervade police discourse, while resistance to its implications and aspects of a culture of special pleading continue alongside. The ways in which these tensions will play out under New Labour's modernization project remain to be seen.

There are at least three far-reaching and profound consequences of managerialization for the public police. The first is that managerialism has been internalized and all other forms of organizational discourse must refer to it. NPM now informs police discourse in sometimes ironic ways. Thus it sounds, superficially at least, incongruous that the Police Federation, the focal point for the 'forces of conservatism' within the police, increasingly uses the language of managerialism to attack reforms, and to press its own case for more resources. Resistance to further managerialization tends to takes place within a managerial framework. These shifting discursive boundaries make this perhaps the most significant marker of the quiet hegemony of NPM discourses. Second, managerialization is driving a programme of civilianization – rather than privatization – of key organizational tasks. Senior officers are deferring and delegating to civilians from both the public and private sectors who take responsibility for 'quality of service' and 'performance review' issues. This trend is likely to gather momentum as the 'Best Value' audit and inspection regimes take effect. This shift to generic management skills further undermines any case for regarding the police as 'unique' and not like other organizations. The third consequence of ongoing managerialization is that it has swept aside a whole tissue of illusions and consoling fictions about the nature of the British police and exposed previously hidden aspects of organizational culture, practice and performance. The 'new performativity' has been centred from above (government pressure for efficiency), below (local performance indicators, community consultation and partnerships), and within the police organisation as the words of many senior police officers attest. Over nearly two decades, NPM discourses and techniques have opened up different conceptions of the organization, delivery and meaning of police work. Despite all its unevenness, the managerialized future does not offer the public police the prospect of security and stability that seemed to exist in the 'golden ages' of either the Keynesian welfare state or of the authoritarian state. As an ongoing process it does not offer periods of relief from pressure. 'Modernization' has become a trope under which the latest form of a potentially ceaseless dynamic for continuous managerialization is occurring.

References

Amis, M. (1998) *Night Train*, New York: Vintage.

Anderson, P. and Mann, N. (1997) *Safety First: The making of New Labour*, London: Granta.

Audit Commission (1990) *Effective Policing: Performance review in police forces*, London: HMSO.

Audit Commission (1991) *Pounds and Coppers: Financial delegation in provincial police forces*, London: HMSO.

Audit Commission (1993) *Helping with Enquiries: Tackling crime effectively*, London: HMSO.

Audit Commission (1994) *Cheques and Balances*, executive briefing, London: HMSO.

Audit Commission (1996a) *Streetwise: Effective police patrol*, London: HMSO.

Audit Commission (1996b) *Local Authority Performance Indicators, Vol 3: Police and Fire Services*, London: HMSO.

Baker, K. (1993) *The Turbulent Years: My life in politics*, London: Faber and Faber.

Clarke, J. and Newman, J. (1998) *The Managerial State*, London: Sage.

Davies, H. (1992) *Fighting Leviathan: Building social markets that work*, London: Social Market Foundation.

Driver, S. and Martell, L. (1998) *New Labour*, Cambridge: Polity.

Feeley, M. and Simon, J. (1992) 'The new penology', *Criminology*, 39: 449–74.

Foucault, M. (1980) 'Power and strategies' in Gordon, C. (ed.) *Power and Knowledge: Selected interviews and other writings*, Brighton: Harvester.

Garland, D. (1996) 'The limits of the sovereign state', *British Journal of Criminology*, 36: 45–71.

Giddens, A. (1994) *Beyond Left and Right*, Cambridge: Polity.

Giddens, A. (1998) *The Third Way*, Cambridge: Polity.

Hall, S. (1979) *Drifting into a Law and Order Society*, London: Cobden Trust.

Hall, S. (1998) 'The great moving nowhere show', *Marxism Today,* Nov/Dec: 9–14.

HMIC (Her Majesty's Inspectorate of Constabulary) (1998) *What Price Policing? A study of efficiency and value for money in the police service*, London: Home Office.

HMIC (Her Majesty's Inspectorate of Constabulary) (1999) *Annual Report, 1998–99*, London: Home Office.

Home Office (1993) *Police Reform: A police service for the twenty-first century* (Cm 2281), London: HMSO.

Home Office (1998) *Reducing Offending: An assessment of research evidence on ways of dealing with offending behaviour*, London: Home Office Report No 187.

Home Office (1999) *Criminal Justice: The Strategic Plan for 1999–2000 to 2001–2002*, London: Home Office.

Horton, C. and Smith, D. (1988) *Evaluating Policework*, London: Policy Studies Institute.

House of Commons (1982) *Efficiency and Effectiveness in the Civil Service*, Report of the Treasury and Civil Service Select Committee, London: HMSO.

Jenkins, K. (1985) *Making Things Happen; A report on the implementation of government efficiency scrutinies*, London: HMSO.

Jones, C. (1993) 'Auditing criminal justice', *British Journal of Criminology*, 33: 187–202.

Kirkpatrick, I. and Martinez-Lucio, M. (eds) (1995) *The Politics of Quality in the Public Sector*, London: Routledge.

Leishman, F *et al.* (1996) 'Reinventing and restructuring: towards a 'new policing order', in Leishman, F. *et al.* (eds) *Core Issues in Policing*, Harlow: Longman.

Loader, I. (1997a) 'Policing and the social: questions of symbolic power', *British Journal of Sociology,* 48: 1–18.

Loader, I. (1997b) 'Thinking normatively about private security', *Journal of Law and Society,* 24: 377–94.

Loader, I. (1999) 'Consumer culture and the commodification of policing and security', *Sociology,* 33: 373–92.

Loveday, B. (1998) 'Waving not drowning: chief constables and the new configuration of accountability in the provinces', *International Journal of Police Science and Management,* 1, 2: 133–146.

McLaughlin, E. and Muncie, J. (1994) 'Managing the Criminal Justice System', in Clarke, J., Cochrane, A. and McLaughlin, E. (eds) *Managing Social Policy*, London: Sage.

McLaughlin, E. and Murji, K. (1995) 'The End of Public Policing?', in Noaks, L., Levi, M. and Maguire, M. (eds) *Contemporary Issues in Criminology*, Cardiff: University of Wales Press.

McLaughlin, E. and Murji, K. (1996) 'Times Change: New formations and representations of police accountability', in Critcher, C. and Waddington, D. (eds) *Policing Public Order: Theoretical and Practical Issues*, Aldershot: Avebury.

McLaughlin, E. and K. Murji, K. (1998) 'Resistance through representation: storylines, advertising and Police Federation campaigns', *Policing and Society*, 8: 367–399.

Metcalfe, L. and Richards, S. (1990) *Improving Public Management*, London: Sage.

Miller, P. and Rose, N. (1991) 'Programming the poor: poverty calculation and expertise' in Lehto, J. (ed.) *Deprivation, Social Welfare and Expertise*, Helsinki: National Agency for Welfare and Health, Research Report No 7.

Morgan R. and Newburn, T. (1997) *The Future of Policing*, Oxford: Clarendon Press.

O'Malley, P. (1992) 'Risk, power and crime prevention', *Economy and Society*, 21: 252–75.

O'Malley, P. (1997) 'Policing, politics and postmodernity', *Social and Legal Studies*, 6: 363–381.

O'Malley, P. and Palmer, D. (1996) 'Post-Keynesian policing', *Economy and Society*, 25: 137–55.

Osborne, D. and Gaebler, T. (1992) *Reinventing Government: How the entrepreneurial spirit is transforming the public sector*, Reading, MA.: Addison-Wesley.

Pollitt, C. (1993) *Managerialism and the Public Services*, second edition, Oxford: Blackwell.

Power, M. (1994) *The Audit Explosion*, London: Demos.

Sheehy, P. *et al.* (1993) *Inquiry into Police Responsibilities and Rewards*, London: HMSO.

Sinclair, I. and Miller, C. (1984) *Measuring Police Effectiveness and Efficiency*, London: HMSO.

Spencer, J (1993) 'The criminal justice system and the politics of scrutiny', *Social Policy and Administration*, 27: 1.

Reiner, R. (1992a) *'Fin de siecle* blues: the police face the millennium', *Political Quarterly*, 63, 1: 37–49.

Reiner, R. (1992b) 'Policing a postmodern society', *Modern Law Review*, 55: 761–81.

Reiner, R. (1992c) *The Politics of the Police*, second edition, Hemel Hempstead: Harvester Wheatsheaf.

Reiner, R. (1995) ' From the sacred to the profane: the thirty year's war of the British police', *Policing and Society*, 5: 121–28.

Rose, N. (1996) 'The death of the social', *New Times*, 9 July: 6–7.

Stenson, K. (1993) 'Community policing as a governmental technology, *Economy and Society*, 22: 373–89.

Stenson, K. (1999) 'Crime control, governmentality, and sovereignty' in Smandych, R. (ed.) *Governable Places: Readings on Governmentality and Crime Control*, Aldershot: Dartmouth.

Waldegrave, W. (1992) *The Reality of Reform and Accountability in Today's Public Services*, London: Public Finance Foundation.

Walker, N. (1995) 'Defining core police tasks: the neglect of the symbolic dimension', *Policing and Society*, 6: 53–71.

Weatheritt, M. (1986) *Innovations in Policing*, London: Croom Helm.

Weatheritt, M. (1995) *Policing Plans: The role of police authority members*, London: ACC Publications.

4

Criminal justice and risk

7

'Entitlement to cruelty':
the end of welfare and the punitive mentality in the United States

Jonathan Simon

> Through punishment of the debtor, the creditor takes part in the
> *rights of the masters*: at last he, too, shares the elevated feeling of
> despising and maltreating someone as an 'inferior' – or at least,
> when the actual power of punishment, of exacting punishment, is
> already transferred to the 'authorities', of *seeing* the debtor
> despised and maltreated. So, then, compensation is made up of a
> warrant for and entitlement to cruelty.
>
> FRIEDRICH NIETZSCHE, *The Genealogy of Morality*

Introduction

In his justly renowned study, *Seductions of Crime*, Jack Katz (1988) argued against the view, presumed by modern deviance theory (especially the influential work of Robert K. Merton), that criminal behaviour was best seen as a displacement for normal objectives of economic and social advancement. Instead, Katz sought to examine specific criminal acts as fun, expressive, and satisfying. This need not be taken as an invitation to ignore the economic distribution of opportunity as a determinant of crime. While class may not determine the motivations for crime, it does create the opportunity structure in which those motivations will be pursued. Indeed, Katz himself argued that for people of means the pursuit of these values through crime would be close to insane because of the availability of sanctioned means to accomplish many of the same kinds of benefits.

This chapter explores the notion of whether it would be profitable for the sociology of the punitive mentality to have its own version of Katz's turn. Much of the current discussion of penal practices in the US presumes that political support for harsh measures reflects a belief by ordinary citizens, manipulated or otherwise, that crime is out of control and the past failure of government to impose certain and stiff penalties is to blame. Most politicians and some academics talk as if this was a rational response to heightened levels of crime and the failure of earlier crime control strategies. Many academics and very few politicians talk as if the dominant ideas and practices of punishment are a displacement of other deeper social objectives or meanings like disciplining the working class, containing the underclass, or expressing a post-Civil Rights era version of keeping the African-American population down. Both views tend to downplay what might be thought of as the middle range aspects of punishment, not individual intentions or macro social structures, but the background of practices, institutions, and meanings against which strategic and expressive conduct by all kinds of agents and actors is intelligible.

In contrast, the approach to punishment modelled in this paper, privileges the 'what' rather than the 'why'. What is in fact produced? What possibilities are opened for action, expression, and imagination? Against the pull of explaining punishment, several tactical and methodological disciplines are borrowed from the work of social theorists like Bourdieu (1993), Foucault (1977), and Garland (forthcoming). First, foregrounding the fragmentary nature of punishment for victims, for specific work forces, like guards or lawyers, for the general audiences of voters, newspaper readers, and other spectators; second, studying the horizontal links that specific penal resources create between particular actors rather than the vertical links that establish their reference to deeper social concerns; third, mapping the lateral movements by which punishments and the legal procedures necessary to carry them out provide satisfaction to those authorizing them, exercizing them, watching them, or merely acting in the highly charged atmosphere they tend to create.

The next part of this chapter ('Cruelty') identifies a specific aspect of the penal field for closer scrutiny, the increasing role of cruelty. One of the most widely noted features of the present conjuncture is the severity of current penality, especially in the United States where the death penalty, life-trashing prison sentences, and shame sanctions (Kennedy forthcoming; Pratt, 1998; Kahan, 1996). Then, in the section headed 'Cruelty and Social Organisations', III, I offer a preliminary analysis of how the moral economy developed by the production of cruelty may fit with the challenges of shaping new strategies of governing subjects under conditions of advanced liberalism (Rose 1999) and the emergence of a risk society (Beck, 1992).

Cruelty

I use the term cruelty for this trend toward penalties that are painful, vengeful, and destructive of the penitent in body as well as life chances. By cruelty I also mean to foreground a feature of the public presentation of these penalties as something more than a belief in the necessity of harsh punishments to provide some crime control benefit, or even to satisfy some philosophically abstracted notion of retribution. By cruelty I mean satisfaction at the suffering implied by, or imposed by, punishments upon criminals, as well as emotions of anger and desire for vengeance taking violence.

Until quite recently it seemed that while these sentiments and mentalities remained an important motivation behind penal practices, they operated against a strong set of cultural norms restraining their expression, norms which seemed to grow more powerful with the advance of modernization itself (Jacoby, 1983). As David Garland noted (1990, 66):

> Punishment continues to be an 'emotive issue', as the politicians say, but in fact our culture imposes heavy restraints upon such emotions, and ensures that the forms and possibilities of their expression are carefully structured and controlled. 'Vengeance', for example, is no longer an acceptable sentiment to be voiced in this context. … In fact 'punitiveness', as such, has come to be a rather shameful sentiment during the twentieth century, at least among the educated elite, so that arguments about prison conditions, severity of sentences, or the justice of the death penalty tend to be couched in utilitarian terms – even when it seems apparent that hard treatment is what is wanted, not 'useful effects'.

In the year 2000, it is far from clear that cruelty or vengeance[1] is no longer an acceptable sentiment and the hold of utilitarian arguments on penal discourse is loosening and changing in its very form. As recently as the 1970s a majority of death penalty supporters cited deterrence as their primary rationale. By the 1990s a majority of death penalty supporters identified statements suggestive of retribution and cruelty as their primary reason for popular support of the death penalty (Ellsworth and Gross, 1994: 26–29).

In fact, the notion of retribution as an abstract requirement of justice is giving way to the ability of specific individuals to obtain satisfaction from cruelty, and is reflected in the prominence that politicians now give to the desires of family members of the victims of violent crime (especially murder) for the emotional satisfaction of a death penalty carried out with dispatch and a minimum of solicitude for the offender. A new kind of state psychology is evident in the frequency with which elected officials invoke the need for surviving loved ones of the victim to achieve 'closure' or move to another stage in their grieving process. This kind of therapeutic culture of punishment may suggest a very different form of subjectivity to those studied by anthropologists and historians of cruelty, but it shares an appropriation of punishment for the work of personal self-fashioning (Miller, 1993; Scheper-Hughes, 1998: 114–15; Greenblatt, 1980). The really disturbing question, both individually and collectively, is just what kind of subjectivity is nourished on such material.

Cruelty has also emerged as a theme within the production of academic knowledge about punishment. A new wave of philosophical retributivists has begun to reimagine punishment as a kind of therapeutic theatre in which the needs of both society and the victim to enact within the subjectivity of the offender feelings of pain and moral shame are satisfied (Hampton, 1984). There is also growing interest among legal theorists for new symbolic punishments that make the humiliation and psychological discomfort of existing sanctions like probation more palpable (Kahan, 1996).

What we call here cruelty is not the only or perhaps even the dominant feature of contemporary developments in penality.[2] Thus far it can be seen most prominently in three types of sanctions: capital punishment, extremely long prison terms (what I call 'life-trashing' sentences), and in a potpourri of sanctions and quasi-sanctions that go by the name of 'shame sanctions'. In addition, each of these has a penumbra of extra-legal actors for whom the cruelty of sanctions creates a flow of power and opportunity.

The death penalty

The death penalty can be thought of as a vast theatre of cruelty in which the scene of execution is only one act. The writing and adoption of a death penalty law allows the legislators of the state, and vicariously their constituents, to experience the satisfaction of pronouncing their preparedness to take the lives of murderers (Zimring and Hawkins, 1986). Each further amendment which 'toughens' that law allows for a repeat of this performance.[3] Some of these amendments are directed at particular types of potential victims to be recognised as esteemed subjects of law, and perhaps to deploy this status in pursuit of other kinds of public benefits (Simon and Spaulding, 1999).

At another end of the system, capital sentencing provides for the families of murder victims to express their desire for cruelty to the offender and to the public through the media. In Miami, for example, it is becoming a common practice for judges to allow victims to speak at the sentencing hearing, prior to the judge's statement of the sentence. This is not testimony for purposes of informing the judge; the decision has already been made. Instead, it is an opportunity, granted to the victim's family by the trial judge, in front of print media and cameras to berate the convicted killer and express their rage.[4]

The experience of cruelty is not limited to the victim's loved ones. To live in a city like Miami where death penalties are issued several times a year is to read headlines in the morning newspaper like the following:[5]

Jimmy's killer gets the chair
Chavez 'forfeited his right to live among us,' judge says

Such speech acts may be largely markers in a game of electoral politics as trial judges, subject to election, seek to link their names with tough on crime sentences. But that political purpose does not exhaust their narrative effects. It would take careful ethnographic research to understand how it changes a speaker to participate in a discursive field in which such speech acts are performed with some regularity.[6]

Life-trashing prison sentences

But while the death penalty is the most expressively cruel sanction, an argument can be made that a new kind of prison sentence also fits the model of cruelty. Characterized by severity of length and the fact that they are often mandatory and lack possibilities for reduction (via parole), the new prison sentences share with the death penalty this quality I would call 'life-trashing'. Prison sentences of forty or fifty years, with no possibility of parole, operate just like the death penalty in shattering any possibility of common ground between agents of punishment and subjects of punishment. Such sentences are also cruel in the sense used here because they are undisguisedly aimed at causing pain and despair in their targets. What judge could realistically say, 'And I hope you come out a better person' to a twenty-year old receiving a fifty-year sentence for drug trafficking? They might as well say, 'You have forfeited your right to live among us'.

Law enforcement as a blood-sport

These life-trashing sentences are connected to a third dynamic of cruelty that is playing out in the expanded police and penal sectors. As agencies of government, police departments, jails, and prisons remain subject to strong legal constraints against displays of cruelty or personal vengeance taking. Some of the embarrassment that for several centuries, at least, attended the administration of punishment remains in the high level of formal neutrality that the law requires its agents to take. The pull of this is more than legal. A salient example is the fact that the word 'correctional' has been retained almost universally by contemporary prison systems even though the rehabilitative ideal that made sense of it has been largely abandoned. You will search the nation in vain for a jail or prison that has officially named itself a 'cruelty centre'.

At the same time and despite intensive bureaucratization of both police and corrections, the persistent pattern of expressive violence by police against arrestees and by prison staff against inmates is growing (Skolnick and Fyfe, 1993; Chevigny, 1995; *Madrid v. Gomez*). This violence may be an effect, in part, of the larger war-like dynamic that is set up by life-trashing prison sentences. A police officer or federal agent seeking to make an arrest that could lead to such a sentence has every reason to view themselves as hunters involved in a lethal blood sport. One must at least explore whether an important attraction to employment in either of these fields is the access to cruelty that it provides.

Popular cruelty-seeking

Beyond the criminal justice system there is a vast and largely unstudied territory of cruelty-seeking in popular culture and everyday life. There are features of popular culture that reveal the appeal of cruelty. Consider MTV's enormously popular program *Celebrity Death Match*.[7] The show features puppet caricatures of celebrities fighting to the death in front of enthusiastic puppet caricature audiences. The show mimics the antics of professional wrestling in which the characters engage in vicious verbal exchanges before engaging in purely staged physical combat.[8] Here the celebrities are chosen because of real or imagined conflicts between them. Although the dramatic violence of the show and its explicit celebration of expressive humiliation and pain are made less morally problematic for the viewers by the fact that it is a cartoon, the combat is far more realistic, and lethal. So far this remains a theme of popular culture. Actual crowds outside executions and trials remain sparse and are highly unrepresentative of the population.

Even harder to measure change in is the broad set of cruelty-seeking conduct by private individuals in private. Criminologists have long suspected that a good deal of crime represents private acts of cruelty. Domestic violence is a recognized example where the batterers almost always view themselves as punishing the battered spouse for any number or 'wrongs'. There is also a substantial body of mail order publications aimed at the person looking to 'get even' with someone, typically an employer or a former spouse.

Cruelty and social organization: the sociology of the punitive mentality

The return of cruelty to respectability as a penal value is, at the very least, an important reversal in what has long been considered one of the master patterns of modernization (Durkheim, 1901; Elias, 1978; Foucault, 1977; Pratt, 1998). The decline of cruelty as a public justification for punishment has been celebrated since the eighteenth century as a central feature of civilization's progress and enlightened, modern values. The emergence of rehabilitation as central purpose of punishment at the beginning of the twentieth century seemed to mark a final victory of these values over traditional purposes, including cruelty. What to make of this counter trend has been of obvious interest to students of penality (Radzinowicz, 1991; Simon, 1997; Pratt, 1998; see the chapters by Hudson, O'Malley, and Stenson and Edwards in this volume). This chapter argues that we resist the temptation to examine these developments under the sign of 'penal regression' (Radzinowicz, 1991). The promoters of what Foucault memorably called 'the gentle way in punishment' (Foucault, 1977) viewed cruelty in punishment as a natural and primitive response to crime, to be replaced by civilization's more refined aims. But in exploring a present in which so many of the Enlightenment's fondest constructs are eroding, we would be badly served by taking over their presumptions. Instead, following recent historians of culture (Miller 1993), I examine cruelty-seeking in contemporary penality as a complex formation of narratives, interpersonal relations, and emotions. From this perspective it is not a desire or drive always present and waiting to make itself heard socially; instead it is the refined product of its own construction process. Instead of seeking to map the political and economic patterns that correspond to the vicissitudes of an instinct, in the Freudian sense, we should map the economy of power in which cruelty has come to have currency (Foucault, 1977).

To help us surface the broadest array of functions that cruelty in penality serves in contemporary society I turn in this section to two sociological theorists most often cited as providing the foundations for an understanding of the punitive mentality and its diminution under conditions of modernity, Emile Durkheim and Norbert Elias.[9] The suppression of the element of cruelty in punishments provided a constitutive problem for the sociology of punishment in modern society (Garland, 1990). Durkheim offered his famous 'laws of penal evolution' to explain this transition. Elias (1978) looked to other issues in the main, but his 'arc of civility' traced an evolution in the sensibilities of modernizing societies that has been productively related to punishment (Spierenberg, 1984; 1991).

Here, however, I want to reverse the logic for which their theories are usually invoked. Rather than explaining the rise of cruelty I want to explore its effects. If one assumes that strong residues of the modernist sensibility keep the subjective value of cruelty underdeveloped, then it is likely that our penal laws and our prisons are turning out more cruelty than our current 'emotional economy' (Miller, 1993: 115) can utilize. The problem is not to explain the production of this surplus (or at least not the only problem) but rather how that surplus will be used up. Will the growing population of felons draw to it strategies and practices that can make use of their stigmatized status?[10] Will it be converted to other uses by those with enough will-to-power to place some other meaning on that stigma? Or will it simply decay into a kind of cultural pollution that no parties are capable of either exploiting or converting? Here it seems to me that we can usefully draw on all the great strands of social theorizing on the punitive mentality, not as explanation for an ongoing change seen, as it were, diachronically, but as the generator of a field of possibilities from which to situate existing formations synchronically.

Durkheim

Durkheim's contributions to the theory of criminal deviance remain more influential than his efforts to theorise penality. This is due in large part to Durkheim's emphasis on penal law as an expression of social solidarity at the expense of a closer study of the way the power to punish is actually organized and exercized (Garland, 1990). Even in his most significant effort to reflect on penal form, the essay *Two Laws on Penal Evolution* (1901), Durkheim fails to examine the character of the changes he describes. Pointing to the historic shift from sanguinary and painful punishments to greater and greater reliance on imprisonment, Durkheim is primarily interested to rehearse his master story about the evolution of social solidarity from mechanical to organic solidarity. From this perspective Durkheim reduces the prison to one dimension, its reduction in severity from the bloody practices of the past. Its positive characteristics remain unsurveyed and irrelevant to his effort to fit the curve of penal evolution to that of social change more generally.

Yet, as Garland (1990) argues, Durkheim's emphasis on the public's response to crime and punishment is an important corrective to treating punishments primarily as instruments of power over those punished. Reconstructed (or perhaps deconstructed) Durkheim remains valuable to thinking about contemporary penal transformations. Punishments are a way of exercizing power on those punished, but also on those who watch or imagine.

For purposes of this chapter I want to briefly catalogue the major variables that Durkheim identifies as driving the level of cruelty[11] in his *Two Laws of Penal Evolution* (1901) and his earlier book, *The Division of Labour* (1893). Durkheim suggested that reduction in the severity of the penal law reflected a fundamental change in the division of labour. The response to crime is a central feature of society's moral order (or *conscience collective* in Durkheim's phrase) which is itself shaped by the division of labour. Societies of relatively simple divisions of labour, with relatively little role differentiation, according to Durkheim, have moral orders focused on uniformity of identity. This moral order, which Durkheim spoke of as 'mechanical solidarity', corresponded to a harshly punitive response to crime. The development of a complex and interdependent division of labour produced a moral order, which Durkheim described as 'organic solidarity', in which the response to crime was both less central overall and less severe, better represented in the restorative law of contracts, property and civil injuries. The bloody rituals of the scaffold reflected the characteristics of the *conscience collective* under mechanical solidarity. Under conditions of organic solidarity justice is increasingly reconceived as restitutive. There is less intense collective emotion and what there is valorizes things like individuality, rationality, and choice, which mitigate against cruelty.

Durkheim's basic story seems to track relatively well the decline in penal severity across most Western societies from at least the eighteenth century on. The emergence of a complex industrial division of labour corresponded to a marked decline in the use of the death penalty and of corporal punishments. It is less clear that the same model can account for the shift back toward severity in recent decades. The division of labour in the sense used by Durkheim has not returned to a state of mechanical solidarity. The diversification of economic functions continues. Indeed accounts of contemporary transformations of economic life associated with the emergence of advanced liberalism suggest an intensification of this process with even the relatively stable occupational patterns of industrial capitalism breaking down in favour of rapidly changing roles and statuses (Beck, 1992).

The state

In the *Two Laws of Penal Evolution*, Durkheim introduces a factor rather ignored in his earlier theory of punishment, that is, the nature of the state. Although Durkheim died before the triumph of fascism in Europe he anticipated both that absolutist states could co-exist with modernist economies and that fascism would result in an intensification of the severity of penal law. In such a society, in effect, the figure of the leader invested penal law with some of the severity demanded by mechanical solidarity.

The case of Hitler and Stalin, or even Castro and Milosovich, suggest how the cult of personality can replace the deity as a source of vengeful demands by the law. But whatever else is going on in the United States today it is difficult to interpret it as a triumph of political authority, at least at the level of our national leaders. One need only consider our recent Presidential impeachment to be sceptical of the view that the punitive trend in American justice reflects the vicarious fear and respect for an idealized and godlike leader.

Religion

In the *Two Laws of Penal Evolution*, Durkheim emphasizes the religious roots of penal severity. Societies of mechanical solidarity tend to concretize their moral order in the form of deities. The violation of law, in such cultures, produces a demand for cruelty on behalf of the offended deity. Leniency in punishment posed a risk of angering the gods and thus bringing retribution against the whole community.

The resurgence of religious practice in the United States over the past three decades, and perhaps more importantly, the increasingly political role of fundamentalist protestant sects in that period, would seem to bear some consideration as a source of cruelty. Durkheim himself had anticipated that the playing out of the secularization trend would be experienced as a levelling off of the trend toward gentleness in punishment. And yet even if these sects are an important source of punitive narratives (and we shall see potential customers for the surplus production of cruelty) they do not seem to operate primarily by displacing a fear of collective punishment. The contemporary growth of religion in the United States emphasizes features of self-improvement and realization over collective norm adherence.

Individualism (rationality and freedom)

In both *Two Laws of Penal Evolution* (1901) and in his earlier book, *The Division of Labour*, Durkheim suggests that the modern division of labour yields a moral order that enshrines quite different values. The nature of the new values, rationality, freedom, individualism, affects the severity of punishments in two ways. First, because these values are less well expressed in penal sanctions than in the institutional vehicles of civil justice. Second, and admittedly Durkheim does not develop this thought much, because the values themselves mitigate punishment. It is in the nature of such a value system to care about the offender as an individual, to question their rationality and freedom. Likewise, subjects that value themselves primarily for rationality, freedom, and individuality, are unlikely to find in cruelty much satisfaction, but rather instead discomfort brought on by empathy with the sufferer.

Individualism does not seem to be in decline even if it no longer can project itself as an inevitable and universal stage of human cultural development. The Taliban may rule Afghanistan (as much as any state can) but much of the rest of the globe continues to cope with an expansion of the various trends associated with individualism, including rationality and freedom. Indeed, some have argued that the nature of individualism has only intensified (Beck, 1992).

Elias

Like Durkheim, Norbert Elias attempted to find in the changing rules of society, an indicator of its state of evolution toward modernity. In his best known book, *The Civilizing Process* (1978), Elias examined etiquette books and other practices of the aristocracy from the thirteenth through the eighteenth centuries. What he found was a consistent pattern of change across a wide range of practices including food preparation, food consumption, and waste expulsion. In all these areas the uniform direction was toward moving the body and its analogies behind the scenes, a growing capacity to take into account the feelings of others, and a distancing of social relations from bodily contact. Closely related was a suppression of violence or even its symbolic portrayal.

Influenced by the work of Sigmund Freud, Elias saw the civilizing process as closely related to the repression of the instincts. Elias' contribution was to see this as linked to the evolution of social organization and social control.[12] On Elias' account the construction of more advanced forms of social organization, largely in the form of the state, parallels the repression of the instincts in the form of manners. The decline in the cruelty of punishment, from this perspective, can be seen as a response to civility norms. Punishments that call for violent attacks on the body of criminals offend the sensibilities of one who has been civilized in two ways: first, by exposing them to sights of the body and of pain that cause profound discomfort and embarrassment to the observer; second, through the capacity of the observer to empathize with the experience of the target of punishment.

Is there evidence of a broader de-civilizing process? Social observers since Herbert Marcuse (1970) have noted the waning of the Freudian concept of 'man'. Instinctual repression, at least the way Freud and Elias thought of it, seems inconsistent with the massive cultural promotion of desire in most advanced liberal societies (Rose, 1999). Sex and drugs and rock and roll may be all some bodies need but they are not what Elias would have thought of as civilized bodies. Likewise the availability of highly expressive violence in the media is clearly increasing and moving to harder core modes as it shifts to other media like computer games.

The homology between psychic and social order presupposes a certain degree of closeness to society. If we learn to sacrifice our own gratification in order to invest the energy in a collective process it must come from a sense of solidarity (with all the sense of obligation that entails). The rise of welfare states in both Europe and North America marked the apotheosis of that development. The welfare state was in some respects a pay-off to people for the hard work of civility. It lifted huge areas of worry off the shoulders of individuals. If you lose your job, if you get hurt, if you get old, we will take care of you (Baumann, 1998: 117).

The larger political and economic strategies of neo-liberalism tend to place many of those burdens back on individuals. What remains of organized forms of social solidarity are further problematized by increased immigration and growing fragmentation of the society into geographically segregated class and race enclaves. These changes may be breaking down the psychical equilibrium that the civilizing process presupposed.

For the period covered by Elias' arc of civility the key transformation in social control was from violent external repression, to disciplinary training and self-control. Modern government could only work by having subjects who had internalized capacity for self-control. Some have argued that this model of governance is giving way to a new one that combines features of disciplinary technology with a more external approach. Clifford Shearing and Philip Stenning (1984) provide the most powerful example, in their essay, 'From the Panopticon to Disney World'. Disney World works by embedding policing and social control right into the landscape and architecture. Other related examples include gated communities, airports, high-tech highways. In these systems punishment is largely replaced by exclusion.[13] If we are becoming postmodern in this way it has a number of implications for the civilizing process. First, the stake of the state and other power elites in the civilizing process may disappear. Since control can be assured externally there is no reason to invest heavily in encouraging people to self-control. Second, self-control may not disappear but it may become privatized so that those who invest in those skills are rewarded by greater access to the goods of society while those who do not are excluded.

More interestingly, perhaps, the civilizing process itself may provide a way of understanding the return to cruelty. The same traits that lead to civility also lead to a greater fear of violence and a greater empathy with victims. These in turn may lead to demands for punishment as a form of security. Because we see punishment as an instrumentally useful security device, we may not respond to it as an act of violence and thus feel embarrassment and empathy. For example, we do not view surgery as violence because we believe it is objectively necessary and we believe it is being carried out in a dispassionate way. Thus while we may fantasize about violently punishing criminals, and simultaneously pack many of them into prisons, we rarely seem to fantasize about the packed prison. HBO's dramatic series, *Oz*, is currently the only television show to include regular images of prison life (and that on a premium channel).

Even if one elected to hold onto Elias' Freudian psycho-sexual model, it is possible to imagine that the very increasing demands of civility could generate support for cruelty toward criminal offenders. Curiously (from Freud's perspective) the trends toward cultural desublimation, lots more nudity, sex, and violence, has paralleled increasing demands for civility in our society. For example, much verbal (and even physical) abuse that was once permitted in the workplace and the family is now seen as socially unacceptable and even legally actionable. The service economy, in contrast to the industrial economy, requires even more emotional labour (Hochschild, 1983) and impression management. The old-fashioned assembly line worker could be as sullen and ill-tempered as they cared to be (within limits). The worker at McDonalds has to be polite and cheery all day long even if they are feeling bad. The old-fashioned assembly line worker could be as sullen and ill-tempered as they cared to be (within limits). The growth of anti-discrimination norms means that there are fewer categories of people who are exempted from the general norms of civility. Traditionally, even late into our own history, there were people one could verbally and sometimes physically abuse without much consequence, including some minorities; children (so long as one's own), wives (so long as one's own). As these have been closed off the criminal remains one of the few targets for venting aggressive drives.

The currency of cruelty

No doubt one could play out a far more sophisticated parlour game of Durkheim and Elias. My point is not, in any event, to dissuade anyone who might seriously construct a social theory proper on the basis of our current penal trends. Indeed an initial pass, at any rate, through applied social theory is useful for the next iteration. There I want to suggest that the phenomena that we begin to surface by running Durkheim and Elias through rewind come into more interesting if not sharper focus when we ask a very different question. What does the cultural production of cruelty do? What kinds of things does it make visible as a form of knowledge? What strategies does it invite?

Neo-mechanical solidarities

Globalization and de-industrialization has led to a kind of crisis of collective conscience of a sort that Durkheim would not really have anticipated but which we can draw on his theory to explore. His evolutionary approach was set at such a high level of abstraction that much was missed as problematic. The division of labour may have changed in ways that have rendered many modernist forms of government less effective. Law and science do not serve to resolve our disputes (Beck, 1992). People in such a moral economy might find a moral order celebrating individualism, rationality, and freedom, largely irrelevant. In Durkheim's sense they might be thrust back onto forms of mechanical solidarities. Only these no longer exist (if they ever did) in the unproblematic ways that Durkheim imagined. Nation, race, class, do not stand at ready to be re-harnessed. Instead we see the invention of new racisms, new nationalisms, new enclave economies.

Cruelty may in fact provide one kind of input to the construction of such postmodern mechanical solidarities. For many young males in or around the underclass, the reconstruction of an honour ethos emphasizing cruelty is readily apparent (Anderson, 1998). For others in the unstable middle tiers of the economy the perception that the moral order of modernity is fraying seems to be correlated to support for cruelty in criminal justice. California's '3-Strikes' law provides an example of the kind of contemporary penal sanction that incorporates cruelty. Although the law was formally defended on the usual grounds of deterrence and incapacitation, its promotion openly incorporated expressive anger against violent criminals against the backdrop of the recent abduction/murder of 12-year old Polly Klass from her middle-class home. Tyler and Boeckmann (1997: 35–36), in their study of why Californians supported the crudely expressive punitiveness of California's '3-Strikes' initiative, suggest that those who feared the breakdown of a common moral order as reflected in the family or in the demographic make-up of the state, were more likely to support the initiative.

Constructing authority

Durkheim tended to treat strong punishments as indicating the presence of an emotionally powerful loyalty to an authority whose command crime repudiates. His basic account, however, lends itself as well to an analysis of punishments as a mechanism for constructing authority (Garland, 1990). Later historians have shown that the ritual production of the criminal law can serve as an important vehicle for establishing the emotional supports for the existing class and political hierarchies (Hay, 1975; Linebaugh, 1992).

Some intellectuals have begun to defend features of contemporary penality linked here to cruelty, precisely in terms of its capacity to build authority. A particularly interesting case is David Gelernter, a professor of computer science at Yale, who since being severely wounded by a letter bomb mailed by 'unibomber' Theodore Kaczynski has begun to write about punishment. For Gelernter, punishment is an essential language of moral community, the death penalty even more so. 'The death penalty represents absolute speech from a position of moral certainty' (1998, 23). Opponents, Gelernter suspects, are not so much appalled by the violence but precisely by the moral certainty which offends the elitist moral scepticism which this class tends to affect.

Despite the overwhelming public support for the death penalty, Gelernter is not altogether sanguine about the capacity of this deep communitarian purpose to be accomplished. Having been tainted by the doubt of intellectual elites the culture is ambivalent about the death penalty, notwithstanding strong support in the abstract:

> The death penalty is hard for us as a community above all because of our moral evasiveness. For at least a generation, we have urged one another to switch off our moral faculties. 'Don't be judgmental!' We have said it so many times, we are starting to believe it. (Gelernter, 1998: 23)

Despite the risk that because of this moral decay the actual emotional responses mobilized by the death penalty are not the moralizing ones, which Gelernter intends, he believes that it is necessary to carry this penalty through because in the end it may create the meaning it now lacks:

> Our attempts to speak with assurance as a community come out sounding in consequence like a man who is fighting off a chokehold as he talks. But a community as cavalier about murder as we are has no right to back down. That we are botching things does not entitle us to give up.

Buddy State

But while neo-conservative intellectuals like David Gerlernter wait for the voice cruelty to become the voice of the stable patriarchically centred moral community, politicians have made a very different use of it. For them the death penalty is almost always an exercise in empathy with victims (I feel your pain) more than in shared sacrifice. The death penalty and other cruel sentences have become a central procedure of what might be called the Buddy State to link it to this remarkably popular genre of movies and to contrast it with varieties of more parental 'nanny' states and paternalistic welfare states.

President Bill Clinton has best defined the Buddy State in the 1990s. Leaders like Margaret Thatcher of the United Kingdom and Ronald Reagan of the United States during the 1980s portrayed the state as the enemy. President Clinton popularized a vision of the state as a kind of helper, not responsible for taking on the risks and burdens of the people but instead for providing guidance, encouragement and the occasional subsidy. When the Buddy State punishes the audience of victims the imaginary political audience would be hard pressed to experience a fearful and awesome presence of the state and its majesty. There is little in either sentencing or execution ritual that currently lends itself to that kind of construction. Instead the message is powerfully one of the state as reliable provider of that lawfully consecrated but private consumed entitlement to cruelty that a conviction for serious crime produces.

Where both the neo-conservatives of the moral community and the neo-liberals of the Buddy State find common ground is in the utility of cruelty for decomposing the forms of governance associated with the social welfare state. Murder, after all, is the perfect vehicle for attacking the socialization of risk in the welfare mode. It effectively symbolizes all of those risks that cannot be managed through the forms of security associated with the modern social welfare state, including insurance, public education, poverty programs and 'city planning' (Ewald, 1986). At the same time violence is taken as evidence of the moral decline visited upon populations secured through welfare modes of governance. This critique was made all the more compelling in the US case by the fact that homicide rates grew dramatically during the 1960s when welfare governance was perceived as expanding rapidly (Wilson, 1975). Cruelty as a kind of government benefit becomes increasingly relevant to individuals who already experience themselves as disaggregated from any social provision. Those who manage to stay afoot on these rapidly shifting currents of the new economy find that the most effective kind of demand for government to take responsibility for risk is about violent crime, and they can be expected to identify with the goal of cruelty against anyone who breaks the rules, and especially those who add to the real risks of material pain, suffering, and death through deploying violence (Baumann, 1998: 117–118).

The resurgence of religious values

Whether or not the cruelty of contemporary penality is driven in any sense by the rising influence of religious activists on American political culture, the prominence of cruelty within penality may feed religion. The case of Karla Fay Tucker is illustrative. Converted to Christ while on Texas' death row, Tucker became a national celebrity when religious conservatives like Pat Robertson appealed for the commutation of her sentence. The telegenic young woman was seen repeatedly on television narrating the truly tragic features of her life through the metaphors of Christian salvation and speaking absolutely sincerely of her readiness to meet her saviour. Although Karla Fay Tucker's religious appeal did not save her life, her moment in the public eye revealed how powerful capital punishment is for religion, and especially Christianity. It is not simply a question of whether Christian values support capital punishment or not (an issue of great contention), but of the way capital punishment enacts symbolic events enormously resonant for religion: the awfulness of sin, the pain and tragedy of death, the possibility of salvation and rebirth. Nor is this limited to conservative Christians like Pat Robertson. We can see the same themes operating in the figure of Sister Helen

Prejean, whose ministry among the condemned was the subject of the hit movie, 'Dead Man Walking' (1995).

Hyper-individualism

Durkheim and Elias both charted the relationship between the rise of individualism and the diminution of cruelty. No doubt a certain mode of Western individualism was embarrassed by cruel punishments with their degradation of the pretences of humanity, but this does not prove an inevitable and unchangeable relationship.

Durkheim recognised that under modern conditions the sanctity of the self could itself become a source of punitive moral outrage. Or to put it in Elias' terms, the rise in humanity in punishment that comes with the rising sense of empathetic identification with the suffering of others, is checked to some extent by the rising identification with the suffering of individuals as victims of crime. It is little wonder that in modern societies murder quickly sets itself as the most essential crime and the last place for a humanizing mercy to take hold.

The relationship between individualism and cruelty seems to change further under conditions of advanced liberalism, and specifically the dismantling of the collectivist forms of social security associated with the now discredited strategies of the social-welfare state.[14] In a world of low taxes and little state welfare function, economic and medical misfortune will be allowed to fall unmediated upon the population. Events like industrial accidents, the birth of a severely deformed child, a violent assault by a stranger or intimate, or the collapse of local economies, will leave adults and children at the mercy of relatives, friends, churches, and businesses, or the very coercive forms of state provision.[15]

In such a world it is not hard to understand how both violence and cruelty become an increasingly important part of the entire economy of power. Where individuals are permitted to suffer the sometimes violent blows of fate with only the most limited and coercive social mediation, those whose actions call for collective outrage must be clearly demarcated from those who face merely hardened social indifference. In such a culture ordinary people acquire a much greater stake in the public distancing of their suffering and their insecurity from that of those whose suffering and insecurity is an official sign of retributive desert, than they had under social welfare modes of governance. In this sense cruelty may become a kind of entitlement distributed by government.

The rise of what Ulrich Beck describes as the risk society also creates conditions where cruelty may become a resource for self-fashioning. The radical decomposition of the community and class contexts in which individualism was held in check during the first industrial phase of modernity leaves a self largely responsible for its own rituals of sanctification, a process he calls 'hyper-individualism'. The suffering of others can be made to reflect the value and esteem of those for whom the suffering is enacted (Simon and Spaulding, 1999). The current invocation of cruelty reflects not only a hardening of attitude against offenders but also a sense of entitlement to the death penalty as a satisfying personal experience for victims, and a satisfying gesture for the rest of the community. The subjective satisfactions produced by the death penalty are sufficient in its own terms.

Conclusion

Social theory may offer us valuable tools for understanding the significance of the reconfiguration of punishment that is taking place in the United States and other advanced liberal societies. The particular purposes of punishment that are emerging today are not simply a problem to be explained by the past but clues to interpret our present. As Nietzsche argued: But every purpose and use is just a *sign* that the will to power has achieved mastery over something less powerful, and has impressed upon it its own idea [*Sinn*] of a function (Nietzsche, 1994: 55).

This chapter has attempted a preliminary analysis of how the increasing level of cruelty discourse in contemporary penal discourse is assimilated and used by existing social formations or those which might come into existence to take advantage of it. Cruelty remains an anathema to many of our most influential narratives of modern self-understanding. At the same time one can see it as a resource for communities, political authorities, and individuals as they strive to establish a new moral economy. As we begin to look closer at the emerging penality of cruelty our interests in its origins should not distract us from discerning what 'meanings' they have in our culture, and how they are invested with and invest different formations of power.

Notes

1   I use the term cruelty, rather than vengeance, to emphasize that the value of suffering may be relevant beyond the usual subjects assumed to have a specific compulsion to seek revenge (say the immediate family of the victim).
2   See O'Malley (1999) for a discussion of the heterogeneity of the penal field.
3   A recent amendment to the Florida constitution, adopted by ballot initiative, titled itself an act to 'save the death penalty' although it was mainly directed at fending off possible judicial challenges to Florida's electric chair.
4   Interestingly this is not a formal part of the statutory procedure but has become a judicial practice.
5   *The Miami Herald*, Tuesday, 24 November 1998, A1.
6   Some evidence for its capacity to provide meaning to membership in the political community is reflected by the intense cultural repugnance produced in Europe by the resurgence of the death penalty in the United States. (*New York Times*, Sunday 9 April, 2000)
7   See Eric Messinger, 'The premise is, poking fun can be a poke in the eye', *New York Times*, Sunday 28 March, 1999: 35.
8   Indeed the enormous popularity of professional wrestling on television generally points to the attractions of cruelty and its discourses. Long limited to a relatively small audience, wrestling is now on for as many as five hours a night during prime time on

cable. Indeed among males, from ages 12 to 34, wrestling now beats Monday night football as the most watched programming. See, Jeff MacGregor, The new pop hero: a mirage of muscle and mean, the *New York Times*, Sunday 28 March, 1999: 35. These shows suggest that cruelty does not need to be limited to socially beneficial acts of punishment carried out by a benevolent state. Indeed, while wrestling used to feature battles between easily recognized good and bad characters (with good reliably triumphing), the new wrestling universe lacks good guys altogether. 'As we enter professional wrestling's late century renaissance, though, everything has changed. Forget good guys; as in real life, there are none. Now there are only characters portraying various degrees of stylish, programmatic badness along a continuum that runs from costumed sociopath to attractively rebellious anti-hero' (MacGregor, *ibid.*).

9   Here I once again draw heavily on David Garland's (1990) reconstruction of modern social theory and its reflections on the transformation of punishment in modern society.

10 This is a set which is already enormously broad, encompassing gangs which can employ those locked into that labor market by their stigma, law enforcement agencies that can demand new resources to manage this stigma.

11 Durkheim did not of course analyse cruelty in the way I am using that term here. I am taking the rather large liberty of treating cruelty as fairly consistent with the larger theme of penal severity, while bracketing the difference for now.

12 Here we can find close links to both Durkheim and Foucault. Durkheim saw the rise of a complex and interdependent division of labour as the key to modernity. He argued that the form of social solidarity created by the modern division of labour was both powerful and more refined (importantly for us not requiring reproduction through gross and public punishments). In some regards Elias is providing a psycho-social explanation of this. A complex division of labour requires people who are capable of carefully managing their relations with others. Manners are an important outward form of this, but they reflect a growing capacity for internal self-control. The transformation of the aristocracy from a warrior elite to a court society marks the emergence of skills in social coordination and the repression of the honor ethos, both keys to modern economic and social relations. The court aristocrats who spend all their time on dress and preparing for social exchange are the model for modern business relations where impression management is key.

Foucault tells a similar story about social control. Once societies were governed through crude and external sanctions. The capacity of rulers to monitor obedience was limited. Rulers relied heavily on dramatic and ritualistic occasions to create lasting fear and loyalty. The disciplines represented a new technology of governance that changed this. They replaced erratic and spectacular rituals with continuous and unobtrusive controls pegged to the individual. Although external in some sense they operate, as the Panopticon metaphor reminds us, by inculcating a capacity for internal self-control.

13 Jock Young (1999) has characterized this as a shift from a culture of cannibalism (deviance must be digested) to a culture of bulimia (deviance must be expelled).

14 Social security here refers not to the specific set of federal programs popularly called 'social security' but the larger body of governmental strategies aimed at socializing the risks of life in industrial society, of which social security in the narrower sense is an example.

15 The form of the prison seems to have been applied early on primarily to debtors, paupers, and vagabonds, rather than robbers and thieves.

References

Anderson, Elijah (1998) 'The Social Ecology of Youth Violence', in Mark H. Moore and Michael Tonry, eds. *Crime and Justice, Vol. 24: Youth Violence*. Chicago: University of Chicago Press.

Baumann, Zygmunt (1998) *Globalization: The Human Consequences*. New York: Columbia University Press.

Beck, Ulrich (1992) *Risk Society: Towards a New Modernity*, translated by Mark Ritter. London: Sage.

Bourdieu, Pierre (1993) *The Logic of Practice*, translated by Richard Nice. Stanford, CA: Stanford University Press.

Chevigny, Paul (1995) *Edge of the Knife: Police Violence in the Americas*. New York: The New Press.

Durkheim, Emile (1901, translated 1973) 'Two Laws of Penal Evolution,' translated by T. Anthony Jones and Andrew Scull, in Stephen Lukes and Andrew Scull eds. (1983) *Durkheim and the Law*. London: Oxford (pp.102–132).

Elias, Norbert (1939, translated 1978) *The History of Manners: Vol. I. The Civilizing Process*, translated by Edmund Jephcott. New York: Pantheon.

Ellsworth, Phoebe C. and Samuel R. Gross (1994) 'Hardening of the Attitudes: Americans' Views on the Death Penalty', *Journal of Social Issues,* 50: 19–52.

Foucault, Michel (1977) *Discipline and Punish: The Birth of the Prison*, translated by Alan Sheridan. New York: Pantheon.

Garland, David (1990) *Punishment and Modern Society*. Chicago: University of Chicago Press.

Gerlernter, David (1998) 'What Do Murderers Deserve?', *Commentary*. April 1998: 21–24.

Greenblatt, Stephen (1980) *Renaissance Self Fashioning: From More to Shakespeare*. Chicago: University of Chicago Press).

Hamptom, Jean (1984) 'The Moral Education Theory of Punishment', *Philosophy and Public Affairs*, 13: 211.

Hochschild, Arlie (1983) *The Managed Heart: The Commercialization of Human Feeling* Berkeley: University of California Press.

Jacoby, Susan (1983) *Wild Justice: The Evolution of Revenge*. New York: Harper and Rowe.

Kahan, Dan M. (1996) 'What Do Alternative Sanctions Mean?' *University of Chicago Law Review*, 63: 591–653.

Katz, Jack (1988) *Seductions of Crime: Moral and Sensual Attractions of Doing Evil*.

Kennedy, Joseph (forthcoming).

Linebaugh, Peter (1992) *The London Hanged: Crime and Civil Society in the Eighteenth Century*. New York: Cambridge University Press.

Marcuse, Herbert (1970) 'The Obsolescence of the Freudian Concept of Man', in *Five Lectures: Psycho-Analysis, Politics, Utopia*, translated by Jeremy H. Shapiro and Shierry M. Weber. Boston: Beacon Press.

Miller, William Ian (1993) *Humiliation and Other Essays on Honor, Social Discomfort, and Violence*. Ithaca: Cornell University Press.

Nietzsche, Friedrich (1994) *On the Genealogy of Morality*, translated by Carol Diethe. Cambridge, UK: Cambridge University Press.

O'Malley, Pat (1999) 'Volatile and Contradictory Punishment', *Theoretical Criminology*, 3: 175–196.

Pratt, John (1998) 'Towards the "Decivilizing" of Punishment?' (unpublished manuscript on file with author).

Radzinowicz, Sir Leon (1991) 'Penal Regressions', *Cambridge Law Journal*, 50: 422–444.

Rose, Nikolas (1999) *The Powers of Freedom*. Cambridge, UK: Cambridge University Press.

Scheper-Huges, Nancy (1998) 'Undoing: Social Suffering and the Politics of Remorse in the New South Africa', *Social Justice*, 25: 114–142.

Shearing, Clifford and Phillip Stenning (1984) 'From the Panopticon to Disney World: The Development of Discipline', in A. Doob and E. Greenspan, eds. *Perspectives in Criminal Law*. Aurora, Ont.: Canada Law Books.

Simon, Jonathan (1997) 'Governing Through Crime', in George Fisher and Lawrence Friedman, eds., *The Crime Conundrum: Essays on Criminal Justice*, pp.171–190. New York: Westview Press.

Simon, Jonathan and Christina Spaulding (1999) 'Tokens of Our Esteem: Aggravating Factors in the Era of Deregulated Death Penalties', in Austin Sarat (ed.) *The Killing State: Capital Punishment in Law, Politics, and Culture*, pp.81–114. Oxford, UK: Oxford University Press.

Skolnick, Jerome H. and James F. Fyfe (1993) *Above the Law: Police and the Excessive Use of Force*. New York: Free Press.

Spierenberg, Pieter (1984) *The Spectacle of Suffering: Executions and the Evolution of Repression from a Pre-Industrial Metropolis to the European Experience*. Cambridge, UK: Cambridge University Press.

Spierenberg, Pieter (1991) *The Prison Experience: Disciplinary Institutions and Their Inmates in Early Modern Europe*. New Brunswick, NJ: Rutgers University Press.

Tyler, Tom R. and Robert J. Boeckmann (1997), 'Three Strikes and You Are Out, but Why? The Psychology of Public Support for Punishing Rule Breakers', *Law and Society Review*, 31: 237.

Wilson, James Q. (1975, second edition 1983) *Thinking About Crime*. New York: Basic Books.

Young, Jock (1999) 'Cannibalism and Bulimia: Patterns of Social Control in Late Modernity', *Theoretical Criminology*, 3: 387.

Zimring, Franklin E. and Gordon Hawkins (1986) *Capital Punishment and the American Agenda*. Chicago: University of Chicago Press.

8

Punishment, rights and difference:
defending justice in the risk society

Barbara Hudson

Introduction: justice, risk and neo-liberalism

The problem with which I am concerned in this chapter is the sense that 'justice' is an endangered concept in the UK, USA, and other similar societies. Apart from a few members of the judiciary, legal theorists, philosophers, and some human rights specialists and civil libertarians, our societies seem to be losing sight of the importance of justice as a regulative ideal. Commitment to justice is weakening; indeed, our societies seem almost to be losing a discourse, even a vocabulary, of justice. What is in danger of being lost is understanding of the difference between 'justice' and 'vengeance'.

We can see lack of commitment to justice very clearly in policies to do with crime and punishment. Mandatory sentencing laws in particular and the reduction of judicial discretion in general diminish the scope for substantive justice in criminal justice proceedings; we also find lack of concern for justice in the absence of substantial opposition to altering the implications of maintaining silence in police interviewing, and to altering the rules of disclosure of evidence because it is thought that too many 'guilty' people are being acquitted by the courts.

'Justice' is now very much less important than 'risk' as a preoccupation of criminal justice/law and order policy; the politics of safety have overwhelmed attachment to justice in the institutions of late-modern democratic polities. If someone, or some category of persons, is categorized as a risk to public safety, there seems to remain scarcely any sense that they are nonetheless owed justice. The vocabulary of justice is almost entirely absent from current debates about sexual offending (in particular); about safety in public spaces; and about penal treatment of those deemed at risk of reoffending. Discussion of crime prevention techniques such as CCTV, for example, show how easily risk to the law-abiding public 'trumps' justice not only to offenders, but also to others who may come into various contemporary categories of suspicion.

'Justice', in popular and political discourse, seems now to be synonymous with 'punishment'. When victims or the public generally, talk of wanting justice, or being denied justice, what is meant is a demand for an offender, or offenders, to be punished, or to be punished more severely. For those, myself included, who seek to identify some quality of justice which is not simply retribution – or vengeance – the quest for an adequate definition is difficult and inconclusive. The jurist Hans Kelsen comments on the elusiveness of an answer to the question of what is meant by 'justice', saying that down the ages the most illustrious of minds have failed to find a definitive answer to the question, 'what is justice?', but have only been able to improve the cogency with which the question is posed (Kelsen, 1996:183).

Most discussions of justice discuss the rules and social institutions necessary to secure justice, rather than attempting any definition of justice itself. Kelsen himself describes it as a 'social happiness'. He explains that he cannot say universally what this happiness involves, he can only say what it is for him. For him, 'justice is that social order under whose protection the search for truth can prosper. "My" justice, then, is the justice of freedom, the justice of peace, the justice of democracy – the justice of tolerance' (*ibid*: 206). This relativistic, almost-definition is compatible with that of John Stuart Mill, for whom 'Justice is a name for certain classes of moral rules, which concern the essentials of human well-being more nearly, and are therefore of more absolute obligation, than any other rules for the guidance of life' (Mill, 1996: 173).

Kelsen's almost-definition is also compatible with my own preferred perspective, which is the American criminologist and moral philosopher Jeffrey Reiman's theory of *justice as reason's answer to subjugation* (Reiman, 1990). While I might not agree with all Reiman's arguments, and while I approach both the necessity of an ideal of justice and the requirements of that ideal from a somewhat different direction, the essentials of his conclusion that the principles of justice are the principles which are necessary to defend humans living in societies against oppression, are ones that I share, and which underpin this chapter.

Whatever their differences of wording, nuance and emphasis, approaches to justice generally refer to two different elements: a quantitative element and a qualitative element; distributive justice, and treatment which meets the requirements of the person being dealt with, treatment which meets the moral claims of the concrete Other. The first requires dealing with people fairly in relation to other people; the second requires dealing with people decently in relation to their own needs, beliefs and desires. These two different principles of justice are often known as *justice as fairness* and *justice as alterity*, and they are more or less equivalent to the principles termed *formal* and *substantive* justice in law. The formal elements of law involve applying legal rules consistently, and therefore if carried out fulfil the requirements of justice as fairness; substantive justice involves making the right decisions, providing the right remedy, for the particular case, and thus corresponds with the principle of justice as alterity.

These two components of justice are in some tension with each other, and the history of penal change reflects shifting balances between them. In the so-called rehabilitation era, substantive justice was emphasized to the detriment of formal justice; in the 1980s the formal elements, justice as fairness, were brought back to the centre, with substantive concerns relegated to very secondary status. As Bottoms has described, an over-emphasis on formal elements comes to look as though criminal justice is concerned only with internal, managerial objectives, and has lost adherence to any external referent (Bottoms, 1995). A rebalancing after the 1980s was almost inevitable, therefore. As we have seen on both sides of the Atlantic, however, the predominant substantive referent of criminal justice in the 1990s turned out to be risk, rather than 'justice'.

The first part of this chapter highlights some developments in penal policy in England and Wales during the 1990s which illustrate this shift from 'justice' to 'risk'. It is not my intention to present an exhaustive description of penal policy changes nor to attempt a comprehensive analysis.[1] On the contrary, I have selected some important developments which exemplify the shift from 'justice' to 'risk' as the primary organizing principle of criminal justice. Although my review of developments is highly selective, I do not believe that the examples are unrepresentative; I do believe that there has been a significant shift from doing justice to managing risk as the goal of law and order and penal strategies.

Next, there is a similarly brief and selective review of the so-called 'governmentality' perspective as it has engaged with, or has the potential to illuminate, late modern society's engagement with crime.[2] This literature focuses on the exercise of governance in the age of regulation by norm, and fits well with many aspects of current trends in crime control and penal policy, so that descriptions of 'new' or 'managerialist' penology draw on many of the same concepts and examples as the governmentality writings (Cohen, 1994; Feeley and Simon, 1994). There are, however, some differences in the trends observed by analysts of the growth of actuarialism in policy spheres such as health, education, and in relation to crime. Furthermore, the governmentality perspective, as Garland has pointed out, neglects important expressive elements in punishment, elements which are of great significance in the shift from justice to vengeance in late-1990s crime policy (Garland, 1997).

This literature, and the work of Foucault on which it draws, also omits to balance the description and analysis of the strengthening and deepening penetration of governance in the name of providing security, with the Enlightenment elaboration of theories of justice and boundaries of legitimate authority which were to set limits to governance. In Foucault's works, and in the works deriving from them, juridical and governmental power are granted an overwhelming puissance uninhibited by considerations of justice. Although, therefore, he gives us warnings of the totalitarian possibilities of power, he gives us little indication of the principles and institutions that need either to be preserved or to be initiated if western liberal democracies are not to become fully-fledged totalitarian carceral archipelagos (Hudson, 1996; Walzer, 1986).

My argument is, then, that if risk management is a legitimate goal of governance, it needs to be framed and limited by respect for the ideal of justice; if governmental power in relation to the risk of crime is enhanced, it needs to be balanced by correspondingly strengthened commitment to justice as regulative limit.

In the final sections of the paper, I turn to some developments that have potential for providing surfaces of emergence for another rebalancing, a shift of the pendulum back towards justice. By far the most important of these is the growing significance of The European Convention on Human Rights, hitherto acknow-ledged by the UK but without force in domestic legislation. The Convention is about to be inscribed into domestic law, and therefore there is the possibility that it could turn from pious but empty words to a real influence on institutions and practices. Current debates about its implications for penal policy are discussed. Most important is the way in which human rights is being adopted as an anchoring principle for criminal justice by influential legal scholars. My own contribution to these developments is to bring together this focus on rights with the literature on difference. The chapter therefore ends with a look at the relational theory of rights found in some, mainly US, legal scholarship (Minow, 1990), and the idea of 'legal guaranteeism' put forward, albeit sketchily as yet, by some European critical criminologists (Cohen, 1998; Pitch, 1995; Van Swaaningen, 1997).

Penal policy in the 1990s – some significant developments

Developments in penal policy in England and Wales since 1993 have been in the direction of greater harshness, expressed in the increasing use of imprisonment. This has been aptly described by Garland as punitive segregation, combined with penal marking: 'Punitive segregation – lengthy sentence terms in no frills prisons, and a marked, monitored existence for those who are eventually released – is increasingly the penal strategy of choice' (Garland, 1999: 8).

This strategy combines, Garland explains, a functional, instrumental logic which is focused on managing the risk of crime, and an expressive logic which makes clear that this is a blaming, stigmatizing strategy which allows the public to vent feelings of vengeance on wrongdoers (Sarat, 1997).

Penal developments in the mid- and late-1990s demonstrated a marked contrast with developments in the late-1980s and early 1990s. In 1988 prison populations had reached what was then a record high, and at that time this high led to attempts to achieve a reduction by introducing clear principles for the allocation of penal sanctions. A series of guideline judgments, white papers, setting of objectives for criminal justice agencies, training for sentencers and other initiatives encouraged penal bifurcation, with prison designated for serious offences and non-custodial sanctions developed and strengthened to provide appropriate penalties for less serious offences (Cavadino and Dignan, 1996; Newburn, 1995). This policy drive culminated in the 1991 Criminal Justice Act, generally regarded as the high-point of influence of the 'justice model' approach in England and Wales. By the time the 1991 Criminal Justice Act was implemented in 1992, the influence of its principles – disseminated through an unprecedented level of training of criminal justice professionals – had already brought about a reduction of prison numbers.

This reduction soon went into reverse, however. Ten years later, in 1998, the new peak in prison populations was apparently responded to by the present (at the time of writing) Labour Home Secretary telling ministers not to 'go on about' prison numbers, as he had no great desire to see them fall. The prison-building programme continues.

The mid- and late-1990s were characterized by the move from the policy-guiding belief that prison, if not used rationally and viewed as a scarce resource, can be an expensive way of making people worse, a view espoused by Douglas Hurd when Home Secretary, to the conviction that 'prison works', a view expressed by Michael Howard during his term as Home Secretary, both in office in a Conservative government. This signals a move from 'just deserts' to 'public protection' as the dominant idea in criminal justice. The move has been codified through a series of Acts of Parliament, but several well-publicized speeches by Michael Howard urging judges and magistrates to give prison sentences freely, meant that legislation has generally been catching up, rather than leading, penal practice.

The trends in prison numbers together with important legislation and policy interventions are summarized in the following table:

Table 8.1   Use of imprisonment, 1988–97

	Total Prison Population Annual averages		Proportionate use of immediate custody	
	Male	*Female*	*Magistrates' courts*	*Crown courts*
1988	48,160	1,789	6.6	49.2
1989	46,843	1,767	5.2	46.6
1990	44,039	1,597	4.4	43.0
1991	44,336	1,561	5.3	44.3
1992	44,240	1,577	4.9	44.3
1993	43,005	1,560	5.9	48.9
1994	46,983	1,811	7.2	52.0
1995	49,068	1,979	8.9	55.6
1996	53,019	2,262	9.3	60.4
1997	58,439	2,675	10.6	60.0

Key legislation (clauses highlighted in Home Office Statistical Bulletins as influencing prison numbers):

(i) Criminal Justice Act 1991, implemented October 1992 – Custody should generally be reserved for the most serious offences; community sentences should play a full role in sentencing; previous convictions should only be taken into account where the circumstances of the previous offence disclosed aggravating factors of the current offence; the court could only combine two offences in considering whether custody or a community sentence was justified; introduction of 'combination orders' (elements of probation, community service and supervision combined in one order); new early release arrangements introduced.

(ii) Criminal Justice Act 1993 – Account may be taken of any previous convictions or of failure to respond to previous sentences and in considering whether custody or a community sentence is justified, the court may look at all the offences currently before it.

(iii) Crime (Sentences) Act 1997 – An automatic life sentence for a second serious violent or sexual offence unless there are exceptional circumstances; a minimum sentence of seven years for an offender convicted for a third time of class A drug trafficking.

Policy speeches (highlighted as influential in affecting sentencing in Home Office Statistical Bulletins):

(i) Michael Howard's announcement of a 27–point plan to reduce crime (1994).

(ii) Michael Howard's speech to the Conservative Party Conference (1995).

Sources: Home Office Statistical Bulletins 30/92; 8/95; 5/98; 18/98

The figures show a clear drop in the prison population from 1988, when there was much debate between Home Office officials and criminal justice professionals, centred on the problem of prison overcrowding. There was a firm policy commitment to reducing the use of imprisonment for routine property crimes, with consensus among policy makers and practitioners on the policy of bifurcation or 'twin-tracking', predicated upon development of tougher community penalties for offences of intermediate seriousness. The 1988 Green Paper *Punishment, Custody and the Community* (Home Office, 1988) articulated this thinking, acknowledging that custody was not the most appropriate penalty for most offences, and should be reserved for the most serious. It acknowledged what Ashworth (1988) referred to as the prison paradox, that prison was at the same time increasingly deplored but increasingly used.

These policy principles were disseminated through the activities of the Judicial Studies Board, as well as circulars and briefings to magistrates and judges. By the time the 1991 Criminal Justice Act came into force, its principles had been well established in practice. After 1993, prison populations rose again, tracking the increasingly tough legislation and speeches of the Michael Howard era. The table demonstrates clearly that the rising prison population of the mid- and late-1990s was due to increasing proportionate use of imprisonment, rather than to greater numbers of convicted offenders. From 1997 the imprisonment rate appears to have stabilized, but it has stabilized at a rate much higher than that of the beginning of the decade.

Lord Windlesham (1993) has characterized these moves as the 'advance' and then 'retreat' of rational policy making; David Faulkner (1996) describes them in very similar terms as the 'light' of research-led, principled policy making in the late 1980s giving way to the 'darkness' of politicized, media-stimulated punitiveness in the 1990s. Anthony Bottoms (1995) in an influential paper has described this retreat from the spirit of 1991 as 'managerial rationalism' being undermined by 'populist punitiveness', a concept which he carefully distinguishes from 'public opinion'. He explains that it is,

> appropriate to speak of politicians or legislatures adopting 'populist punitiveness' policies, for these are political stances, normally adopted in the clear belief that they will be popular with the public (and usually with an awareness that, in general and abstract opinion polls, punitive policies are favoured by a majority of the public....). Hence, the term 'populist punitiveness' is intended to convey the notion of politicians tapping into, and using for their own purposes, what they believe to be the public's generally punitive stance. (Bottoms, 1995: 40)

David Garland (1996) has shown the tensions between these two tendencies, which he characterizes as a managerialist approach that acknowledges that high crime rates are now accepted as normal, so that they cannot be 'defeated' only managed; and the punitive, war-on-crime mentality which urges politicians to proclaim that something must be done – in the American phrase which has crossed the Atlantic – 'we can make a difference'. Unlike Windlesham and Faulkner, however, Garland shows the two tendencies not as succeeding each other, but as co-present. Whilst he is undoubtedly correct that the two tendencies are co-present, and probably ever-present, Windlesham and Faulkner are also right in that the balance between managerial rationalism and populist punitiveness can shift, and that the balance shifted to such an extent between the late 1980s and mid 1990s that the penal character of the two periods is quite different.

In a more recent paper Garland carries his analysis further, and gives more attention to the change in penal climate than in his 1996 paper. He points out that an important factor in the shift of penal policy has been the changing allegiances of professional elites, from supporting leniency and understanding offenders, to joining in the call for firm action (Garland, 1999). To a large extent, 'progressive' professional thinking has moved from penality to crime prevention, with the liberal rhetoric of 'community safety' making this more appealing to those who want to be on the side of power and policy relevance without losing their sense of themselves as on the side of the powerless, now identified as those whose lifestyles are circumscribed by fear of crime. The support of liberal professionals such as probation officers – and some academics – for innovations such as electronic tagging, victim impact statements, child curfews and child jails, has revealed a massive shift in attitudes.[3] This support is predicated upon the change from offenders to community as locus of professional concern.

Proportionality and risk

> It is now possible to contend that we live in a 'risk society'. … in which the demand for knowledge useful in risk definition, assessment, management and distribution is refiguring social organisation. Discourses of risk penetrate a range of institutions and have bearing upon how the criminal law institution and its operatives think and act. … There is a drift in the public agenda away from economic inequality to the distribution and control of risks. The values of the unsafe society displace those of the unequal society. (Ericson and Carriere, 1994: 102–3)

Bifurcation of penalties between prison and community represents penal bifurcation in another sense: bifurcation between the principles of proportionality and risk management. In the late 1980s and in the 1991 Criminal Justice Act, proportionality was by far the dominant principle, with risk the exceptional approach; in the later 1990s, risk has become more and more the main idea in criminal justice. When Douglas Hurd spoke of the ineffectiveness of prisons, he was talking about effectiveness in reforming offenders; when Michael Howard asserted that 'prison works', he was not thinking of any beneficial change to prisoners – he meant that prison works in risk control terms, that prison works by keeping offenders away from the public.

The 1991 CJA prescribed proportionality to be the overwhelming consideration in most cases. It provided for two kinds of exception to proportionality. Section 1(2)b allowed for custody to be imposed where seriousness of the current offence does not warrant, and Section 2(2)b allowed for custodial terms longer than warranted by the offence – in both cases this is allowed only if necessary to protect the public from serious harm. As the decade progressed, risk became a more prominent theme, with more indeterminate life sentences, so that parole or conditional release subject to risk assessment replaced the automatic release associated with determinate sentences.

Community penalties, too, have become more dominated by the idea of risk (see Clear and Cadora, Chapter 3 this volume). In the 1980s, the probation service saw itself as a provider of 'alternatives to custody' for offences of intermediate seriousness. Its objectives and its procedures were oriented to intervening according to levels of seriousness – services introduced 'gravity of offending' scales to help them with their recommendations to court, and the social background inquiry was replaced with the justice-model pre-sentence report. Assessing seriousness and responding to it were the operational parameters for probation. Day centres, community service and other community penalties were also geared to providing a graduated community response to seriousness. This approach was codified in the 1991 Criminal Justice Act, according to which community penalties were to incorporate degrees of restriction of liberty, and community sentences were to be imposed such that the amount of restriction of liberty reflected the seriousness of the offence. As the 1990s have progressed, community penalties too have become dominated by risk. Assessing 'risk of reoffending' has displaced assessing 'gravity of offence', and the probation service now describes its objectives in terms of 'risk management' (Roberts and Domurad, 1995).

An interesting question is 'which risks, what harm?' the newly risk-dominated criminal justice system is targeted at. In 1991 the understanding was that departures from proportionality were only justified to protect the public from 'serious harm', danger, as commonly understood. Section 31(3) of the 1991 Criminal Justice Act defines 'serious harm' as 'death or serious injury'. By 1996, the objective of risk management as defined in the white paper *Protecting the Public: the Government's Strategy on Crime in England and Wales*, was to protect the public from 'dangerous and persistent criminals' (Home Office, 1996).

Persistent offending (especially by young persistent offenders) had been the theme of one of the main 'moral panics' of the mid-1990s. The discovery of young offenders with extensive criminal records ('rat boy' in Newcastle upon Tyne, 'one boy crime wave' in Nottingham, Sunderland and elsewhere) as well as 'bail bandits' – people offending whilst on bail – were luridly reported in the tabloid press (Williams, 1993). Such stories meshed with the popularity in police and policy circles of the belief that much crime is the result of a small number of offenders. As Simon (1996 and Chapter 7 in this volume) points out, the two great contributions of criminology to penal policy in the 1990s have been victim surveys and research to identify persistent offenders. Victim surveys have constituted crime rates as object of knowledge, and thereby objects of policy intervention, whilst persistent offender profiling has provided a prime tactic for tackling high crime rates. 'Punitive segregation' of persistent offenders thus becomes the counterpoint to 'preventative partnerships' as the means of reducing crime rates (Garland, 1999). The two strategies are, therefore, not so much opposed or contradictory, as complementary. By 1996, risk of reoffending had become as important a theme as risk of serious physical harm: prevention of primary victimization becomes the responsibility of the individual citizen as potential victim; prevention of repeat victimization emerges as the main responsibility of state crime control apparatus.

Although not clearly stated in legislation or policy documents, the distinction between violent and non-violent offences has been a key to much thinking on criminal justice in England and Wales. Penal reformers in the 1980s consistently referred to the numbers and proportions of property offenders in prison; policy and legislation innovation throughout the decade bifurcated parole and remission, restricting early release for violent offenders and extending it and making it automatic for property offenders; strengthened community penalties were aimed largely at burglars and other property offenders. By 1996, this distinction was either blurred, or less important.

Although the 1991 Criminal Justice Act left definitions of seriousness largely to the courts, the spirit of the Act was clearly to separate violent and sexual offences, which were assigned to the risk track, from property offences, assigned to the proportionality track, a separation accomplished by the concept of serious harm. The inclusion of 'psychological injury' in the definition of serious harm in the 1991 Act had left the way open for non-violent offences to be on the risk track, but it was generally understood that this mainly applied where property offenders targeted unusually vulnerable victims, such as the elderly, who might be specially traumatized by the offence. The coupling of 'dangerous' and 'persistent' in the later legislation makes the distinction between violent and non-violent offences far less significant.[4]

An interesting case is that of burglary. This was the offence most innovatively and rigorously targeted for the more robust 'alternatives to custody' in the 1980s. If the expectation is that custody is for violent offences, then most burglaries would not lead to imprisonment. The framing of the 1991 Act seems almost tailor-made to allow for burglary to be generally below the 'so serious that only a prison sentence will suffice' threshold, with exceptional above-commensurate sentences for cases with specially vulnerable victims. Burglary is a high-recidivism offence, so the battles between justice-model advocates and politicians and others over the significance to be accorded to previous convictions are particularly meaningful for burglary. If risk of reoffending is the primary criminal justice theme, then most burglaries can be expected to lead to imprisonment. Sentencing trends (as usual, somewhat in advance of the legislation) reflect this (see Table 8.2).

The 1997 Crime (Sentences) Act put burglary firmly on the risk management rather than proportionality track, by including it in mandatory sentencing provisions. By USA standards, a mandatory sentence of three years' imprisonment for a third offence might not seem particularly draconian; the significant point of principle, however, is that it is unusual for England and Wales to have mandatory minimum sentences rather than mandatory maximums, and this provision put burglary on the same track as violent and sexual offences, rather than with other routine property offences. The Bill was going through Parliament at the time of the change of government from Conservative to Labour; when it completed its legislative passage, although the new government left the burglary provision on the statute, the provision was not implemented alongside the others. It has, however, since been implemented.

What is happening to the idea of 'danger' (as opposed to 'risk') is that it is

Table 8.2 Percentage use of imprisonment for burglary, 1988–97

	Crown Court		Magistrates' Court	
	Under 21	*21+*	*Under 21*	*21+*
1988	*	63	*	16
1989		60		15
1990		56		14
1991		56		15
1992	48	55	11	14
1993	55	60	16	18
1994	61	66	17	22
1995	66	70	18	27
1996	72	78	19	28
1997	67	78	18	31

*Figures for under-21s custody rate by offence and court type are not shown separately for the years before 1992. However, overall percentage custody rates for 1988–90 show that the trend was similar:

	1988	*1989*	*1990*
14–16	10.1	8.3	6.6
17–20	18.2	15.3	12.9

Source: Home Office Statistical Bulletins 30/92; 18/98.

shifting from acts to people. As many commentators have noted, commission of an act is no longer required as evidence of being dangerous or risk-posing. Dangerousness, risk-posing, is a property of a data self which is constructed out of the possession of designated 'risk factors'. Conviction for an offence occasioning or threatening serious physical harm as the criteria for adverse risk assessment has been replaced by 'categorical suspicion' (Marx, 1988). People are assessed as risk-posing on the basis that they display 'whatever characteristics the specialists responsible for the definition of preventive policy have constituted as risk factors' (Castel, 1991: 285).

There are many ways in which we can see that sense of a necessary connection of punishment/exclusion to an actual act, is being lost. As in the USA, there has been much concern about sex offending, particularly paedophilia, and schemes for compulsory supervision and community notification have been introduced. Debates around these issues reveal little grasp of how firm the connection should be between actual crimes and penalization, with no professional consensus about how long periods of supervision and notification of change of address should be. The prevailing sense of the mood in England is that once convicted, or even suspected, a sex offender is to be criminalized virtually for life. Recent proposals concerning disclosure of offences to potential employers covered people who have been arrested or accused of sex offending, not just those who have been convicted; a television programme and subsequent reaction to it made no distinction between paedophiles who had been recently convicted or recently released, and others who had been without arrest or conviction for periods of up to thirty years.

A new proposal from the present Home Secretary is that persons declared 'dangerous' by psychiatrists should be subject to detention – possibly for life – even without a criminal conviction. Two notorious cases have fed this particular panic. A few years ago a young music teacher, John Zito, was murdered by a schizophrenic man. His wife, Jane, is extremely articulate and has led a campaign for the enforcement of compulsory treatment of the mentally ill. This campaign and the official response might have remained at the level of enforcement of treatment in the community, but for a more recent case in which Michael Stone was convicted of the murders of Lynne and Megan Russell, the wife and daughter of a university lecturer, and the attempted murder of the other daughter. The conviction is extremely shaky, and may well be the next big 'miscarriage of justice' case. Evidence based on testimony of convicted offenders, hoping for extra remission as reward for co-operation, that he had 'confessed' to the crime in prison conversation, was the basis of the prosecution case. This testimony was supported by some circumstantial, but no forensic or eye-witness evidence. Michael Stone, however, is diagnosed as having a severe personality disorder, but because of negative assessment under the 'treatability' criterion, could not be detained in the absence of a criminal conviction, under present legislation. The opinion of most of those who have dealt with him is apparently that even if the evidence in the case is weak, he is *the sort of person* who would have committed such a crime, and is extremely dangerous. Details of the proposed legislation have not yet been worked out, but there is considerable public and political support for the idea.

These examples of sex offenders and personality disordered persons demonstrate that adoption of the principle of risk management as the dominant goal of crime control, not only blurs the distinction between violent and non-violent offending, but also blurs the distinction between offender and suspect.

Understanding penal strategies – the relevance of the 'governmentality' perspective

Contemporary penal developments have been discussed in relation to Giddens' writings on modernity, particularly as reflecting a withdrawal of trust in government institutions (Bottoms, 1995). They fit the framework of Feeley and Simon's (1994) *new penology*, which emphasizes displacement of a penal discourse concerned with individual motivation and moral character by that of the management of aggregate crime rates; which replaces humanistic knowledges with statistical and actuarial technologies; and which is oriented to risk rather than justice.

In their review of the degree of penetration of new penology into penal strategies, Feeley and Simon (1995) comment that the managerialist approaches of new penology have not given forth any new understandings of the offender, comparable to the positivism's *homo criminalis* which underpinned the rehabilitative penal strategies of the first two-thirds of the twentieth century's response to crime (Pasquino, 1991), or the more recent rational choice offender consistent with desert approaches. Present penal strategies, in fact, depend on two criminal characters: the dangerous classes, consistent with strategies targeted at aggregates, at crime rates rather than at the reform of individual, socially deprived delinquents; and the persistent offender, the target of selective incapacitation/exclusion policies. As Simon himself has subsequently pointed out, these characters are the perennial targets of crime control strategies, and constituting them as the objects of knowledge is the *raison d'être* of criminology (Simon, 1996). Prediction studies merge these two penal characters, so the fact that the search for the persistent offender has led to rising imprisonment, rather than to containment of prison population rates because identification of the few high-rate offenders allows for community punishment and control of the many low-rate offenders, is hardly surprising. The promise of prediction studies leading to high crime reduction with low prison population increases, is something of a political deceit. The factors identified by persistence studies are factors shared by many of the underprivileged: socio-economic deprivation; low family income and high family size; frequent unemployment; broken homes and early parental separation; criminal, anti-social and alcoholic parents (Farrington, 1997). Present policies are very much the policies of containment of the underclass, with spectacular criminals – the very persistent and the very dangerous – highlighted in political/public discourse to keep morale in the war on crime at its heightened levels.

The analyses by Simon, Garland, and to some extent Bottoms, draw on substantially the same Foucauldian framework as the 'governmentality' literature of Miller, Rose and others (Gordon, 1991; Miller and Rose, 1990; Rose, 1996; Rose and Miller, 1992). These penologists generally, and Garland (1997) in a paper directly engaging with the governmentality perspective rather than drawing upon it, have said that this literature, though having considerable relevance to the problem of crime and its control, is not in itself sufficient. Stenson has been a sympathetic critic of the governmentality perspective as applied to crime control, although he has recently taken issue with some of the work of Garland and Simon (Stenson, 1999). Specifically, Stenson calls for a more dynamic, updated understanding of sovereignty, which can better accommodate the facts of crime control.

I would agree with Stenson's view, especially in relation to punishment. State power is being extended, not reduced, in the sphere of punishment and, I would argue, in relation to other strategies of crime control as well. Prisons are being built, more courtrooms are being built, discretion of professionals is being restricted, with more power accruing to state legislatures, especially in relation to sentencing. The police, the probation service, the Crown Prosecution Service, are all becoming more rather than less centralized, with centralizing tendencies exercised through funding controls, through amalgamations of local services, through government-level setting of objectives, and through inspections.

Some of the phenomena described by the governmentality scholars vis-à-vis other spheres of life are apparent in relation to crime. O'Malley's 'private prudentialism' at first sight appears to be apposite: more and more people are joining groups such as neighbourhood watch; more and more estates have private security systems; more and more communities are hiring or forming their own patrol groups (O'Malley, 1992). Yet such personal activism usually translates into demand for more state activism, not less. The situation with regard to crime is in this respect quite different from that of other aspects of social life where the insurance template applies: with education, health and pensions, for example, people are buying private provision and opting out of state provision. With crime and punishment, privatization is an adjunct to, not an alternative to, state provision.

Private and government-at-a-distance action has fed the state with more offenders to punish. A good example is the use of CCTV to identify people committing crimes: in some of the most recent funding rounds, the provision of evidence for prosecution is placed above deterrence as an objective. Private and community activism in the field of crime control is enlarging the possibilities of crime control, supplementing rather than replacing state resources. What seems to be happening is a 'rolling out' rather than a 'rolling back' of the state (Clarke, 1996:15).

Crime prevention policies and practices appear to be blurring the boundary between private and public realms; they are, therefore, perhaps best understood as analogous to the volunteers, befrienders and other ancillary control personnel in earlier depictions of net widening (Cohen, 1979; 1985). The new schemes are often described as providing extra 'eyes and ears' for the police; they are also providing extra pieces of evidence for prosecutors, and new 'clients' for the social control network. Just as juvenile justice projects in the 1960s and 1970s were criticized for drawing non-delinquents or 'pre-delinquents' into the control network, the same is happening with new prevention strategies. The Crime and Disorder Act dissolves the boundary between crime, disorder and nuisance, with the new local authority/police partnerships targeted at nuisance offences such as littering and dog-fouling, as well as 'incivilities' by young people. One of the things this indicates is that analysis of punishment needs to be reconnected to wider analyses of social control.

I have argued that the features of control and punishment I have mentioned above, suggest that for the governmentality perspective to be useful for understanding developments in penal policy, the nature of 'distance' as in the term 'governing at a distance' needs to be further investigated (Hudson, 1998a). It is curious that although so many of the writers in this perspective are British, and although their main theoretical inspiration is French, much of the work on crime, risk and neo-liberalism seems to over-generalize from American experience.

In England, the Home Office holds most of the power in matters of crime and punishment, usually with the police as its lead agency in the community. 'Community notification' of the release or relocation of sex offenders, for example, means notification to the police, not to community groups; guidelines and training for 'community' CCTV schemes are police-led. Although each region of Britain has its own police force, chief constables and other senior appointments have to be approved by the Home Office; funding is from the Home Office; objectives are given by the Home Office; statistical returns are to the Home Office. The same is true of the Probation Service, and the Crown Prosecution Service. Juvenile justice, which used to be largely a matter for local authority social service departments, has recently been reorganized with the establishment of juvenile justice boards which follow the same organizational pattern as police and probation. Analysis of involvement with crime, punishment and disorder needs to have much more specificity in its analysis of the relations between states, local governments, communities and private individuals and agencies. In spite of certain tendencies shared by the advanced, late-modern liberal democracies, there are important cultural and material differences in their approaches to the provision of welfare, security and order.

The meaning and nature of 'regulation by norm' need to be carefully examined in the sphere of crime and punishment. 'Normalization' as a penal aim of the rehabilitative policies of the pre-1980s has been abandoned in favour of risk management; present policies are also no longer normalizing in the sense that though they accept crime as a normal event of everyday life, criminals are now regarded as 'different' rather than normal. The main impetus of current penal policy is exclusion rather than normalization: exclusion by lengthy imprisonment; exclusion from certain venues on release via notification schemes or electronically monitored curfews.

Risk management techniques which have apparently brought down aggregate crime rates and which have made it more possible for individuals to reduce the risk of their own likelihood of victimization have done nothing to appease the demand for tough, exclusionary punishment policies. Not very long ago, proponents and observers of 'new penology' and 'the engineered society' expressed the hope that the development of new, depersonalized techniques of crime control aimed at prevention and unconcerned with the moral well-being of offenders would reduce dependency on criminal justice, which would become perceived as 'an anachronism whose agents serve only to shoot the wounded after the battle is over' (Marx, 1995: 227), and that the moral distance between offenders and other community members would diminish (Simon, 1988). On the contrary, rational approaches to control of crime rates and harsh punishment policies have developed hand in hand.

Garland (1990) has rightly insisted on the importance of the symbolic role of punishment. The increasing toughness of punishment and its centrality in thinking about crime in spite of the spread and increasing effectiveness of crime prevention techniques, cannot be explained by governmentality theory (see the chapters by O'Malley and Stenson and Edwards in this volume). Despite having congruence with many aspects of community crime prevention programmes, the governmentality perspective appears too functionalist to offer an understanding of penal policy; at most it offers a descriptive framework which matches some of its features.

An analytic perspective that makes sense to me is that of 'authoritarian populism' and 'drift to law and order' developed by Stuart Hall (1980, 1988), and by sociologists such as Paul Gilroy (1987) to explain the criminalization of Afro-Caribbeans, in the 1980s. The coupling of 'the free economy and the strong state' (Gamble, 1994) seems to state the case particularly plausibly. The laissez-faire economics of the new right in the 1980s are said to pose dilemmas for governments/leaders wanting to project themselves as strong leaders. If the creed for economic policy is non-intervention, letting the markets decide, then how do leaders show themselves to be strong and dynamic, making a real difference to the lives of citizens? Crime has been a sphere of social life chosen for active government: hence the barrage of 'something needs to be done' messages to the public; dramatization of individual (and quite rare) crimes such as the James Bulger murder, and particularly the constant spate of legislation and government initiatives (Hay, 1995).

This perspective offers an understanding of neo-liberalism that seems to me to fit the case of penal policy extremely well, with its construction of a succession of 'suitable enemies', constituted as 'different' and targeted for exclusion. Nils Christie (1993) adds a material dimension to this ideological account, suggesting as he does that the correctional-industrial complex has replaced the military-industrial complex as the ending of the Cold War has reduced the need for military spending and as heavy industries have declined in the most advanced economies. Crime control has been one of the principal areas of economic growth in recent years, and many companies which used to specialize in making military equipment are now making equipment for crime control. Prisons are important sources of local employment, especially where manufacturing industries have declined.[5] Christie's *Crime Control as Industry* provides a good description of contemporary Britain. The map of closed coal-fields and the map of new prisons fit together extremely well, and we can contrast the availability of finance for prison building with the lack of funding for protecting and developing industries threatened with closure. If the goal of those in power was crime prevention, the priorities would surely be the other way round!

Simon's (1997) concept of 'governing through crime' goes a considerable way towards bringing these perspectives together. Using 'Megan's Law' (the sex offender registration and control legislation, first introduced in New Jersey in 1994 after the death of Megan Kanka, a seven-year-old girl raped and murdered by a released sex-offender and subsequently adopted in many states) as a case study, Simon shows that not only does contemporary crime exhibit many of the features of 'governmental rationality', but he also highlights the special resonance of crime in the popular and political mind. Preoccupation with crime is such – for various material, ideological, and also cultural/psychological/experiential reasons – that it both allows and demands the sort of extension of state and civil powers, and the degree of suspension of liberty, that western liberal democracies have usually only tolerated in war-time.

Defending justice

Foucault and the writers developing his perspective and concepts have shown us the technological possibilities of modernity for repression, and demonstrated that the logic of governance in the age of regulation by norm involves utilizing techniques and disciplines which constitute dichotomies of normality and deviance. Hall, Gilroy and others have demonstrated the groups currently being defined as 'dangerous other', and revealed the ideological impetus to this enterprise of demonization and exclusion. In a series of powerful works Bauman (1989, 1993) has warned us of the dangers of defining groups as 'dangerous other' and excluding them from the community of those entitled to justice. Contemporary events show us – if we need to be shown – that events such as the German extermination of the Jews cannot be looked at as one-off aberrations. There may be differences in scale and technological sophistication, but the instinct to describe the stranger (including the cultural stranger, who may simultaneously be one's neighbour), as dangerous alien other is strong and ever-present. As well as events in Rwanda, Burundi, Sierre Leone, and closer to home in former Yugoslavia, in our own countries racial violence, the suspicious categorization of most refugees as probable 'bogus asylum seekers', should alert us to the need to keep alive a vigorous commitment to justice, and to address the intellectual task of reformulating our theories and institutions of justice to meet the challenges of the politics of safety. As I have argued, however, present developments in penality show a frightening absence of any commitment to 'justice'.

It is my belief that reinvigorating a commitment to justice necessitates first and foremost, bringing together the ideas of *rights* and *difference*. This section of the paper therefore focuses on two developments:

- first, the incorporation into domestic jurisdiction of the European convention on human rights;
- second, the growth of a literature of recognition of difference.

The European Convention on Human Rights

A recent debate among legal theorists has been concerned with the extent to which developments in penal policy represent a shift in the balance between Packer's *due process* and *crime control* models (Duff, 1998; Packer, 1969). These models are in some ways a legal equivalent of governmentality theory's designation of the juridical and the disciplinary. Tadros succinctly pinpoints the key distinction between juridical power, which is directed at acts; disciplinary power, directed at individuals; and governmental power, which is directed at groups of individuals (1998:78).

It is generally held that criminal justice systems in many western countries shifted very much towards due process in the 1980s, and have shifted back towards crime control in the 1990s. During the so-called rehabilitation era of the 1960s and early-1970s, penal strategies were principally targeted at offenders as individuals, whilst in the 'just deserts' era of the late 1970s and 1980s, attention was focused on the acts the offenders had committed, with proportionality and consistency the primary values expressed in policy and legislation. In the 1990s, as the 'new penology' writers describe, groups and aggregates have assumed more importance as the objects of penal strategies, and control of crime rates rather than fair and consistent sanctioning is the principal penal objective.

Some writers have objected to the presentation of the two models as dichotomous, arguing that crime control is the overall aim of criminal law and criminal justice, whilst due process is concerned with procedure (Ashworth, 1979). Others, however, observing changes over the past two decades, maintain that Packer's formulation points up some useful distinctions, and that the models represent the two polarities of a basic and enduring tension within criminal justice. The current debate sees the two models not so much as expressing competing aims, but as representing different sets of values; the question then becomes the extent to which the values of due process may be allowed to restrict the aim of crime control (McConville, Sanders and Leng, 1997; Sanders and Young, 1994). In previous works I have followed Braithwaite and Pettit (1990) in seeing the two clusters of values as *goals* and *constraints*, which like the current legal version of the debate, prompts the question of the right balance between them (Hudson 1993, 1995). The tension between goals of crime control and values of due process can be seen in the disagreements between politicians and senior lawyers about mandatory sentencing and other issues.

Crime control displacement of due process values is also apparent in changes in procedures in recent years. It has been thought (by police and politicians) that too many professional criminals are escaping justice because of their manipulation of proceedings, and there has come to be a widespread view that rules of evidence and rules of disclosure have tipped the balance too far in favour of defendants. Some changes in procedure have redressed the balance, the most important being altering the implications of remaining silent under police questioning. The right to remain silent still exists, but its exercise can now be taken as inference of guilt. There was almost no popular or political opposition to this change: in terms of my present theme, it does seem that in general, British society now places crime control above due process.

While the old adage that it is better for ten guilty persons to go free than for one innocent person to be convicted seems to have very few adherents now, there also seems to be disturbingly little concern for upholding the principle that the prosecution should have to prove guilt, rather than the defendant having to prove innocence. It is interesting that the civil suit in the O. J. Simpson case prompted a newspaper article from one of Britain's leading lawyers, Sir Louis Blom-Cooper, who had formerly been thought of very much as a liberal, to the effect that greater use of civil procedures should be considered here (Dershowitz, 1997). There is a danger that we could be moving towards combining civil law standards of proof with criminal law penalties. Some of the provisions of the Crime and Disorder Act – the proposal about people with dangerous personality disorders, and some proposals which seek to put people who have been suspected of, or cautioned for, sex offences on the same footing as those who have been convicted with regard to their civil rights – are worrying steps in this direction.

Andrew Ashworth (1995) has argued that human rights should become the anchor of criminal justice, superseding any idea of 'balance' between crime control and due process. For him, human rights should be an absolute constraint on criminal justice in pursuit of crime control goals. Ashworth seeks to establish a firm normative foundation for criminal justice processes in the European Convention on Human Rights. The Human Rights Act 1998, which comes into force in October 2000, provides for the incorporation of this convention into British domestic legislation, something which has been campaigned for vigorously by human rights groups. Ashworth's is a substantial contribution to the defence of justice, and its significance for substantive justice is that it incorporates recognition that 'due process' might not of itself embody human rights.

The rights Ashworth defends are mostly to do with process rather than sentence, and important though these are, they leave unresolved key questions about rights not to be punished excessively, and not to be punished for possible future offences. This latter right – the right not to be punished for acts which one has not (yet) done but may (or may not) do if at liberty – is the principle of 'just deserts' penal theory which is threatened by the shift to risk as the key penal principle, and which needs robust defence in the interests of 'justice'. The requirement that a conviction by a court must precede punishment (Article 5(1)(a) of the European Convention) looks as though it may cover this situation, but this is doubtful, since most provisions for more than commensurate detention are defined as 'protective detention' rather than 'punishment'.

Similarly, interpretation by the European Court of the requirement that there be 'sufficient connection' between sentence and subsequent detention has made it clear that the self-declared objectives of the relevant legislature constitute such connection (Henham, 1998: 599). Henham considered the likely impact of this legislation on the non-commensurate detention of mentally disordered offenders and those defined as dangerous, and points out that Article 5 allows for the detention of persons with infectious disease, those of 'unsound mind', alcoholics, drug addicts or vagrants. There is no precision given to standards of proof or diagnosis of being of unsound mind. He concludes rather bleakly that,

> the Convention adopts a minimalist approach to questions concerning the legitimacy of state sentencing policy and the protection of individual rights and, since no protection exists in domestic law against the potential injustices described, the maintenance of fundamental rights against procedural unfairness in this context has no foundation. (*ibid*: 600)

Challenges to the European Court on the basis of breaches of human rights have been procedural rather than substantive: in the case of Thompson and Venables, the boys who killed the toddler James Bulger, for example, the main challenge was that the use of standard criminal proceedings rather than welfare/juvenile procedures was oppressive, and unfair because the boys were not likely to be able to understand and instruct their legal representatives in the way that adults would be. There has also been a successful challenge to the Home Secretary's altering the tariff period of the boys' detention; again a procedural issue rather than on the basis that the detention might simply be too long.

What has caused some consternation in governmental and professional penal circles is the possibility that aspects of prison regimes might be held to be in contravention of the Convention. The Convention provides that secondary legislation can be declared in contravention if it is not clearly mandated by primary legislation: the regrettable but perhaps predictable response has been hastily to transfer some issues of regimes and proceedings from secondary to primary legislation. There has not been a new Prisons Act, but various other Acts have contained clauses to do with prisons. These have largely gone unremarked in debate about the main provisions of the Acts concerned. For example, section 57 of the Crime and Disorder Act – where most attention has been given to the new Anti-Social Behaviour Order – provides that remand prisoners should normally give evidence in pre-trial proceedings by video link rather than by court appearance, and that magistrates are to provide explanations if, exceptionally, they do not use this process. The distinction in the Convention between primary and secondary legislation supports Henham's view of minimalism of likely impact of the Convention with respect to state sentencing policy.

The Convention could make a difference beyond its technical provisions, however, if it encourages the growth of a rights culture among the judiciary, penal practitioners, and above all, policy makers. Penal progressives in eastern Europe are placing considerable emphasis on the Convention to support the need for reform; successive UK governments having copied so much that is reprehensible in US penal innovation, penal reformers could well learn from their US counterparts who have used constitutional rights to challenge excessive, inhumane and discriminatory punishments.[6]

Justice, rights and difference

Western theories of justice are based on a philosophy of identity. Philosophers construct their subject of justice by abstracting from actual personalities, social groups, contexts and situations, qualities which all people share. That which is shown to be universal is the ability to exercise rational will. This universal rational subjectivity is notably represented in Kant's theory of the transcendental subject, and Rawls' reasonable person. Such a subject is presumed able to act on general principles rather than subjective impulses, to speak as 'the voice from nowhere', representing the common good over sectional interests. Questions of justice are then cast as what principles and what social institutions would be acceptable to all such rational beings, *qua* rational beings rather than as representatives of communities of interest (Rawls, 1972). Impartiality and objectivity are primary virtues for this 'justice as fairness'.

Philosophical expulsion of difference is reflected in law's model of the abstract subject of law, with all legal subjects constructed as equal in their possession of agency and free will. This assumption of sameness has been the focus of critique by postmodernists, for whom the abstract universal turns out to be the characteristics associated with the white, western citizen of the Enlightenment, and feminists, who point out that the so-called universal norm is in fact predicated on the middle-aged, middle-class male. Philosophical critiques (Bauman, 1993; Cornell, 1990; Young, 1990) of theories of justice predicated upon a logic of identity have thus paralleled the arguments of feminist and Marxist critics of law in action (Kerruish, 1991; MacKinnon, 1989; Smart, 1995). Law based on this logic of identity is castigated for its lack of appreciation of alternative standpoints, and for its failure to recognize that what it presumes to be universal is in fact very partial.

The move to risk orientation has brought difference very much to the fore in penal policy. Current penal strategies recall the old 'social defence' strategies, aiming to separate high risk from low risk offenders, the dangerous from the normal; their logic is thus the opposite of proportionality's precept of treating like offences similarly. One very significant implication of this is that if the aim is no longer to punish fairly, to treat like offences the same, then 'discrimination' loses any meaning. Discrimination is a term whose meaning is entirely dependent on a norm of equality. Under a risk rationale, however, someone assessed as higher risk should be punished more – kept away from the public for longer – than someone assessed as low risk. Norval Morris has shown us what this might mean in relation to race:

> Criminals X and Y had identical criminal records and had committed identical crimes, but X was not a school dropout, X had a job to which he could return if not sent to prison, and X had a supportive family who would take him back if allowed to do so, while the unfortunate Y was a school dropout, was unemployed, and lacked a supportive family. And let us suppose that past studies reveal that criminals with Y's criminal record and with his environmental circumstances have a base expectancy rate of 1 in 10 of being involved in a crime of personal violence. While no such calculations have been made for criminals like X, it is quite clear that they have a much lower base expectancy rate of future violent criminality. I suggest that Y should be held longer than X based on these predictions ... As a matter of statistical likelihood, X is white and Y is black. (Morris, 1994: 257)

We have seen the mass incarceration of black Americans accelerate as penal strategies have shifted from the desert ideal of 'doing justice' to a risk-oriented 'new penology' concerned with preventing the risk of reoffending, and with managing a 'dangerous' underclass of people who are assumed to be likely to become more rather than less criminal as they grow from youth to adulthood. Morris was envisaging risk as an occasional departure from a predominantly proportionate system; his allowance of departures from equal, proportionate distribution of punishment because of considerations of dangerousness takes on a new import if the due process ideal of justice-as-fairness is abandoned. The 1991 Criminal Justice Act approximates Morris's formulation; the post-1993 developments with their movement towards risk as the dominant principle part company with the principle of equal penal treatment. These developments thus expel 'discrimination' whilst they re-centre 'difference'.

In the UK we have not, perhaps, had the same rise in proportion of black prisoners as in the USA. This is because many of the so-called 'underclass' in Britain's degenerated cities are white. The over-penalization and over-criminalization of black youth continues, but what has happened in Britain is that as the war on youth crime has escalated, the custodial response which young black people suffered in the 1980s, in comparison with the increasing use of intensive intermediate treatment and similar penalties for young white offenders, has been extended to the white, workless young men of London, Birmingham, Leeds, Liverpool, Manchester, Newcastle and other cities. Disturbances in Oxford, Cardiff and Newcastle in 1991 were by white youths, and so were interpreted in a crime rather than a racial tension frame of reference. These events meshed with stories of 'one boy crime waves', and fitted the underclass stereotypes of youths as uninterested in work, content to live on benefits topped up by the proceeds of crime. The circumstances specified as 'risk factors' to identify young people likely to become hardened criminals are the characteristics of the so-called underclass, black and white. In the UK, risk penality has led to injustice for all youth, with the penal treatment of young black men becoming the template for the treatment of all impoverished youth.

Feminist criminologists and legal theorists have for a long time been arguing that treating people the same is not necessarily treating them all equally in the sense of giving them equal consideration (Carlen, 1990; Hudson, 1998b). 'Woman-wise penology' was proposed as an alternative to the equality-as-sameness of the just deserts era, an approach to equality which in practice meant fitting women into a penal system designed for men. Arguments for reducing or even abolishing imprisonment for women have been predicated on the low numbers of women committing violent offences.[7] Any decrease in the significance of the violence/non-violence divide, therefore, has implications for the punishment of women. Hannah-Moffat (1999) describes the development of new risk assessment guidelines in Canada, which, she says, recast what were formerly 'needs' as risk factors. I understand that the women's policy section of the Prison Department in the UK is working on a similar development now.

The rising imprisonment rates for women which were seen in the 'justice era' were described as 'equality with a vengeance' (Daly, 1994). We may be about to see something similar now, a new twist of equality with a vengeance, in terms of risk. If conventional risk assessment scales tend to identify women as low-risk, the invention of these new scales seems to mean that comparisons among women rather than among all criminals will enable populations of women offenders to yield a 'fair share' of high-risk individuals. This might seem fair enough, but the whole risk/new penology strategy is predicated on male criminality: it is male crime that is the major social problem; it is male crime that causes such widespread fear of crime; moreover, it is male patterns of criminality on which criminological theories about career criminals, persistent criminals, and underclass criminal values are based.

Considerations of race and gender, and also varying social and economic conditions of offenders, pose what Martha Minow describes as 'the dilemma of difference':

> When does treating people differently emphasize their differences and stigmatize or hinder them on that basis? And when does treating people the same become insensitive to their difference and likely to stigmatize them on *that* basis? (1990: 20)

Minow explains that law's usual categories distinguish the normal from the abnormal, the capable from the incapable, and the autonomous from the dependent. In terms of the present discussion, those who are defined as normal, capable, autonomous, are dealt with in juridical mode, with their deeds responded to consistently and fairly, without their whole selves being investigated and placed under continuing control. The abnormal (the dangerous), the incompetent (the mentally disordered) and the dependent (those whose legal identity is a function of their relationships – children and, to an extent which varies with time and place, women) will be dealt with by disciplinary mechanisms (surveillance, institutional care, preventive detention, psychotropic medication, and maybe even expulsion or elimination). The problem is that present institutions presume similarity, and see difference as a difficulty which will be encountered from time to time, and for which special arrangements need to be made. These special arrangements (preventive incarceration, for example) will generally be worse than the normal arrangements, because difference – however statistically normal, given for example that half the population is female, or that the factors associated with persistent offending are shared by a large proportion of the male, economically marginalized population – is treated as an aberration or deviation.

There are plenty of examples which show the deficiencies of the unitary standpoint. We can think of the struggle to gain recognition for a feminist account of domestic violence: the male question is always, 'why didn't she leave'?, while feminist understanding shows that women in a situation of serious and long-lasting abuse cease to think of themselves as active agents with the capacity to make things happen to improve their situation. Another example is the distinction between regulation of alcohol and cannabis: consumption of alcohol, the recreational drug-of-choice for most middle-aged white persons, is not of itself illegal, whereas consumption of cannabis, the recreational drug-of-choice for many Afro-Caribbean communities and for many young people, is illegal without any accompanying dangerous or anti-social behaviour.

Difference is denied in those who come within the definition of normal, capable and autonomous, and is repressed in those who are defined as abnormal, incapable or dependent. The boundaries of inclusion as 'the same' change from time to time, but the cost of successful challenges to designations of difference is false identification with an unacknowledged norm. Thus the price for women of challenging the paternalism, infantilism and lack of acknowledgement as persons rather than possessions of men, has been to be treated the same as men; the price for minority ethnic groups challenging prejudice and lack of legal equality is denial of their cultural specificity and insensitivity towards their needs and sensibilities.

Attempts by feminists or others to question law's male-centredness, to acknowledge female or black standpoints, may widen categories and definitions, but they do not disturb the univocity of ideas and institutions of justice. They merely add more types of people to those who can be included in the identity of reasonable person. Such advances may broaden the definition of sameness, but they do nothing to solve the problem of difference. For every dimension of difference that is encompassed within the circle of similarity, new definitions of difference will be discovered. Genetics, psychology and new versions of positivist criminology are prolific in giving us new categories of difference: the attention-deficit child, the sexual predator, the bad parent, the persistent offender, the bogus asylum-seeker, are new labels which put those to whom they are ascribed outside the constituency of justice as fairness.

A difference which is crucial to current penal strategies is that of victim/offender. Ashworth's concern to secure a rights-based approach to justice is prompted in part by the growth of victim concerns as influences on sentencing as well as mandating better provision of victim services (Ashworth, 1996). The rights-based approach advocated by Ashworth, Henham and others still has in mind the rights in standard cases to be secured to standard offenders and standard victims. Even where they have in mind 'different' groups such as mentally disordered offenders, these writers are envisaging procedural rights which will obtain in these *sorts* of cases. But as Lacey makes clear, emphasis on procedural rights and fairness does not guarantee substantive justice, a just outcome in the individual case (Lacey, 1987: 225). Consideration of the balancing of victim and offender interests shows that this standard case/difference as exception to be *coped* with, cannot provide satisfaction to all parties. If an offender is dealt with more harshly than someone convicted of a similar offence, because of some greater-than-standard impact on the victim, then that offender will believe him/herself to have been unjustly treated; if some special circumstance means that an offender receives less than the 'going rate', then the victim will feel that s/he has been denied justice.

What needs to happen to promote substantive justice is the development of a rights-based approach which is predicated on difference, on conflicts of rights that will be generated by individual cases. Elsewhere I have developed the theme of reconstruction of theories and institutions of justice based on difference (Hudson, 1998c). For this to happen, criminal proceedings would have to become more like the discursive procedures of restorative justice, underpinned by the process model of Habermas's discursive rationality (1984, 1987). The problem with many formulations of restorative justice, however (and indeed the weak point of Habermas's formulation, according to some critics) is that it still presumes that the outcome of discourse will be a consensus (Benhabib, 1986). Contemporary recognition of so many claims on justice – the offender, the victim, the community – forces acknowledgement that such consensus is not generally possible. Once the subject of justice is given back his/her social context and flesh-and-blood reality, it is clear that difference is the standard case, and that differences are routinely irreducible: criminal justice needs to find ways of balancing legitimate but competing or conflicting rights.

Universal statements of human rights such as the United Nations Declaration of Human Rights, and attempts to interpret them as a practical guide to governance such as the European Convention are only starting points, and should lead to the development of a jurisprudence of rights geared to deciding conflicts and upholding rights in specific cases. Minow and others (1990) provide an important first step towards thinking what such a jurisprudence would be like, and towards bringing discourses of rights together with discourses of difference, by advocating a relational approach to rights. Rights dilemmas are relational difficulties – the respective rights of victims and offenders; the balance of rights of the individual offender to limited punishment and the rights of communities to concern for their safety; the rights of a female offender to have the difference of her circumstances from the male penal norm recognized; the right to recognition of male and female perspectives on what constitutes 'provocation'; the right to recognition of affluent and poor perspectives on what constitutes economic 'coercion'; the recognition of black as well as white perspectives on what constitutes racial motivation.

The developing perspective of legal guaranteeism (Van Swaaningen, 1997; Hudson, 1998c) seeks a role for formal law in guaranteeing the rights of the different parties in individual cases. A starting point for writers in this perspective is recognition that at present, criminal law due process offers better protection of the rights and liberties of those defined as dangerous, as criminal, than other processes of social control. This certainly seems to be true at the moment in the response to sexual offending and to youth crime. Those classified as different or dangerous need protection by a criminal justice system that is respectful of their rights, against a potentially vengeful community. In the past, proponents of ideas such as restorative justice or abolitionism have had to deal with the argument that communities would probably not provide adequate controls on offenders, or censure sufficiently strongly; now, perhaps, the argument is that they would not be sufficiently temperate.

Legal guaranteeism is as yet little developed, and not so far sufficiently detailed nor clearly enough differentiated from the standard due process model. As I envisage, the role of the legal adjudicator would be to identify what rights are endangered in particular cases or (with discursive justice processes) in particular deliberations, and need to be safeguarded. This would mean that the task of law would be to make sure that rights which we hold in general, are protected in individual cases, as well as being operative in the framing of penal and protective legislation. It might mean, for example, the right of an offender not to have a 'cruel and unusual punishment', or to punishment without conviction (see Simon, Chapter 7 in this volume). This would extend beyond sentencing to the administration of penalties: the length and extensiveness of community surveillance of sex offenders; the degree of interventiveness of probation supervision, as well as issues such as parole decision-making are in need of active rights-thinking.

Although human-rights based legal guaranteeism needs substantial theoretical elaboration and also needs the accumulation of a substantial body of case law, its aim is clear. The objective is to establish a system such that human rights can 'function as a moral standard which sets limits to purely instrumentalist law enforcement, while leaving enough space for normative pluralism in a democratic society' (Van Swaaningen, 1997: 239). Much work remains to be done to develop a jurisprudence of rights, and to bring this together with the growing politico-legal theorization of difference. Such work is vital, however, if 'justice' is to survive, even as an aspiration, in the risk society. For risk society to be a society where justice sets limits to power, a vibrant culture of rights, and a non-repressive respect for difference, are pre-requisites.

Notes

1   See for example Dunbar and Langdon (1998) and Windlesham, (1993) for detailed descriptions of policy changes; Bottoms (1995), Cohen (1994) and Garland (1996 and 1999) for analysis of their import and cultural meaning.
2   This perspective is selected because of the topic of the symposium for which the chapter was originally prepared as a presentation. For a review of other analyses of the place of 'risk' in contemporary criminal justice policy, see Hudson (2000).
3   There are, of course, some exceptions. Rutherford (1996) has been a consistent critic of developments in relation to youth offending, whilst several prominent lawyers and legal theorists have been strongly opposed to major provisions of the 1998 Crime and Disorder Act. Such opposition, especially from lawyers, has been reviled as 'silly' by the present Home Secretary, Jack Straw, and is within the purview of Prime Minister Tony Blair's attacks on 'the forces of conservatism'.
4   Ralph Henham (1998) points out that robbery using a knife, which would come under the definition of a violent offence for the purposes of section 2(2)b of the 1991 Criminal Justice Act would not qualify as a 'serious' offence under the 1997 Crime (Sentences) Act which legislated the 1996 white paper.
5   Proposals to locate a prison ship off the coast of Dorset, and to convert outdated holiday accommodation in a seaside town in Lancashire, have been discussed by local officials and residents entirely in economic terms – whether they are desirable developments because of the jobs they will create, or undesirable because of the tourists they may deter, tourism/leisure being the only other industry in contemporary Britain which has expanded to the same extent as crime control.
6   On a visit to Hungary, I witnessed the vitality of commitment to European human rights standards among academics, officials, lawyers and prison governors; the use of rights-based legal challenges is beginning to happen more frequently in England. For example, the Howard League for Penal Reform has mounted challenges to the imprisonment of under-18s under anti-discrimination and child protection provisions.
7   'Abolition', in this context, means treating imprisonment as an exceptional measure for exceptional cases, rather than the penal norm, rather than in the more fundamental sense of abolition of categories such as 'crime' and 'punishment' associated with some, mainly European, theorists.

References

Ashworth, A. (1979) 'Concepts of Criminal Justice', *Criminal Law Review*, 26: 412–27.
Ashworth, A. (1988) 'Criminal Justice and Criminal process', *British Journal of Criminology*, 28, 2: 241–53.
Ashworth, A. (1995) 'Principles, Practice and Criminal Justice', in P. Birks, ed. *Pressing Problems in the Law, Vol. 1: Criminal Justice and Human Rights*, Oxford: Oxford University Press.

Ashworth, A. (1996) 'Crime, Community and Creeping Consequentialism', *Criminal Law Review*, 43: 220–30.

Bauman, Z. (1989) *Modernity and the Holocaust*, Cambridge: Polity Press.

Bauman, Z. (1993) *Postmodern Ethics*, Oxford: Blackwell.

Benhabib, S. (1986) *Critique, Norm and Utopia*, New York: Columbia University Press.

Bottoms, A. (1995) 'The Philosophy and Politics of Punishment and Sentencing', in C.M.V. Clarkson and R. Morgan, eds. *The Politics of Sentencing Reform*, Oxford: Clarendon Press.

Braithwaite, J. and Pettit, P. (1990) *Not Just Deserts*, Oxford: Oxford University Press.

Carlen, P. (1990) *Alternatives to Women's Imprisonment*, Milton Keynes: Open University Press.

Castel, R. (1991) 'From dangerousness to risk'.in G. Burchell, C. Gordon and P. Miller, eds. *The Foucault Effect: Studies in Governmentality*, Chicago: University of Chicago Press.

Cavadino, M. and Dignan, J. (1996) *The Penal System: An Introduction*, second edition, London: Sage.

Christie, N. (1993) *Crime Control as Industry: Towards Gulags Western Style*, London: Routledge.

Clarke, J. (1996) 'The Problem of the State after the Welfare State', in M. May, E. Brinsden and G. Craig, eds. *Social Policy Review*, London: Social Policy Association.

Cohen, S. (1979) 'The Punitive City: Notes on the Dispersal of Social Control', *Contemporary Crises*, 3: 339–63.

Cohen, S. (1985) *Visions of Social Control: Crime, Punishment and Classification*, Cambridge: Polity Press.

Cohen, S. (1994) 'Social Control and the Politics of Reconstruction' in D. Nelken, ed. *The Futures of Criminology*, London: Sage.

Cohen, S. (1998) 'Intellectual Scepticism and Political Commitment: the Case of Radical Criminology', in P. Walton and J. Young, eds. *The New Criminology Revisited*, Basingstoke: Macmillan.

Cornell, D. (1992) *The Philosophy of the Limit*, New York: Routledge.

Daly, K. (1994) *Gender, Crime and Punishment*, New Haven, Conn: Yale University Press.

Dershowitz, A. (1997) *Reasonable Doubts: The Criminal Justice System and the O.J. Simpson Case*, New York: Touchstone.

Duff, P. (1998) 'Crime Control, Due Process and the 'Case for the Prosecution': A Problem of Terminology', *British Journal Of Criminology*, 38, 4: 611–15.

Dunbar, I. and Langdon, A. (1998) *Tough Justice: Sentencing and Penal Policies in the 1990s*, London: Blackstone Press.

Ericson, R. and Carriere, K. (1994) 'The Fragmentation of Criminology', in D. Nelken, ed. *The Futures of Criminology*, London: Sage.

Farrington, D.P. (1997) 'Human Development and Criminal Careers', in M. Maguire, R. Morgan and R. Reiner, eds. *The Oxford Handbook of Criminology*, second edition, Oxford: Clarendon Press.

Faulkner, D. (1996) *Darkness and Light: Justice, Crime and Management for Today*, London: Howard League for Penal Reform.

Feeley, M. and Simon, J. (1994) 'Actuarial Justice: the emerging new criminal law', in D. Nelken, ed. *The Futures of Criminology*, London: Sage.

Feeley, M. and Simon, J. (1995) 'True Crime: The New Penology and Public Discourse on Crime', in T.G. Blomberg and S. Cohen, eds. *Punishment and Social Control: Essays in Honor of Sheldon L. Messenger*, New York: Aldine De Gruyter.

Gamble, A. (1994) *The Free Economy and the Strong State: The Politics of Thatcherism*, second edition, Basingstoke: Macmillan.

Garland, D. (1990) *Punishment and Modern Society*, Oxford: Oxford University Press.

Garland, D. (1996) 'The Limits of the Sovereign State: Strategies of Crime Control in Contemporary Society', *British Journal of Criminology*, 36, 4: 445–71.

Garland, D. (1997) ' 'Governmentality' and the problem of crime: Foucault, criminology, sociology', *Theoretical Criminology*, 1, 2: 173–214.

Garland, D. (1999) 'The Culture of High Crime Societies: the social preconditions of the new politics of crime control', paper presented at the *Conference on Crime, Neo-Liberalism and the Risk Society*, John Jay College of Criminal Justice, New York, April (forthcoming in *British Journal of Criminology*, vol. 30, 2000).

Gilroy, P. (1987) 'The Myth of Black Criminality', in P. Scraton, ed. *Law, Order and the Authoritarian State*, Milton Keynes: Open University Press.

Gordon, C. (1991) 'Governmental Rationality: an Introduction', in G. Burchell, C. Gordon and P. Miller, eds., *The Foucault Effect: Studies in Governmentality*, Chicago: University of Chicago Press.

Habermas, J. (1984 and 1987) *The Theory of Communicative Action, Vols. 1 and 2,* Boston, Mass: Beacon Press.

Hall, S. (1980) *Drifting into a Law and Order Society*, London: Cobden Trust.

Hall, S. (1988) *A Hard Road to Renewal*, London: Verso.

Hannah-Moffat, K. (1999) 'Moral agent or actuarial subject: Risk and Canadian women's imprisonment', *Theoretical Criminology*, 3, 1: 71–94.

Hay, C. (1995) 'Mobilization through Interpellation: James Bulger, Juvenile Crime and the construction of a moral panic', *Social and Legal Studies*, 4: 197–223.

Henham, R. (1998) 'Human Rights, Due Process and Sentencing', *British Journal of Criminology*, 38, 4: 592–610.

Home Office – Acts of Parliament

  1991 *Criminal Justice Act*, London: HMSO.

  1997 *Crime (Sentences) Act*, London: HMSO.

  1998 *Crime and Disorder Act*, London: HMSO.

Home Office – Statistical Bulletins

  30/92 *Cautions, Court Proceedings and Sentencing England and Wales 1991*, 28 October, London: Home Office.

  8/95 *The Prison Population in 1994*, 27 April, London: Home Office.

  5/98 *The Prison Population in 1997*, 26 March, London: Home Office.

  18/98 *Cautions, Court Proceedings and Sentencing England and Wales 1997*, 17 September, London: Home Office.

Home Office – White and Green Papers

  1988 *Punishment, Custody and the Community*, London: HMSO.

  1996 *Protecting the Public: The Government's Strategy on Crime in England and Wales*, London: HMSO.

Hudson, B. (1993) *Penal Policy and Social Justice*, Basingstoke: Macmillan.

Hudson, B. (1995) 'Beyond proportionate punishment: Difficult cases and the 1991 Criminal Justice Act', *Crime, Law and Social Change*, 22: 59–78.

Hudson, B. (1996) *Understanding Justice: an introduction to ideas, perspectives and controversies in modern penal theory*, Buckingham: Open University Press.

Hudson, B. (1998a) 'Punishment and Governance', *Social and Legal Studies*, 7, 4: 553–60.

Hudson, B. (1998b) 'Doing Justice to Difference', in A. Ashworth and M. Wasik, eds *Fundamentals of Sentencing Theory*, Oxford: Clarendon Press.

Hudson, B. (1998c) 'Restorative Justice: the Challenge of Sexual and Racial Violence', *Journal of Law and Society*, 25, 2: 237–256.

Hudson, B. (2000) 'Balancing risks and rights: dilemmas of justice and difference', paper presented at the *Colloquium on Risk and Criminal Justice*, Cardiff University, 18 and 19 May.

Kelsen, H. (1996) 'What is Justice?', in J. Westphal, ed. *Justice*, Cambridge: Hackett Publishing.

Kerruish, V. (1991) *Jurisprudence as Ideology*, London: Routledge.

Lacey, N. (1987) 'Discretion and Due Process at the Post-Conviction Stage', in I.H. Dennis, ed. *Criminal Law and Justice*, London: Sweet and Maxwell.

MacKinnon, C.A. (1989) *Towards a Feminist Theory of the State*, Cambridge, Mass: Cambridge University Press.

McConville, M., Sanders, A. and Leng, R. (1997) 'Descriptive or Critical Sociology: the choice is yours', *British Journal of Criminology*, 37, 3: 347–58.

Marx, G. (1988) *Under Cover: Police surveillance in America*, Berkeley: University of California Press.

Marx, G. (1995) 'The Engineering of Social Control: The search for the silver bullet', in J. Hagan and R.D. Peterson, eds. *Crime and Inequality*, Stanford, Calif: Stanford University Press.

Mill, J.S. (1996) 'On the Connexion between Justice and Utility', in J. Westphal, ed. *Justice*, Cambridge: Hackett Publishing.

Miller, P. and Rose, N. (1990) 'Governing economic life', *Economy and Society*, 19: 1–31.

Minow, M. (1990) *Making All the Difference*, Ithaca, N.Y.: Cornell University Press.

Morris, N. (1994) 'Dangerousness and Incapacitation', in R.A. Duff and D. Garland, eds. *A Reader in Punishment*, Oxford: Oxford University Press.

Newburn, T. (1995) *Crime and Criminal Justice Policy*, London: Longman.

O'Malley, P. (1992) 'Risk, power and crime prevention', *Economy and Society*, 21, 3: 252–275.

Packer, H. (1969) *The Limits of the Criminal Sanction*, Stanford, Calif: Stanford University Press.

Pasquino, P. (1991) 'Criminology: the Birth of a Special Knowledge', in G. Burchell, C. Gordon and P. Miller, eds., *The Foucault Effect: Studies in Governmentality*, Chicago: University of Chicago Press.

Pitch, T. (1995) *Limited Responsibilities: Social Movements and Criminal Justice*, English edition, London: Routledge.

Rawls, J. (1972) *A Theory of Justice*, Oxford: Oxford University Press.

Reiman, J. (1990) *Justice and Modern Moral Philosophy*, New Haven, Conn: Yale University Press.

Roberts, J. and Domurad, F. (1995) 'Re-engineering Probation: lessons from New York City', *Vista*, 1, 1: 59–68, Worcester: Association of Chief Officers of Probation.

Rose, N. (1996) 'The Death of the Social? Refiguring the territory of government', *Economy and Society*, 25, 2: 327–389.

Rose, N. and Miller, P. (1992) 'Political power beyond the state: problematics of government', *British Journal of Sociology*, 43: 173–205.

Rutherford A. (1996) *Criminal Policy and the Eliminative Ideal*, inaugural lecture, University of Southampton, 8 October.

Sanders, A. and Young, R. (1994) *Criminal Justice*, London: Butterworths.

Sarat, A. (1997) 'Vengeance, Victims and the Identities of Law', *Social and Legal Studies*, 6, 2: 163–190.

Simon, J. (1988) 'The ideological effects of actuarial practice', *Law and Society Review*, 22, 4: 771–800.

Simon, J. (1996) 'Criminology and the Recidivist', in D. Schicor and D.K. Sechrest, eds. *Three Strikes and You're Out: Vengeance as Public Policy*, Thousand Oaks, Calif: Sage.

Simon, J. (1997) 'Governing through Crime in a Democratic Society', paper presented to New York University Law School, January.

Smart, C. (1995) *Law, Crime and Sexuality: Essays in Feminism*, London: Sage.

Stenson, K. (1999) 'Crime Control, Governmentality and Sovereignty', in R. Smandych, ed., *Governable Places: readings in governmentality and crime control*, Aldershot: Dartmouth.

Tadros, V. (1998) 'Between Governance and Discipline: the Law and Michel Foucault', *Oxford Journal of Legal Studies* 4 (Spring): 75–103.

Van Swaaningen, R. (1997) *Critical Criminology: Visions from Europe*, London: Sage.

Walzer, M. (1986) 'The Politics of Michel Foucault', in D. Couzens Hoy, ed. *Foucault: A Critical Reader*, Oxford: Basil Blackwell.

Williams, B. (1993) 'Bail bandits: the construction of a moral panic', *Critical Social Policy*, 37: 104–112.

Windlesham, Lord (1993) *Responses to Crime. Vol. 2 Penal Policy in the Making*, Oxford: Clarendon Press.

Young, I.M. (1990) *Justice and the Politics of Difference*, Princeton, N.J: Princeton University Press.

5

The media, crime and risk

9

Casino culture:
media and crime in a winner–loser society

Robert Reiner, Sonia Livingstone and *Jessica Allen*

> When the (capital) development of a country becomes a by-product of the activities of a casino, the job is likely to be ill-done.
>
> JOHN MAYNARD KEYNES

Introduction: from riskophobia to riskophilia – the coming of casino culture

Deviance, crime and control have become defining issues of our time. In Britain 'law and order' only became prominent party political matters in the final quarter of the twentieth century (Downes and Morgan 1997), but now crime, fear of crime, and competing policies aimed at containing them, are central to public policy debate. A pivotal part of the political success of New Labour in Britain was its 'tough on crime, tough on the causes of crime' pledge. Labour's £250m Crime Reduction Programme and the 1998 Crime and Disorder Act represent significant efforts to deliver on this, although views differ on the prospects of success. The rapidly shifting, increasingly ambiguous boundaries between 'deviance' and 'normality' are the storm-centre of raging 'culture wars', throughout the world.

The conventional popular and political understanding of this is that we have – for disputed reasons – become beset by ever more numerous and ever more serious crimes. This is of course what the official crime statistics indicate. In Britain recorded crime has increased by an average of 5.1 per cent per year since 1918, and recorded violent crime by 6.4 per cent per year since 1947 (Home Office, 1999: 3). In 1999 the Home Office recorded over 5m notifiable offences, ten times the 1950 figure and fifty times the pre-1920 level (*ibid*: 2). In the US although recorded crime rates are generally lower than twenty years ago, that still leaves them much higher than they were fifty or one hundred years ago (Currie, 1998).

The popular and political reactions to crime and justice are of course much more complex than a straightforward reflex of crime statistics. Perceptions of crime bear an extremely problematic relationship to any official statistical measures of crime rates, as the vexed debate about the 'rationality' and meaning of public 'fear of crime' demonstrates (Sparks, 1992). In any event, as most criminology textbooks spell out, official crime rates are dubious reflections of trends and patterns in offending (Maguire, 1997).

The problematic nature of official crime statistics of any kind has tended to be ignored in recent debate, partly because of the hold of new realist perspectives. Even more important has been the influence of national crime surveys (such as the British Crime Survey and the US National Crime Victimization Survey) in the last two decades. Although these have demonstrated unequivocally the huge volume of unrecorded crime that exists, the overall trends in survey-estimated and officially recorded victimisation have been similar, creating a climate of greater confidence in official statistics. It is likely, however, that the congruence between officially recorded and victim survey statistical trends results from some historically peculiar characteristics of the last twenty years (such as virtually saturation reporting of the most common property offences). They do not constitute a vindication of official crime statistics as a measure of crime trends in general.

In Britain there is certainly much evidence that the decline in recorded crime rates in the 1990s was largely a product of changes in victim reporting and police recording behaviour, paradoxically arising from pressures generated by very high rates of crime (Reiner 1996, 2000). Victims of property crime have been reporting a diminishing proportion to the police because of concern about the insurance consequences of claims, whilst the police have recorded a declining proportion of crimes made known to them as they have become subject to more stringent performance measurement. More generally research on policing continues to suggest that recorded crime rates are highly manipulable in response to political and other exigencies (H.Taylor, 1998, 1999).

Nonetheless, despite the continuing limitations of recorded crime statistics as evidence of this, it seems clear that we do now live in what can be called a 'high crime society' (Garland, 2000). Crime is a central political and popular concern, and security strategies pervade the routines of everyday life. Debate rages about how to explain the growth of crime rates, and whether and how they might be controlled, with contrasting diagnoses reflecting different political and moral perspectives. Although politicians and some journalists tend to favour single factor explanations, understanding recent changes in crime and criminal justice requires analysis of all the complex and perplexing social, economic, political and cultural developments of the last few decades. There have been some recent attempts to offer synthetic accounts of how the resurgence of free market economics, consumerism, increasing individualism, declining deference, the information technology revolution, and other processes have reconfigured crime and criminal justice (for example Garland 1996, 2000; Currie, 1998; I.Taylor, 1999; Young, 1999; Reiner, 2000).

One of the most influential theorizations of the current stage of social development (which has become increasingly applied to issues of crime and justice) is the concept of the 'risk society', the key theme of this volume. For all the proliferation of risk discourses, inside and outside the academy, there is much ambiguity about what is involved. The pioneering analyses of 'risk society' (notably Beck, 1992) do not refer to issues of crime or disorder, leaving even more interpretive latitude for those who seek to apply the concept to criminology and criminal justice. There is a particular ambiguity about how far the notion of 'risk society' implies a change in the extent or nature of risk, as distinct from new cultural sensibilities and techniques of seeking to achieve security.

With regard to the kinds of risks on which Beck concentrates (physical dangers of various kinds such as environmental and food hazards) it is implausible to see them as more threatening in some absolute sense than the dangers of 'class society' or earlier social formations. Rather the point is that they are 'manufactured' as opposed to 'external' risks (Giddens, 1998: 27–8). In addition one of Beck's central points is that in 'risk society' the threats are global and face everyone more or less equally. Although there may be attempts by the wealthy and powerful to gain positions of advantage in the 'distribution of bads' these are largely futile.

None of these features of the seminal 'risk society' analyses apply straight-forwardly to crime and criminal justice. Arguably there *is* in an absolute sense more danger of criminal victimization now than in earlier stages of modernity (although fear of crime is often seen as being disproportionate to 'objective' measures of risk). Crime has always been a 'manufactured' rather than 'external' risk, in that its incidence is socially constructed – although a key feature of popular and media conceptions is the criminal as 'outsider'. Although we do know from victimization surveys that crime disproportionately hits the more vulnerable sections of the population, it nonetheless is a threat that faces all social strata, even if more powerful or affluent groups do increasingly seek to buy more adequate provisions for security.

The concept of 'risk society' connotes not only a shift in the nature of risk, but also an alteration in cultural sensibilities, and above all, in strategies for dealing with risk (see Sparks, Chapter 10 in this volume). Here the analysis has parallels with other influential conceptualisations of the contemporary period, such as theories of postmodernity and neo-liberalism. Perhaps the key themes are the decline of the grand narrative of progress – the hallmark of modernity – and the 'death of the social' (Rose, 1996; Stenson, 1998). Problems are not seen as having fundamental causes that can be ameliorated by collective policy. Rather they are regarded as either the product of chance or of individual action. The state and its agencies are problems not solutions. Remedies cannot be found in social policy but by changing the behaviour of the people responsible, and by individual self-help strategies such as insurance or personal protection. Problems and solutions are de-moralized, de-mystified, secularized. Events are judged problematic not in terms of absolute moral codes but because they risk causing harm to us, or to those we identify or at least empathize with. Actions are good not because they embody virtue but because they work.

Individuals are held responsible for their fates, in a 'winner-loser culture' (James 1995). In an increasingly deregulated global market place, where there is a continuous proliferation of new millionaires and new paupers, the stakes are ever higher. The National Lottery is the quintessence of this new casino culture. Instead of the cradle to grave security of a welfare state the ideal is winner takes all, and the compensation for the substantial risk of losing is the scintilla of hope of being that winner. Some thirty years ago when he constructed his magisterial theory of justice (as what has proved to be an intellectual Custer's Last Stand defence of the welfare state) John Rawls could still assume with some plausibility that people were risk averse (Rawls, 1973: 152–161). This riskophobic culture has clearly been replaced by a riskophiliac one. The media play a pivotal role in reproducing this, celebrating the winners as celebrities and devaluing any styles of life other than spectacular consumerism.

In relation to crime and criminal justice this is reflected in many changes of the last quarter of the twentieth century. The optimistic paradigm that crime could and would be conquered by social progress and rehabilitation of individual offenders, which dominated policy from the late nineteenth century until the 1970s (Garland, 1985, 2000), has been eclipsed by a combination of more pragmatic and more punitive responses. This has been underlined by an aggressive analytic 'know-nothingism' epitomised above all by James Q. Wilson's scornful dismissal of the idea of social 'root causes' of crime in favour of a tough administrative realism. The 'rehabilitative ideal' has been replaced by incapacitation, general deterrence and revenge as the purposes of penal policy.

Criminals now are to be condemned and contained, not understood and changed. 'Tough on the causes of crime' means a variety of what David Garland has dubbed 'criminologies of everyday life': pragmatic routines to minimize opportunities for offending such as situational crime prevention and targetting 'hot spots' (Garland, 1996). Without a social dimension, individual target-hardening becomes a burgle-my-neighbour tactic; problem-oriented policing becomes problem-suppressing policing. The police are no longer custodians and symbols of public tranquillity and virtue, but compete in a commercialized marketplace for security with other (mainly private) suppliers (South 1997; Johnston 2000). Customers (private and governmental) choose the best deals from a 'pick'n'mix' policing bazaar (Reiner, 1997a: 1038–9). Crime becomes a practical hazard not a moral threat. The criminal justice system operates increasingly in actuarial terms of seeking to calculate and minimize risks pragmatically rather than achieving broader ideals of justice (Feeley and Simon, 1994; see chapters by Simon, Hudson, O'Malley, and Stenson and Edwards this volume).

This chapter attempts to assess the role of mass media representations of crime and criminal justice in relation to the above changes. It does so by considering the implications of our historical study of mass media representations of crime and criminal justice since the Second World War, and of audience perceptions of these. This research was supported by a grant from the Economic and Social Research Council of Great Britain (no. L/210/25/2029), for which we thank them. In the next section we consider briefly the long-standing and wide-ranging debate about the media–crime relationship, which informed the research. Then we describe the research methods we used. The fourth section offers some key findings about the changing content of mass media representations of crime, whilst the fifth section looks at audience perceptions drawing on our focus group interviews. Finally, the conclusions consider the relationship between mass media representations and the rise of risk discourse about crime and criminal justice policy.

The media-crime debate

Anxiety about media representations of crime has flourished for as long as the modern media of communication have existed. It has been particularly prominent in various discourses about why crime rates and patterns have changed since the Second World War (although such respectable fears have a much longer ancestry-cf. Pearson, 1983). The most familiar of these discourses is that of moral decline and fall: the media are blamed for sensationalizing deviance, glamourizing offending, and undermining moral authority and social controls.

Anxieties about the media have also figured in liberal and radical discourses about crime and criminal justice changes, although with very different concerns and inflexions. A common theme is that media representations unduly accentuate the risks of crime, fanning public anxieties, and thus bolstering support for more authoritarian criminal justice policy and practice.

There is a large research literature on media representations of crime, and their sources and possible consequences. However, virtually all empirical studies examine only one period in time, although some have collected data comparing a few different years (e.g. Roshier, 1973; Sumser, 1996). The sole exception is one recent study of the content of American television and cinema over the last half-century, which provides useful material on changing crime and law enforcement images (Lichter, Lichter and Rothman, 1994; Powers, Rothman and Rothman, 1996).

Our research analysed the changing content of the main British media concerning crime over the period since the Second World War, and how audiences interpret these changes. The data cannot directly assess the extent to which changing media representations of crime are causally related to crime or fear of crime. To the extent that parallels are found between developments in media images and patterns of crime or fear of crime, the causal interpretation of this is complex.

Previous content analyses have shown that media representations vastly exaggerate the risks and seriousness of crime, as well as the success of the police and criminal justice system in combatting crime. Many studies do indeed find associations between media consumption patterns and various measures of fear of crime (Howitt, 1998: chap. 4). Heavy viewing of TV crime fiction, for example, is linked with more fearful perceptions of crime and support for authoritarian solutions (Signorielli, 1990: 96–102). Readers of newspapers which present violent crime stories more frequently and more sensationally express more fearfulness in response to survey questions (although not in behavioural manifestations such as not going out after dark), even controlling for age, gender and socio-economic status (Williams and Dickinson, 1993).

The problem lies in deciding what causal relationship can be inferred from these associations. Do media crime stories cause fearfulness, or do more fearful people read or watch more? Given that the majority of stories, especially in the past, feature 'happy' endings with crime and conflict resolved neatly, perhaps they reassure rather than disturb viewers who are already fearful due to personal or vicarious experience of actual victimization (Wakshlag, Vial and Tamborini, 1983). Or do particular life experiences or social positions, such as living in high-crime areas, generate more risk, heightened anxiety, *and* more media consumption?

Our reviews of the voluminous existing research literature on these issues led us to the conclusion that the most plausible model is a dialectical one. There is a continuous process of interaction between changing media representations and patterns of criminality, perceptions of crime risks, and criminal justice policy and practice (Livingstone, 1996: 31–2; Reiner, 1997b: 216–9, 224–5). Different life positions and experiences intertwine in complex ways with the reception of media texts, which quantitative content analyses can hardly penetrate, requiring interpretive approaches more sensitive to the subtleties of analysing meaning.

Our aim was to gather historical and interview data which could test the validity of particular elements of the competing discourses about the part the media have played in the changes in criminality and justice since World War II. These discourses all assume particular accounts of how media images have changed. For example, the conservative discourse of moral decline presumes that the media *have* become increasingly focussed on crime, present offenders in more attractive ways, and portray the criminal justice system less favourably. The fear of crime debate by contrast assumes that the media increasingly exaggerate the risks of victimization. Historical content analysis is necessary to assess such claims.

We will argue that the historical content analyses and the focus group discussions we conducted converge in suggesting a particular picture of the changing discourse about crime and criminal justice, both in the public arena constituted by the mass media, and in everyday life and experience. In many ways this parallels the themes of the 'risk society' analyses considered above. Criminality is no longer seen as an offence against the hallowed and absolute norms of a common culture, but as a pragmatic matter of one individual harming another. This process is reflected in a transformation of representations of the moral status of offenders, the criminal justice system, victims, punishment, and fear of crime. Moral status is no longer automatically conferred by a role in the social order; it is subject to negotiation and constructed anew by particular narratives. The police and criminal justice system are not seen as guardians of a social order so much as regulators of risk to potential individual victims. They are often perceived as threatening rather than reassuring.

Research methods

Our study examined representations of crime and criminal justice in three mass media from 1945 to 1991. We also looked at audience understandings of, and relations to, the media representations. Clearly we could not examine all mass media, due to practical constraints of availability and resources. We focussed on the two media which have been most prominent throughout the twentieth century, cinema and newspapers, and the pre-eminent medium of the post-war period, television.

The historical content analyses

The cinema research combined a generic analysis of all films released in Britain since 1945 (which included an increasing proportion of US films over the period), and detailed quantitative and qualitative content analyses of box-office hits. The latter were chosen as approximating the most influential films of the period. For television, we focussed on fictional crime series. The ephemeral character of television news presents insuperable problems of non-availability for the study of long-term changes in content. The press study analysed representative samples of stories from the *Times*, the British newspaper of record for most of the period, and the *Mirror*, a paper which contrasts with it in terms of both market (tabloid versus quality) and politics (left of centre versus right). Although inevitably limited, this is a larger sampling across media and time than hitherto found in the criminological research literature.

What counts as 'crime' is, of course, subject to enormous definitional and conceptual debate and difficulties. For the purposes of this research a straightforward legal positivist definition was adopted: we took a 'crime' in a media narrative to be any act which appeared to violate English criminal law (at the time of the story).

In the quantitative analyses of our data we adopted a three-stage periodisation: 1955–64; 1965–1979; and 1980–1991. Clearly any single year cut-off points are fairly arbitrary. However, this broad three-fold division corresponds to the picture given by most histories of the period since the end of the Second World War. The first period is one of post-war recovery, merging into what is usually seen as an era of unprecedented mass affluence, consumerism, and political and social consensus. The middle period – the 'sixties' – sees the continuation of mass affluence and consumerism. However, it was widely experienced as a time of conflict, change, and questioning of traditional patterns of morality, authority, sexuality, and relationships between generations and ethnic groups. The third period sees the attempts by the Reagan and Thatcher governments to combine a return to earlier moral certainties with neo–liberal economic policies. In the end the latter tended to undermine the former, although 'culture wars' about morality, gender and family continue to rage. What became increasingly clear was that there had occurred a profound break in social and economic development during the 1970s, whether this is interpreted primarily in terms of late or postmodernity, risk society, globalization or other competing theorizations. We began the research with this rough periodization in mind, but translated it into the precise three periods we used for the quantitative analysis after this appeared to fit the emerging data most coherently.

Film   The film study was based on two different samples. A random 10 per cent sample of all films released in Britain since 1945 was drawn from a source which also provided synopses of these (*Film Review* which has been published annually since 1944). This sample was coded by genre to calculate the changing proportion of crime films (i.e. with narratives centred on the commission and/or investigation of a crime), and the extent to which there were significant representations of crime in other films. A smaller sample of 84 films was drawn randomly from the 196 crime movies since 1945 that had been listed amongst the top box-office hits in Britain. These were viewed and analysed in detail to assess qualitative changes.

The press   The press study also used two related samples. To assess the proportion of crime stories a random 10 per cent sample of all 'home news' stories since 1945 in the *Times* and the *Mirror* was coded. A more detailed qualitative analysis was conducted for a smaller random sample of stories. Ten days were selected randomly for both newspapers for every second year since 1945. In those issues all front-page stories, editorial or op-ed items, and letters concerning crime were analysed, as were the most prominent crime news stories on the home news pages.

Television   The television study examined all the top twenty television programmes for every year since 1955 (when audience ratings first became available). These were coded according to genre to see the changing proportions which were focused on crime or criminal justice.

Audience reception of crime media

Historical study of how audiences interpret mass media representations of crime and criminal justice clearly raises profound methodological difficulties. Our project combined methods from oral history with audience reception methods, using homogeneous focus groups to interpret specific media contents. The key dimension of analysis was age, although we also considered gender, ethnicity and class. Audience age indexes two phenomena: position in the life course and generation.

Selected examples of images and texts were used to stimulate focus group discussion of the media in relation to crime, social change, and notions of authority and responsibility. After a pilot group discussion, sixteen focus groups (of approximately 20, 40, 60, and 80 years of age, each separated by gender and into two rough class groupings)were recruited from seven locations in the south-east of England (covering urban, suburban areas). Ninety-six people were interviewed in all.

The changing content of media representations of crime

Crime narratives and representations are, and always have been, a prominent part of the content of all mass media. Our study attempts to assess the long-term trends in crime content since the Second World War. For the cinema and newspapers we measured the proportion of all narratives which were primarily crime stories. We also estimated the proportion that had significant crime content, even if not primarily focused on crime. The absence of change in the quantity of crime represented would not falsify any claims about possible relationships between trends in media content and developments in crime and criminal justice. Nonetheless a significant increase or decrease would be of considerable interest in examining the validity of the different discourses about the media/crime link. For example, an increase in crime stories might be seen as related to the rise of crime risk discourse.

In our random sample of cinema films there did not appear to be any significant pattern of change in the extent of representation of crime. There is no clear trend for the proportion of crime films to either rise or fall, although there are many sharp fluctuations in individual years around this basic steady state (Allen, Livingstone and Reiner, 1997). Crime has clearly been a significant concern of the cinema throughout the post-war period (and probably before that as well). In most years around 20 per cent of all films released are crime films.

The results of the analysis of a random sample of newspaper stories between 1945–91 suggest a more complex picture. By the end of the period the proportion of stories about crime had increased considerably. In the *Mirror* the average proportion of stories which were centrally about crime in the years 1945–51 was 9 per cent, whilst in the *Times* it was 7 per cent. By 1985–91 this had risen to 21 per cent for both papers (the drawing level of the two papers suggests the general process of tabloidisation of the *Times*). The proportion of stories about the criminal justice system or policy (as distinct from specific crimes) also rose in both papers. It had increased from an average of 2 per cent in the *Daily Mirror* between 1945–51 to 6 per cent between 1985–91, and from 3 per cent to 9 per cent in the same periods in the *Times*. Whilst newspapers' concern with crime and criminal justice appears distinctly higher in the last period of our study than the first, the years in between show a marked pattern of cyclical fluctuation around this overall rising trend.

Changes in levels and patterns of offending, or of fear of crime, cannot be attributed to a sheer quantitative increase in crime content in the media. This has not occurred at all in the cinema, although there has been some increase in crime content in newspaper stories. This is nowhere near as marked or as continuous as the rise in recorded crime but it may be a factor in increasing concern about crime, as well as a reflection of it. Changes in the way that crime narratives are constructed are more significant than their sheer quantity.

Media crime patterns

Our analysis of cinema films distinguished three types of crime in terms of their function within the narrative (Allen, Livingstone and Reiner, 1998). Adapting Hitchcock's terminology for the object that is pursued in a story, we call the crime providing the primary focus or motive for a story the 'McGuffin'. 'Consequential' crimes are those which are necessary adjuncts of this, either before or after (for example in order to escape capture). 'Contextual' crimes are those which are represented in the narrative but are not related to the 'McGuffin' (for example the bank robbery Clint Eastwood encounters while munching a hamburger in *Dirty Harry*).

Throughout the period 1945–91 the most frequent 'McGuffin' was homicide, but to a slightly diminishing extent: in 50% of crime films between 1945–64; 35% for 1965–79; 45% 1980–91. Property crime 'McGuffins' virtually disappeared: 32% of films 1945–64; 20% 1965–79; only 5% 1980–91. Sex-related 'McGuffins' (e.g. rape or prostitution) have become more frequent, although still rare: 3% 1945–64; 10% 1965–79; 15% 1980–91. Drugs have shown a curvilinear pattern: 2% 1945–64; 10% 1965–79; 5% 1980–91.

The extent of violence depicted in the presentation of the 'McGuffin' has increased considerably. The proportion of films in which it was associated with significant pain rose from 2% 1945–64; 20% 1965–79; to 40% 1980–91. This has consequences for the typical representation of offenders, victims, police and the criminal justice system.

The representation of consequential crimes has changed even more markedly. Between 1945–64 14% of films depicted no consequential crimes, 43% showed one, and 43% featured multiple consequential crimes. After that there are hardly any films without consequential crimes, and over 80% feature multiple offences of this kind. The extent of violence depicted in these crimes has also multiplied considerably. Whereas between 1945–64 74% of films had consequential crimes involving little or no violence, and only 5% featured significant levels of violence, by 1980–91 these proportions had changed to 16% and 47% respectively.

The representation of contextual crimes is the most striking change. Contextual crimes have proliferated, connoting a society pervaded by generalized crime risks. Between 1945–64 32% of films had no contextual offending at all, 9% showed just one contextual crime, and 59% had multiple crimes of this type. By 1980–91 only 15% of films showed no contextual crimes, and 80% featured multiple offences unrelated to the central narrative. An increasing proportion of contextual offences are violent and/or sex- and drug-related, and a diminishing proportion are property offences (as with the 'McGuffin' crimes). The extent of violence portrayed in these offences has increased. In 1945–64 90% had no or only minor violence, by 1980–91 these proportions had changed to 29% and 65% respectively.

Overall then our findings show that although murder has always been the most common 'McGuffin' crime in films, there is over our period a diminishing proportion featuring property crime, and an increase in the representation of violent crimes of all kinds. The extent of violence inflicted in these offences has sharply increased. The large rise in the depiction of consequential and especially contextual offences implies a picture of a society much more threatened by all pervasive risks of violent crime.

Our sample of newspaper stories shows a rather similar pattern of change. Murder (including attempts) is the most common single offence type throughout the period, although to a slightly increasing extent. It accounted for 20% of all newspaper crime stories between 1945–64; and 28% in both the later periods analysed, 1965–79; 1980–91. In newspaper stories the most rapidly increasing single type of crime reported was terrorist offences: 0.7% of stories 1945–64; 5.3%

1965–79; 8.8% 1980–91. Overall there was a clear shift from stories featuring property crimes (such as burglary and car theft) to offences against the person, including homicide, assault, and sexual offences. The proportion of stories reporting property offences went down from 20% in 1945–64; to 12% 1965–79, and 8% between 1980–91. Offences against the person stories rose from 33% between 1945–64; to 44% 1965–79; and 46% 1980–91.

This means that the standard research finding that the media over-report violent and sexual offences disproportionately (Reiner, 1997b: 199–203) requires some qualification. This has indeed been true throughout the post-war period, but the extent of the imbalance has increased markedly. Stories purely about property offences have virtually disappeared. Almost half of all crime-related news stories are now about violence and/or sex.

Criminal justice

The representation of the criminal justice system and its agents has changed in substantial ways. However, on most dimensions the representation of criminal justice alters in a curvilinear pattern. Variables are at their highest or lowest in the middle years (1964–79) of our period.

The cinema research shows an increasing prevalence of criminal justice agents as heroes (or at any rate the central protagonists) of narratives, although this is subject to something of a U-shaped pattern. The key aspect is the rise (and partial fall) of police heroes. The police are the protagonists of only 9% of films between 1945–64, but 50% of those between 1965–79, and 40% of those between 1980–91. There was a continuous decline in amateur investigator heroes: 36% 1945–64; 5% 1965–79; none 1980–91. Victim-related protagonists clearly increased, but also in a curvilinear pattern: 13% in 1945–64; none 1965–79; 25% 1980–91. Overall there is a clear decline of amateur sleuths in favour of criminal justice professionals, especially the police, and an increase in victim or victim-related heroes. The police predominance is especially marked in the middle period, although substantial more recently as well. The rise of police protagonists is structurally related to the representation of crime risks as all pervasive, and hence requiring a bureaucratic organisation of professionals to contend with it.

Overall the representation of police protagonists has become less positive over time, although there is a clear curvilinear pattern. Critical and negative images are most common in the period 1964–79, although they are more frequent in 1980–91 than 1945–64. This applies both to the success and the integrity of the police protagonists.

The police and criminal justice system are portrayed as slightly less successful over time. Throughout the period the overwhelming majority of movie crimes are cleared-up. However, there is a marked change in how this is achieved. In the first period 1945–64 the most common method of clear-up is that the offender is brought to justice: 39%. In the two later periods this becomes very infrequent (15% 1965–79, 10% 1980–91). The most frequent method of clear-up becomes the killing of the offender – in 35% of films 1965–91.

The police come to be represented more frequently as vigilantes than as enforcers of the law. In 89% of films between 1945–64 the police remain within the parameters of due process of law in their methods, but they break these in 80% of films between 1965–79, and 67% from 1980–91. The police are also shown as more likely to use force, both reasonable and excessive force. Between 1945–64 the police protagonists are not shown using force in 54% of films, and in 40% the force used is reasonable and proportionate (e.g. minimal self-defence). Only in 3% of films were they shown using excessive force. But this is shown in 44% of films from 1965–79, and 25% from 1980–91.

The police protagonists are represented as entirely honest in personal terms in 89% of films between 1945–64; but only in 67% between 1965–79, and 77% 1980–91. In no films in the early period are they shown as seriously corrupt, but they are in 13% of films 1965–79, and 15% 1980–91. They are shown as engaged in petty corruption in 11% of 1945–64 films; 20% between 1965–79, and 8% between 1980–91. They are also represented as increasingly personally deviant (in terms of such matters as excessive drinking, swearing, and extra-marital sexual activity).

The criminal justice system is also portrayed as more divided internally. Conflict within police organisations features in only 15% of films 1945–64, but 79% from 1965 to 1979, and 56% 1980–91. Conflict between criminal justice organisations, such as the police and the courts, also becomes more frequent. It is represented in only 20% of films 1945–64, but 70% from 1965–91. Police officers themselves become more internally divided: conflict between buddies occurs in only 9% of films 1945–64, but over 50% thereafter.

Similar trends can be found in newspaper representations of criminal justice. The increasing proportion of stories about criminal justice in itself is an indication of the more politicized and controversial character of criminal justice issues. News stories in which the police are mentioned critically have increased (6% 1945–64; 10% 1965–79; 17% 1980–91). Stories with approving or even neutral accounts of the police have declined. Approving stories were just over 11% from 1945–79, but only 6% from 1980–91. Neutral mentions declined from 13% to 11% and then 8% through the three periods (the police were not mentioned at all in about 69% of crime news stories in all three periods).

The police and criminal justice system are represented in news stories as less successful in dealing with crime, especially in the middle period. Between 1945–64, 23% of news stories feature crimes which are not cleared up, but this rises to 37% from 1965–79, although there is a slight decline thereafter to 31%. Crime is explicitly represented as out of control in a growing minority of news stories: 3% 1945–64; 6% 1965–79; but 13% 1980–91.

Criminals

We have not uncovered any significant trends in the portrait of the personal characteristics of offenders. Throughout the period they are predominantly middle-aged or older (though there is a small tendency to portray young offenders more frequently), white (although the proportion of ethnic minority offenders is increasing slightly in both fiction and news stories), and male (confirming earlier studies). One way our findings challenge previous content analyses is that we find that only a minority of stories feature middle or upper-class offenders. This does not change significantly over time.

Criminals are overwhelmingly portrayed unsympathetically throughout the period, in both fiction and news. There is little change, and what there is suggests an increasingly unfavourable image of offenders. For example, they are shown using excessive or sadistic force in an increasing proportion of films (80% between 1980–91 as compared to 50% 1945–64). They are portrayed as committing crimes because of external causal pressure in a decreasing minority of films (30% 1945–64; around 15% thereafter). Increasingly they are represented as purely evil and enjoying their offending (from around 60% 1945–64 to 85% 1980–91). Films in which some sympathy is shown for offenders have declined over time: 40% 1945–64; 20% 1965–79; 15% 1980–91.

This predominantly (and slightly increasingly) unfavourable portrayal of offenders goes against the claim that crime has been stimulated by more sympathetic media representations. However, crime is represented as increasingly rewarding. In 91% of films between 1945–64 'crime does not pay' in that the offenders are unsuccessful and/or apprehended. After 1965 this is only true in 80% of the stories – although this still suggests an overwhelming message about the folly of offending (especially in the light of the low and diminishing clear-up rates found in official statistics).

Victims

Probably the clearest and most significant changes we have found are in the representation of victims. Victims have moved from a shadowy and purely functional role in crime narratives to a pivotal position. Their suffering increasingly constitutes the subject position or the *raison d'etre* of the story (mirroring the 'discovery' of, and increasing concern about, victims in criminal justice systems around the world – cf. Rock 1990; Zedner, 1997). In the film sample, no concern is evinced for the plight of the victim in 45% of cases 1945–64; 35% 1965–79; but only 11% 1980–91. Victimization is shown as having traumatic consequences in 74% of films between 1980–91, 40% 1965–79, but only 25% 1945–64. Victims are increasingly represented as the protagonists of films, that is to say as the principal subject position. They are protagonists in 56% of the films were they are presented as characters at all (as opposed to corpses or case files) between 1980–91, but only 26% 1965–79, and 16% 1945–64.

News stories also increasingly present the plight of victims in sympathetic or concerned terms. This was found in 11% of stories 1945–64, 18% 1965–79, and 24% 1980–91.

Audience perceptions of media representations of crime

The popularity of crime media

In the interviews, people varied in which type of crime fiction they enjoyed (if any). Young women were particularly keen on media which are realistic and offer them information about the nature, consequences and prevention of crime. These were appreciated as informal instruction about the actuarial risks and how to limit them. Men preferred action plots, with fast pace, special effects and humour. Most people were ambivalent about press crime reporting, wanting to know but not to be voyeuristic. Older people recalled past media largely in terms of notorious events, prominent drama series, television and film stars and little was recalled of specific narratives. Young people showed little interest in past media.

Perceptions of past crime media

Despite age and other differences, respondents were remarkably consensual in their characterization of the post-war period. This consensus tells a story of change in which crime representations (and society generally) shift from the 'pre-sixties' days, of little, mild crime where difficult issues were largely hidden, crime was largely nonviolent and the police were your friends. After the 'sixties' crime is much more prevalent, media images more explicit and upsetting, violence has increased and police are themselves more distant and more violent.

This shift is interpreted, again consensually, as a transition in morality. An era when good and bad were clearly distinguished and authority structures were respected (a culture of discipline), has been replaced by one in which the boundary between good and bad has blurred, criminals are sympathetic and authorities are corrupt (a culture of disrespect and desubordination).

However, the generations differed markedly in their relation to and evaluation of this. Older people tell a story of decline – the do-gooders in the 1960s upset the proper social order. Media representations are now too much 'in your face', voyeuristic and disrespectful of authority. Young people, on the other hand, tend to see this as a story of progress. They are optimistic, because they welcome the media championing civil rights in areas like gender, sexuality and ethnicity, the greater legitimation accorded to alternative viewpoints, and are glad that controversial issues are no longer hidden. They approve of the idea that morality should be decided by context, and respect must be earned, not given automatically to those in certain social roles.

Life course also mattered. What is most striking is that people are almost universally positive about the media they encountered during their youth (and into their mid-thirties), irrespective of whether this was, in fact, media from the 1950s, the 1970s or the 1990s. With the exception of the youngest group, people were far more tolerant of the media from before they were born than they are of media from later in their adulthood. The importance of life course suggests that the media of one's youth set the interpretive framework, the expectations for subsequent experiences of media.

Positioning the audience in relation to crime

Respondents continually 'commute' (Liebes and Katz, 1995) between a concrete concern with crime in the media and crime in everyday life. They also commute between a concern with the concrete, such as who commits what kinds of crimes, and the moral (what does this say about the moral and social order?). This suggests that everyday perceptions of crime in society provide a salient context within which media crime is interpreted; conversely, media crime triggers thoughts and feelings that are central to daily life.

Audiences seem more powerfully positioned in relation to crime media according to their perceived positioning in relation to the risks of crime and criminal justice. Particularly in our early period, crime media typically offer audiences the subject position of 'criminal justice protagonist', the criminal becomes 'other', and the victim is virtually invisible. However, 'real world' crime offers three subject positions: police/law enforcer, criminal and victim, and our different groups perceived the media through the lens of these.

Those aged 80 perceived media throughout the period, not only through the lens of their youth (the culture of respect), but also through the lens of their present-day perceived vulnerability, as potential victims of crime. The loss of a culture of respect weakens their identification with authorities. While both the media and everyday experience tell older people that they are muggable, our youngest groups felt they were continually portrayed as 'dangerous youth', potential perpetrators of crime. Thus they welcome a civil rights focus and the questioning of police authority.

Recalling that each generation is most positive about the media of their youth, we suggest that young people are positive about present-day media because they, like it, are ambivalent about police heroes, seeing themselves as often positioned as suspected criminals in daily life. Their desire is to understand both sides through the media, to question both authority and the criminal.

Gender and generation

This picture is cross-cut by gender. Unlike the men, young women are aware of their potential victim status, particularly their vulnerability to male violence, and so they welcomed coverage of such crimes. The oldest women shared their generation's pessimism, yet also expressed some approval of the destruction of the 'fairy tales' of their youth – the glamourous images of femininity and masculinity which some perceived to have trapped and distracted them.

The youngest women, on the other hand, shared their male peers' scepticism about the criminal justice system and so turned to reliance on themselves, not the authorities. Their orientation to media was actuarial and risk-related. It centred on how media provided information and opportunities to think through situations offering self-protection, through realistic assessments of risk. It was mainly if police heroes are female or feminized (as in *Silence of the Lambs* or *Cagney and Lacey*) that younger women showed some approval or identification with the criminal justice system.

Neither younger nor older men in our groups would accept views of themselves as potential victims. Rather the older men accepted the proffered identification with the protagonist, typically a law-enforcement hero. Younger men were particularly interested in forms of crime media in which the criminal was as much a focus as the law enforcers and in which the moral boundaries between the two were ambiguous or unresolved. Some saw the police as presenting them with more risks of trouble than criminals did.

Conclusion: from morality tales to calculated risks

The media representation of crime since the Second World War exhibits a clear periodization in terms of three ideal-type narrative structures. The first post-war decade is a period of consensus and social harmony in representations of criminal justice. Crime stories – news as well as fiction – present an image of society as based largely on shared values and a clear yet accepted hierarchy of status and authority. Crime was as defined by Durkheim: it united all healthy consciences to condemn and extirpate it. Criminals were normally brought to justice: crime did not pay. The forces of law always got their man. The criminal justice system was almost invariably represented as righteous, dedicated, and efficient.

During the mid-1960s the dominant mode of representation of crime and justice shifts discernibly. The values and integrity of authority come to be questioned increasingly. Doubts about the justice and effectiveness of criminal justice proliferate. Increasing prominence is given to conflict: between ethnic groups, men and women, social classes, even within the criminal justice system itself. Whilst street-cops more frequently feature as protagonists, they are often morally tarnished if not outright corrupt. However, the increasing criticism of the social order and criminal justice is from a standpoint of reform, the advocacy of preferable alternatives.

Since the late 1970s another shift is discernible, the advent of what could be called a post-critical era. Stories are increasingly bifurcated between counter-critical ones, which seek to return as far as possible to the values of consensus, and those which represent a hopelessly disordered beyond-good-and-evil world, characterized by a Hobbesian war of all against all. It is this division of narratives which accounts for the curvilinear pattern of many variables: there is some attempt to restore the values of the past, challenged by those which portray the exacerbation of the conflicts of the middle period.

Underneath the shifts in the mode of representation of concrete aspects of crime and justice, however, can be discerned a more fundamental shift in discourse, encompassing both media representations and popular discussion (as captured in our focus groups). This echoes the themes of the 'risk society' discourse outlined earlier. There is a demystification of authority and law, a change in the conceptualization of criminal justice from sacred to secular. Pragmatism and contingency push out moralistic certainties.

The marked changes in the representation of victims are the clearest emblem of the new risk discourse in popular cultural conceptions of crime. Crime moves from being something that must be opposed and controlled *ipso facto* – because the law defines it thus – to a contested category. Crime *may* be wrong, but this is a pragmatic issue, turning on the risk of harm to individual victims that audiences sympathize or empathize with, not from the authority of the law itself. The moral status of characters in a story (news or fiction) is no longer ascribed by their formal legal role. It has to be established from scratch in each narrative, and turns on who causes serious suffering to the victims occupying the subject position. Increasingly the latter may be the legally defined offenders, represented as victimized by a criminal injustice system.

However, the majority of narratives continue to work to justify ultimately the criminal justice viewpoint, although this has to be achieved by demonstrating particular harm to identifiable individual victims. In this sense the media both continue to reproduce a more complex and brittle order, and to function as sources of social control. Above all they reflect the increasing individualism of a less deferential and more desubordinate culture. Media narratives traditionally performed the ideological work of reconciling tensions between the values of individualism and community, suggesting a dynamic interdependence between them. Plots rescued individualism from tipping over into egoism as regularly as their rugged individualist heroes came in the end to act as saviours of social order (Bellah *et al*, 1996: 144–7). In the risk discourse which has come to prevail, however, heroes are merely the fittest individuals in a struggle for self-preservation.

References

Allen, J., Livingstone, S. and Reiner, R. (1997) 'The Changing Generic Location of Crime in Film: A Content Analysis of Film Synopses', *Journal of Communication* 47:89–101.

Allen, J., Livingstone, S. and Reiner, R. (1998) 'True Lies: Changing Images of Crime in British Postwar Cinema'. *European Journal of Communication* 13: 53–75.

Beck, U. (1992) *Risk Society.* London: Sage.

Bellah, R., Madsen, R., Sullivan, W., Swidler, A. and Tipton, S. (1996) *Habits of the Heart,* second edition. Berkeley: University of California Press.

Currie, E. (1998) *Crime and Punishment in America.* New York: Holt.

Downes, D. and Morgan, R. (1997) 'Dumping the "Hostages to Fortune"? The Politics of Law and Order in Post-War Britain' in *The Oxford Handbook of Criminology*, edited by M. Maguire, R. Morgan and R. Reiner, pp.86–134. Oxford: Oxford University Press.

Feeley, M. and Simon, J. (1994) 'Actuarial Justice: the Emerging New Criminal Law' in D. Nelken (ed.) *The Futures of Criminology*, pp.173–201. London: Sage.

Garland, D. (1985) *Punishment and Welfare.* Aldershot: Gower.

Garland, D. (1996) 'The Limits of the Sovereign State: Strategies of Crime Control in Contemporary Society'. *British Journal of Criminology* 36: 1–27.

Garland, D. (2000) 'The Culture of a High-Crime Society'. *British Journal of Criminology* (forthcoming).

Giddens, A. (1998) 'Risk Society: the Context of British Politics' in J. Franklin (ed.) *The Politics of Risk Society.* Cambridge: Polity.

Home Office (1999) *Information on the Criminal Justice System: Digest 4.* London: Home Office Research and Statistics Directorate.

Howitt, D. (1998) *Crime, Media and the Law.* Chichester: Wiley.

James, O. (1995) *Juvenile Violence in a Winner-Loser Culture.* London: Free Association Books.

Johnston, L. (2000) *Policing Britain.* London: Longman.

Lichter, R. S., Lichter, L. S., and Rothman, S. (1994) *Prime Time: How TV Portrays American Culture.* Washington DC: Regnery Publishing.

Liebes, T. and Katz, E. (1995) *The Export of Meaning: Cross-Cultural Readings of Dallas.* Cambridge, UK: Polity.

Livingstone, S. (1996) 'On the Continuing Problem of Media Effects' in *Mass Media and Society*, edited by J. Curran and M. Gurevitch, pp.305–24. London: Arnold.

Maguire, M. (1997) 'Crime Statistics, Patterns, and Trends: Changing Perceptions and their Implications' in *The Oxford Handbook of Criminology*, edited by M. Maguire, R. Morgan and R. Reiner: 134–88. Oxford: Oxford University Press.

Pearson, G. (1983) *Hooligan.* London: Macmillan.

Powers, S. P., Rothman, D. J., and Rothman, S. (1996) *Hollywood's America: Social and political Themes in Motion Pictures.* Boulder: Westview.

Rawls, J. (1973) *A Theory of Justice.* Oxford: Oxford University Press.

Reiner, R. (1996) 'The Case of the Missing Crimes' in *Interpreting Official Statistics*, edited by R. Levitas and W. Guy, pp.185–205. London: Routledge.

Reiner, R. (1997a) 'Policing and the Police' in M. Maguire, R. Morgan and R. Reiner (eds) *The Oxford Handbook of Criminology.* Oxford: Oxford University Press.

Reiner, R. (1997b) 'Media Made Criminality' in *The Oxford Handbook of Criminology*, edited by M. Maguire, R. Morgan and R. Reiner, pp.189–231. Oxford: Oxford University Press.

Reiner, R. (2000) 'Crime and Control in Britain', *Sociology*, 34(1): 71–94.

Rock, P. (1990) *Helping Victims of Crime.* Oxford: Oxford University Press.

Rose, N. (1996) 'The Death of the Social?', *Economy and Society,* 25: 321–56.

Roshier, B. (1973) 'The Selection of Crime News by the Press' in *The Manufacture of News*, edited by S. Cohen and J. Young, pp.40–51. London: Arnold.

Signorielli, N. (1990) 'Television's Mean and Dangerous World: a Continuation of the Cultural Indicators Project', in N. Signorielli and M. Morgan (eds) *New Directions in Media Effects Research*, pp.85–106. Newbury Park: Sage.

South, N. (1997) 'Control, Crime and 'End of Century' Criminology' in Francis, P., Davies, P. and Jupp, V. (eds.) *Policing Futures.* London: Macmillan.

Sparks, R. (1992) *Television and the Drama of Crime.* Buckingham: Open University Press.

Stenson, K. (1998) 'Beyond Histories of the Present', *Economy and Society,* 29: 333–52.

Sumser, J. (1996) *Morality and Social Order in Television Crime Drama.* Jefferson: McFarland.

Taylor, H. (1998) 'Rising Crime: the Political Economy of Criminal Statistics Since the 1850s', *Economic History Review,* LI: 569–90.

Taylor, H. (1999) 'Forging the Job: a Crisis of Modernization or Redundancy for the Police in England and Wales 1900–39', *British Journal of Criminology,* 39: 113–35.

Taylor, I. (1999) *Crime in Context: a Critical Criminology of Market Societies.* Cambridge: Polity.

Wakshlag, J., Vial, V., and Tamborini, R. (1983) 'Selecting Crime Drama and Apprehension About Crime', *Human Communications Research* 10: 227–42.

Williams, P. and Dickinson, J. (1993) 'Fear of Crime: Read All About It? The Relationship Between Newspaper Crime Reading and Fear of Crime', *British Journal of Criminology,* 33: 33–56.

Young, J. (1999) *The Exclusive Society.* London: Sage.

Zedner, L. (1997) "Victims' in *The Oxford Handbook of Criminology,* edited by M. Maguire, R. Morgan and R. Reiner, pp.577–612. Oxford: Oxford University Press.

10

'Bringin' it all back home':
populism, media coverage and the dynamics of locality and globality in the politics of crime control

Richard Sparks

Introduction

Most observers of contemporary penal politics would agree that the fascination of mass media with crime and punishment is in some way involved in sustaining the prominence of these issues in contemporary public life. They may also agree that the media play some part in inflaming the passions and anxieties that surround these questions. But do we know how best to integrate these (perhaps rather commonplace) observations into our understandings of the place of crime and punishment in the culture and politics of 'risk societies'? How, for instance, are these troubling questions received and used by people in the everyday settings of their lives? Some current views of these matters neglect such questions, while others may overstate or oversimplify them. Here I try to address some connections between punishment, populist politics and 'place' in a way that treats questions of communication as central.

Recent work in the social analysis of penality often seems to disclose a contradiction between ostensibly very different tendencies in the politics of punishment and social control in late modern societies. On one hand we find the development of apparently dispassionate, unemotive and increasingly technically ingenious means of reducing criminal opportunities, defending targets and reducing risk of loss. These gadgets, gizmos and innovations, which come to pervade everyday life and to attend every transaction, arouse some suspicion for their potentially intrusive or exclusionary character. But more influentially they are praised by their advocates for their gift of light and unobtrusive regulation and for focusing rigorously on the practicalities of prevention and loss reduction in ways that improve upon and even sometimes dispense altogether with the costly, inefficient and at times oppressive paraphernalia of traditional criminal justice interventions (Felson, 1998).

On the other hand stand all those measures that derive their appeal precisely from their passionate and emotive character. Here we encounter the calls to arms, the campaigns and 'wars', the demotic gestures, the slogans and the promises that also litter the contemporary penal landscape and which seem to promise to recover those more antique elements of meaning and force that we demand of the penal realm. The litany of such sightings (from the electric chair, by way of the boot camp to the crowd mobbing the police van) is too long and even perhaps by now too familiar to rehearse properly here (see Simon, 1995 and Chapter 7 in this volume; Pratt, 2000). Of course, between the strictly pragmatic and technicist and the purely symbolic and demagogic there is a great array of actual practices of varied and hybrid form, partaking in differing degrees of the instrumental and the impassioned (Garland, 1990: 187).

A number of commentators offer signposts through this labyrinth. Garland (1996) opposes the undemonstrative problem solving of the 'new criminologies of everyday life', such as situational crime prevention, to the state's 'hysterical counter-reaction' in reclaiming the power of sovereign command. Punishment here is the empty promise of the 'hollow state' – the actual business of crime prevention lies primarily elsewhere (see also Bauman, 1998). Bottoms (1995) draws a related distinction between 'managerialism' and 'populist punitiveness'.[1] Others are variously more demonstrative or more cautious. Pratt diagnoses a more radical historical hiatus. Now, on the post-modern side, he argues, many of the scruples and rationality claims characteristic of modernist penologies are being pushed aside in favour of more direct appeals to public sentiment and an increased willingness to tolerate humiliating, destructive and symbolically charged penalties (Pratt, 2000: 138–9). O'Malley, conversely, declines such totalization. The disparate developments that bemuse us find their sense not in a drastic transition into post-modernity but rather within a 'substantively political' logic. That logic is provided by the ideological hegemony of the New Right. In this perspective the endless inventiveness of the free market and the austere moralism of neo-Conservatism come as a package, but a 'volatile and contradictory' rather than a coherent or tidy one (O'Malley, 1999 and Chapter 5 this volume). I incline towards O'Malley's view of the matter, but want to extend the discussion in the following way.

O'Malley wants to reinstate some sense of political agency in what otherwise seems to be a somewhat unengaged and diffuse series of commentaries, in which the recent politics of crime and punishment appear as inevitably and irremediably incoherent. Here the janus-faced character of contemporary penal politics arises because the relative stability of former settlements is prised apart by the contradictory but 'relatively autonomous' forces of the logic of risk management and the rhetoric of punitiveness. This is what we will call, adapting O'Malley, the bi-polar account. O'Malley's correction to this view is that both of these apparently contrary trends find a home under the capacious umbrella of contemporary conservative politics. The volatility of contemporary crime control politics can thus be understood, O'Malley argues, without reference to such large but somewhat inchoate themes as the emergence of post-modernity (O'Malley, 1997: 376–7; 1999: 192). Amongst other things this enables O'Malley to argue astutely that developments that sit on the risk management side of this dialectic are in no sense politically neutral. Rather these are also in certain respects politicized – they are 'moral inventions' (see also Rose, 2000).

My particular focus in this chapter is on the role of communications media in promoting and entrenching some of the stances, slogans and vocabularies characteristic of, and arguably dominant in, penal politics – especially where penal questions have arisen as contentious issues in national, electoral political competition. Especially this, but not exclusively. For to raise the question of how penal politics (broadly the disposition of arguments about how, whom and how much to punish) arise as contentious issues within a certain political culture and at a certain time is both to attempt to sharpen one's sense of how their 'mediatization' works *and* to displace the media from a position of solitary pre-eminence at the dead centre of any explanatory account. Put crudely, there is no useful way of appraising the mobilization of penal questions in political arenas (and hence no way of accounting for much of what has actually resulted at the level of practice) without reference to the characteristic formats and preoccupations of the media. But conversely there is no way of grasping how those media become effective, in terms either of the strategic interventions of political actors or the situated reception of their messages by audiences in the ordinary circumstances and predicaments of their everyday lives without regard to extant cultural traditions, economic contingencies and institutional arrangements that exceed the scope of the media as such.

Suppose then that we address some of the questions that O'Malley and others have posed from this slightly different point of departure. Suppose for the moment that instead of focusing principally on the institutional histories of criminal justice and penal systems, or indeed on the promulgation of certain substantive ideological positions, we take as central the networks, forms and formats through which know-ledge, understanding, commitment and belief on such matters are circulated and exchanged. This is hardly a revolutionary suggestion – after all the study of 'crime and the media' has been a prominent sub-field of criminology and the sociology of social control for thirty years or so. However, I want to suggest that the project of grasping certain of the questions that have lately become central to the theoretical sociology of punishment – sovereignty, governance, risk, legitimation and the rest – specifically in their communicative aspects has become ripe for renewal. These are all key terms of art in the social analysis of penality, as they are in other related fields of social enquiry. They are among the terms that we are bound to use when we want to try to relate penal politics to politics 'proper' – that is, to grasp its englobement within the larger movements of the regulatory and administrative cultures and struggles for influence and ascendancy that characterize our times. In view of the often incendiary nature of penal issues, and the vehemence and indignation that attach to particular stories and controversies (see further Ericson *et al*, 1991; Anderson, 1995; Beckett, 1997), the questions of how those topics enter public discourse and popular culture and, moreover, how they are received and appropriated by viewing, listening, reading and interacting publics are by no means trivial. Moreover, I want to suggest that some such effort of situated understanding is one of the means whereby the hiatus that O'Malley identifies between the larger diagnoses of speculative social theory and the 'middle range' arenas of comparatively sensitive and empirically grounded research may be overcome.

In our attempts to get to grips with the special features of recent penal politics risk has become a key term. Yet, as I have suggested in my opening remarks, the penal politics of 'risk societies' can include many diverse and often contradictory themes and developments (see also O'Malley, 2000: 30). In my view, the unsatisfactory features of the 'bi-polar account' spring from a tendency to give undue priority to one or other of two main understandings of risk, namely an instrumental/managerial one and an alarmist/rhetorical one. For this reason there is often an explanatory hiatus between accounts of risk-as-instrumental-judgement and risk-as-distorted-perception, or as I prefer to express it, between calculation and representation. Insofar as I propose any ways through this thicket it is to favour those accounts of risk that encourage us to hold their calculative and representational 'faces' simultaneously in view, a balancing act in which I find some of Mary Douglas's remarks in *Risk and Blame* particularly helpful. I suggest in this regard:

- that our grasp of how the media cover crime and punishment is enhanced by situating it in relation to the wider domain of communication about risk (including its overlaps and formal similarities with communications about other topics such as, for example, industrial accidents, nuclear hazards, genetic modification and so on); and
- that the reception by people of media stories about crime and punishment is best grasped ethnographically and *in situ*, in which case many public responses that are commonly deprecated by criminologists and others as 'irrational' or 'hysterical' tend to become substantially more intelligible (though not for that reason less intractable or politically problematic).

It therefore seems to me that thinking again about the connections between media, fear and reception may help us to clarify our stances on the social character of risk and, in turn, contribute to our analytic grasp of some of our current predicaments with regard to the politics of punishment and blaming.

Populism as style and technique

In particular I want to begin by focusing here, as Bottoms (1995) and others have advised, on the problem of 'populism'. The notion of populism appears to present itself as peculiarly apt to the discussion of many instances of political intervention and platform rhetoric on crime and punishment. But just what is entailed in using this term? And how precise and consistent are our uses of it? For example, to draw only two examples from recent British penal politics, does it mean the same thing when applied to Michael Howard's 'Prison Works' campaign and to New Labour's interventions on 'crime and disorder'?

I suggest that we frequently use the notion of populism in an inadequately specified and theoretically thin fashion. We apply it in a general way to many things that we dislike – demagogic gestures, alarmism, 'punitiveness'. Used in this way the notion of populism contains a series of unflattering attributions – the cynicism, opportunism and short-termism of politicians who 'play to the gallery'; the irrationalism, prejudices and deep-dyed conservatism of the public. And of course the battlefields of penal politics are littered with examples that seem to lend themselves to this kind of commentary. So wherein lies the problem? Briefly (although the point bears expansion), populism is a term with a lengthy and chequered history; one that denotes a range of parties, postures and social movements – some of them self-identifying as radical-democratic in orientation. Its sense, or at least whatever its current substantive content seems to be, shifts with context. More specifically, for the purposes of the present discussion, it is a term in quite frequent use in current criminological discussion – mainly to denote the emotive, punitive, morally conservative, impassioned side of the bi-polar account outlined above. I suggest that we instead reserve the term populism to refer to a certain set of *styles or techniques* that are now somewhat pervasive in many branches of journalism, marketing and political communication. Seen in this way it is impossible to argue that there are two (or indeed more than two) distinct tendencies in recent penal developments, only one of which is 'populist'. Rather, the relationship between the technical (managerial, risk-oriented) and the popular would seem to be rather more complicated than this. Indeed, some students of political communication argue that it is precisely the increasing technical complexity of many governmental and administrative processes that generates the need to redescribe them in populist language, or conversely which drives the battle for popular legitimacy onto themes and topics that can be so described.

My first proposition therefore is that we think of the relation between the technical and the popular in political communication about crime and punishment (as in other kinds of risk communication) as (to paraphrase Giddens) a mutually involved duality rather than as a dualism. I go on to argue, secondly, that once we begin to take seriously the communicative aspects of penal politics the relations between the global and the local 'sides' of this duality also become more tricky, since what is often involved in populist forms of penal politics is the attempt by political actors to localize and concretize what otherwise look like inaccessibly global or abstract issues. I therefore also argue, thirdly, that we should pay more sociologically imaginative and perhaps by the same token more generous attention to the local appropriations of and mobilizations around penal controversies and other risky topics, since these often look far more situationally intelligible when seen in this light. Finally, if only sketchily and inconclusively, I revisit the question of whether populism in this context must inevitably be reactionary. Can there be a populist penal politics of the left?

Populism and the opacity of contemporary politics

Canovan (2000) argues that populism is one of the inevitable modes of contemporary politics. In her view the very complexity and hence 'opacity' of the 'backstage' practices of governance is itself one of the conditions that favours politicians' recurrent tendency to resort to populist gestures. In place of a candid admission of the often tedious, arcane and unsatisfactory realities of contemporary political and administrative life we find a preference for 'sound-bites', 'spin' and slogans. Thus:

> Ideology, which reduces the complexity of politics to dogmatic simplicity, is ill-fitted to deal adequately with [these] intricacies,[2] and yet ideology is indispensable in mass politics...[But] the ideology of democracy is full of populist themes that belie the current trend of democratic politics, stressing sovereignty and will against compromise and accommodation, popular unity against multiplicity, majority against minorities, directness and transparency against complex and intricate procedures. The paradox in other words, is that while democracy (more than any other political system) *needs* to be comprehensible to the masses, the ideology that seeks to bridge the gap between people and politics misrepresents (and cannot avoid misrepresenting) the way that democratic politics necessarily works. This contradiction between ideology and practice is a standing invitation to raise the cry of democracy betrayed, and to mobilize the discontented behind the banner of restoring politics to the people.

This observation seems highly redolent of some observed features of the penal realm in recent times – colonized by 'managerialist' systems and 'actuarial' procedures of opaque sophistication yet quite unable to break free for long from the pull of emotivism and sloganizing. At the same time it suggests an assessment that is less simple, less terminal and less hyperbolically expressed than that of empty demagoguery in reaction to ebbing sovereignty or any other species of 'endism' (Gamble, 1997). Instead we may hope to develop an understanding that holds the backstage-administrative and the frontstage-rhetorical aspects of the scene simultaneously in view but which is also capable of noticing the distinct terms on which their various component features cohabit at different times.

Perhaps this seems obvious. Certainly the most effective accounts of the implication of media in criminal justice (for example, Hall *et al*, 1978; Ericson *et al*, 1991) have never been exclusively media-centric in their assumptions. Rather their concern has always been with the filtration of images, agendas and preoccupations relayed through media into the larger domains of cultural and political exchange, with all the complications (and often confusion and obscurity) that then ensue with regard to allegations or attributions of specific kinds of 'influence' or 'effect'. To begin with warnings and admonitions ought then to be unnecessary. Two kinds of reduction, it seems clear, are tempting but better avoided. On the one hand there is the style of analysis which treats the detailing of media 'contents' or 'mythologies' (depending on methodological preference) as a largely self-sufficient activity, and which tends to enter grand and mostly unsustainable generalizations about their hold on public opinion or their ideological predominance. 'Social construction' is the totemic catch-phrase here. On the other side stand all those positions, whether presented as critical or mainstream/pragmatic, which treat crime and punishment as largely instrumental domains of action and for whose proponents media analysis is a decorative adjunct or afterthought (an *et cetera* clause introduced at will to explain [away] remaining oddities or irrationalities that cloud the account).

Yet, how exactly to work in another (one hesitates to say 'third') way between and against each of these temptations has never been quite so clear. A *locus classicus* of this problem, I suggest, is provided by debates on 'the fear of crime', and in a moment I enter a few reminders about this important (but generally stymied and inconclusive) question. I do so, however, not out of any attachment to going over old ground but rather because public fears, apprehensions, anxieties and passions towards crime and punishment are a special case of a more general issue, namely the nature of communication and deliberation about risky topics. Moreover, I suspect that some of the same dichotomies, hindrances and confusions that have dogged the 'fear' debate are in danger of being reproduced in current social analysis of risk.

Media, fear and risk communication

The question of 'fear of crime', and of the media's role in instigating or channelling fear, has been a perennial debating point in criminological and policy debate since at least the late 1960s. Many of the positions staked out in these discussions are well known and need not be rehearsed here. On one hand stand the allegations associated with (some uses of) the notion of 'moral panic' and (some versions of) social constructionism: i.e. that there are disparities or disproportions between real risks and expressed fears; that these stand in need of explanation; and that mass media hype and/or political exploitation are responsible. On the other (a certain polemical form of) 'realism' insists that (at least for some people, in some places) there is no such gap: fear has its 'rational kernel' and to suggest otherwise is offensive, a complacent talking-down of the scope of real experiences and predicaments. I have explained elsewhere (Sparks, 1991, 1992) why I think this stand-off will not do, and the debate has in any case to some extent moved elsewhere. What emerges instead from the more convincing accounts of media preoccupations with crime is that the object of enquiry ought not simply to be 'fear' *tout court* but rather a broader grasp of the relaying, sponsorship and discussion of certain (perhaps at first sight more inchoate) conceptions of crime and punishment and their associated vocabularies of diagnosis, commentary, attribution, blame and censure.

Some such move is evidently necessary if the object of inquiry is not (or no longer simply) the social distribution of 'fear' but rather the implication of media in *politics* – i.e. in favouring, or underwriting, or on occasion consciously promoting, certain strategies of intervention into an inventory of problems predominantly understood in a certain way. This is what I take to be amongst the lasting implications of Hall *et al*'s (1978) account in *Policing the Crisis*, namely that the coming-to-prominence of a particular way of understanding and explaining the 'mugging' phenomenon could not be understood in isolation from the naturalization of its proposed solutions, and moreover that such solutions were never merely about reducing muggings but also about the restoration of state capacity and authority. More currently, the account that Ericson *et al* provide in

Representing Order of the usual business of mass media in focusing discussion on 'what is out of place: the deviant, equivocal and unpredictable' (1991: 4) indicates convincingly that the activity of representing ('visualizing', 'symbolizing', 'authorizing', 'staging' and 'convincing') is intrinsically concerned with the question of 'order' – where order is conceived in terms of 'morality, procedural form and social hierarchy' (1991: 1) – and in turn that the activity of representing order in the news takes the domain of law as paradigmatic of authority and legitimacy (1991: 7–10). For Ericson *et al* this makes the media not merely the receptacles, bearers or channels of reports but rather 'an active *agency* of social control, stability and change', and part and parcel of the unceasing processes of social exchange that constitute the 'symbolic politics of order' in our kind of society.

So far, so (relatively speaking) familiar. The points I want to go on to develop now, though, are the ones that seek to establish more securely the connections between media and the risk politics of penality in the advanced liberal economies. The contributions of Hall and of Ericson *et al* urge a move from 'content' to rhetoric in grasping the nature of media involvement in penal politics and, I would add, from 'fear' to risk in comprehending their filtration into political and cultural exchange. But in order to tickle out the implications of this we need, first, to situate the analysis of crime-in-the-media within a broader understanding of risk communication and, second, to develop a more sophisticated language for dealing with the public reception of and engagement with risky topics.

Given the prominence of discussions of risk in recent criminology and sociology of punishment debates the concept itself, and the points of comparison between risks of crime and other societal risk debates, have until recently received relatively little explicit discussion. Yet such comparisons are illuminating, both because of the similarity of some of the problems that arise in different sectors and because of the differences in the ways that they have been rethought. For example, it has often been the case (and certainly in the early stages of debates on specific topics) that sharp differences arise between 'hard science' and 'culturalist' (or social constructionist) positions in ways that replicate quite closely the dichotomies apparent at times in 'fear of crime' discussions. And parallel allegations of public irrationality (and/or ill-informedness) occur in fields as diverse as nuclear safety and industrial accidents, genetic engineering, road safety and so on. In each instance lively sub-fields of risk-perception studies have arisen, the more sophisticated of which can usefully inform understanding of public fears and feeling about crime (for example the oft-made distinction between 'dread', 'catastrophic' and 'chronic' risks), at least to some extent.

More importantly for the present discussion, however, is the increasingly widespread discovery of the persistence and embeddedness of risk controversies. Even in fields less manifestly socially constructed than news of crime such disputes are by no means usually resolved simply by the provision of more (and ostensibly more reliable) information. Often the reverse is the case. Disputes about risk are quite rarely closed by the mere flourishing of conclusive evidence, though they are sometimes forgotten, normalized or neutralized through strategic compromise. Not uncommonly they settle into persistent oppositions between parties with incommensurable outlooks and commitments. Recent discussions about the promises and risks of genetic modification of food would seem to provide a major case in point. Perhaps we are discovering that in a runaway and pervasively uncertain and unsettling world, in which the 'centres' of political power, authority and legitimacy have themselves become uncertain and obscure – in other words the condition that Bauman characterizes as 'ambient insecurity' – we may be apt to redefine our relations to politics increasingly in terms of our risk positions. We may also tend to redefine our identifications with our fellow citizens in terms of what we still take ourselves to share, prominent among which are our 'commonalities of anxiety' in respect of crime. If nothing else we have in common (with at least some other people) that we are (actually or imaginatively) at risk of this; feel we know how that might feel; and stand together in our antipathy to those who do that sort of thing.

The wide world, crime and the media (and the sense of place?)

To recap: I suggest that in order to grapple adequately with the risk politics of crime and punishment we also need to address the question of risk communication. This also requires that we address the *reception* side of that problem. How do these topics filter into the consciousness of people in the ordinary settings of their lives? How are they appropriated by those people? How are generic vocabularies and imageries rendered relevant, meaningful, concrete, applicable? Perhaps in this way we gain some researchable sense of how some of the grander questions of current social theory relate to anyone's lived experience – how, in other words, they are brought 'home'.[3]

In a characteristically engaged and trenchant paper Ian Taylor argues (*inter alia*) that most currently influential accounts of economic and cultural change operate at 'far too generalized and indeed too global a level' (Taylor, 1997: 59 and see Stenson and Edwards this volume) to be informatively applied to the detail of local cases and experiences. (To borrow Stones's [1996] useful terminology, they are the product of theorists working at the level of the 'floater' rather than the 'player'.) Taylor reserves particular censure for the 'highly fashionable embrace' (1997: 61) of social theories of risk as a poor substitute for participation by social scientists in the public sphere properly so called. I want to develop further the interrogation of these generalizing claims of social theory, and to assess its uses in understanding current social responses to crime and punishment. My assessment is in some respects closely akin to Taylor's rather negative one. On the other hand, I think that a fuller and more formal exposition of some of the leading positions discloses that they can nevertheless be turned to use, provided that they can sustain a dialogue with some still challenging discoveries of local difference and specificity.

Current social theory wrestles with the transformative consequences of modernity and produces ambivalent views on the fate of 'place' (Lash and Urry, 1994). The terms of art invented or borrowed in attempts to characterize the distinctive contours of the present include such notions as 'globalization', 'detraditionalization' (Heelas *et al*, 1996), 'risk society' (Beck, 1992) and the 'disembedding' of social relations which seems such a pervasive consequence of modernity (Giddens, 1991). Some readings of such notions would appear, at least initially, to license a certain cosmopolitan indifference to questions of place – but this is sharply disputed (see in particular the debates collected in Featherstone and Lash, 1995). On one side stand those perspectives which, in responding to what are in equal measure some of the most exciting and dismaying aspects of 'global modernities', see place as having been more or less evacuated (as 'phantasmagoric' in Giddens's [1991] view). In some versions of this argument the global flows of capital and culture usher in a largely borderless world, and 'hollow out' not merely the nation-state but also the place-specificity of forms of everyday life. On the other are those who view 'globality' rather as a condition of '*divergent* modernization' (Robertson, 1995), a process which produces not sameness but rather many new 'particularizations' (and in so doing discloses the recalcitrant survival of many kinds of difference in local culture and identity, albeit in altered and hybridized form) (Featherstone and Lash, 1995). All parties see 'place' as having been decisively reconfigured in late modernity – infiltrated and transformed by economic and cultural forces that escape and exceed the traditional constraints of geographical boundaries. The question here is whether this means that place is simply of terminally declining importance. I think that for certain purposes, of which interpreting public anxieties about crime and disorder is one, this is not the case – at least not in any simple sense.[4]

I propose that some of the more perplexing and seemingly anomalous discoveries of the 'fear of crime' literature (especially those which have given rise to the extended and in the main unhelpful debate on the rationality or otherwise of public responses to the perceived risks of crime) become substantially more intelligible in the light of a thicker contextual understanding of place. Similarly, I suggest, the translation of mass media discourse on crime and order into the form of locally-relevant stories and accounts (a process of interpretation which I see as characteristic of their reception) provides a particularly eloquent, and often highly emotively charged, instance of the 'appropriation' of generic media forms by receivers (Thompson, 1996). Local controversies about 'nuisance youth', or the legitimacy of using force to defend one's property, or about the release of imprisoned sex offenders, or about the responsiveness of police to reports of racist violence and an array of other issues share these features.

Giddens (1991) argues that each of us is willy-nilly caught up in globalizing trends that we can neither control nor escape. The resulting awareness of powerlessness is dismaying, and can lead to a disabling sense of 'engulfment' for the individual. Yet the same developments make possible forms of autonomous self-development undreamed of by earlier generations. The world that is coming into being has many ambiguities, not least of which is the paradox between, on the one hand, the 'huge reduction in life-threatening risks' for most inhabitants of developed societies achieved by the development of 'abstract systems' (insurance, health screening, financial services and the rest) and on the other a high level of risk-awareness such that it 'becomes less and less possible to protect any lifestyle, however pre-established, from the generalized risk climate' (1991; 126).

In Giddens's view the immersion of self in place is no longer feasible – the traditional bond between intimacy and proximity has been broken. We are closer to our distant friends and relations with whom we communicate by phone and email than to our neighbours. We of course continue to seek security (provided in part by the studied uneventfulness of much of everyday life) and we invest trust in the reliability of our routines and expectancies. But our 'protective cocoon' involves the reflexive construction of a reasonably coherent 'narrative of self-identity' and 'commitment to a certain form of lifestyle' (together with its material comforts and supports) rather than investment in place-specific custom or authority. Amongst the aspects of experience which are reconfigured under such conditions is the one at issue here, namely the relation between the individual lifespan and place (or, to put it another way, 'home' (see also Robertson, 1995)). Giddens asserts that:

> Place becomes phantasmagoric. While the milieux in which people live quite often remain the source of local attachments, place does not form the parameter of experience; and it does not offer the security of the ever-familiar which traditional locales characteristically display....
>
> Place thus becomes much less significant than it used to be as an external referent for the lifespan of the individual....Where a person lives, after young adulthood at least, is a matter of choice organised primarily in terms of the person's life-planning.... Of course, as with all such processes dialectical forms of counter-reaction are possible... [But] only when it is possible to gear regular practices to specifics of place can re-embedding occur in a significant way: but in conditions of high modernity this is difficult to achieve. (Giddens, 1991: 147).

And Giddens also argues (in equally grudging tone):

> Everyone continues to live a local life...yet the transformations of place, and the intrusion of distance into local activities, combined with the centrality of mediated experience, radically change what 'the world' actually is....Localities are thoroughly penetrated by distanciated influences, whether this is regarded as a cause for concern or simply accepted as a routine part of social life. (*ibid*: 188).

For Giddens it follows that 'No one can easily defend a secure "local life" set off from larger social systems and organizations' (*ibid*: 184). However, the fact that no one in late modern societies can 'easily' defend a 'secure local life' does not mean that they do not attempt so to defend it. Indeed, I would argue that anxiety about the *inability* to secure the borders of one's place against threatening incursions (or even greatly to influence its economic and other prospects) is precisely what much talk about place, including some forms of 'fear of crime' discourse discloses (cf. Taylor, 1995). Such 'crime talk' (Sasson, 1995) is in fact peppered with local allusions and often pervaded by a nostalgic yearning for lost community recounted in the form of narratives of change and decline.[5] In this respect, at the level of lived experience, the tribulations of place are of the essence of the anxieties of Giddens's late-modern citizens including their apprehensions about crime and threats to social order and, not least, the effectivity of the ways in which the latter are caught up in media imagery and not infrequently exploited in populist law and order political campaigns. I return to this argument below.

Writing from a similar perspective, J.B. Thompson (1996) focuses more directly upon the transformative role of the media in contemporary social life. In Thompson's view the media radically re-order (but do not abolish) our relations to place and tradition. They alter the 'interaction mix' of social life (1996: 87), making available diverse forms of information and 'symbolic goods' that are not dependent on face-to-face proximity, thereby creating new possibilities for 'self-formation' (*ibid*: 233) and changing forever the nature of 'publicness' (*ibid*: 127) and prospects for democratic deliberation (*ibid*: 245). Thompson is more sensitive than many commentators to the situated and interpretive nature of media reception and the 'appropriation' of mediated messages in practical contexts of daily life (*ibid*: 11). Whilst the media disrupt the traditionally assumed relation between membership of a 'public' and spatial location (*ibid*: 233, 245) and make possible the discovery of 'despatialized commonalities' (*ibid*: 231–2), the relationship between mediated and lived experience remains complex. The role of tradition in social life is, for example, reconfigured by the media and 'dislodged' in some degree both from its encompassing centrality and its connection to place but not thereby dissolved entirely. Traditions can be reinvented and many traditions (such as ceremonials of national identity like Presidential inaugurations and football finals) are carried by the media rather than destroyed (*ibid*: 197) and these remain 'territorial' if no longer 'local'. What results is *inter alia* a new set of relations between what is distant and what is close (*ibid*: 35), determined as much by the 'relevance structure' (*ibid*: 229) of the receiver as by spatial proximity.

I have argued above that it might be possible to extend and revise Giddens's views on security and anxiety in late modern societies to illuminate some aspects of 'fear of crime talk' and thereby also to rethink some of the ironies of place under such conditions. It is worth noting that the most cited thing about Meyrowitz's exceptionally interesting book *No Sense of Place* (1985) is its evocative title (as distinct from its argument) – and that the assumption of placelessness that it apparently encodes risks becoming part of the *vulgata* of much current media analysis. In fact Meyrowitz states that his title is actually a complex pun on both key terms: sense meaning both 'logic' and 'perception' and 'place' encapsulating both social position and physical location (1985: 308).

In our local study of crime discourse in an English town Evi Girling, Ian Loader and myself have explored a similar idea, namely that much everyday crime talk involves accounts both of the place in which one immediately resides (its remembered pasts, its present problems and its possible futures, and that the intensity of such preoccupations varies in relation to one's personal and financial investments in that place), and more broadly of one's place in the social hierarchies of modern Britain (Girling *et al*, 2000). We have argued in that study that Giddens's own account of the tribulations of place and of the 'compromise package' of security in late modernity can in fact be extended to illuminate the fretful concern with the risks of crime that characterizes many contemporary societies, one aspect of which may be (for some) a defensive and territorial orientation towards one's 'own place'. If, as Giddens argues, the 'frontiers of sequestered experience' (criminality included) are 'battlegrounds' then the intrusion of unmastered or unassimilable behaviour is likely to be seen as especially threatening. This suggests a certain intensity in the demand for order and, moreover, a high expectation upon the responsible 'expert systems' to deliver it. As Giddens further comments, behaviour which is not 'integrated into a system' is thus especially likely to be seen as 'alien and discrete' (*ibid*: 150). It is thus unsurprising if fears of crime figure quite highly amongst the worries of Giddens's late modern citizens, especially as regards behaviour in public places: and it may be possible to theorize criminologists' traditional concern with 'incivilities' in these terms. Indeed, if as Giddens states, places are reflexively 'chosen' by us late moderns to accord with our 'lifestyle' preferences and our painstakingly constructed sense of ourselves, this might well serve to make us only the more anxiously defensive of them, and engender a febrile sensitivity to (and intolerance of) *any* incursion on their cultivated sense of peace and order.[6]

One insightful, and potentially more place-sensitive, treatment of relevant issues may be found in Mary Douglas's cultural theory of risk. Crime can serve as one of those forms of 'danger on the borders' (Douglas, 1992) which gives form to a community's sense of itself and its distinctiveness from others. But it may also provoke anxieties that turn inwards, towards a sense of division from others who are socially and geographically close. In Douglas's view the identification of particular sources of threat and blame refracts a given community's dispositions towards order and authority:

> There is no way of proceeding with analysing risk perception without typifying kinds of communities according to the support their members give to authority, commitment, boundaries and structure. (Douglas, 1992: 47).

It follows that studying the connections between risk, fear and blame can never be simply a matter of quantitatively cataloguing dangers and assorting responses to risk into boxes marked 'rational' and 'irrational' (Sparks, 1991). This view may help us to understand why the social discourse of crime and punishment still 'falls into antique mode' (Douglas, 1992: 26) and refuses to shed 'its ancient moral freight' (*ibid*: 35). But it may also, at the level of the life-world of the individual citizen, help us to comprehend why such concerns continue to be understood in relation to place, long after some social theorists have declared the obsolescence of that category.

Of course one problem that 'members' may face especially acutely under late modern conditions is knowing where the 'boundaries' are to be drawn and whom they are to exclude. That problem is most complex, as Douglas recognizes, when it concerns those who are (at least spatially) proximate and raises the possibility of a fissioning of 'community'. In these respects (perhaps indeed in every respect) risk is irredeemably moral and unavoidably emotive and controversial. One reason for continuing to study media portrayals of crime and punishment, therefore, is that public appropriations of and mobilizations around risk controversies exemplify some of the most difficult issues in current social theory, namely those of the relations between locally lived experience and of global change. Media stories do not only 'disembed' events from place. Rather they ripple outwards and back and *re-present* stories, threats, challenges and controversies to us.

If, as Ericson *et al* (1991) aptly argue, news discourse generally visualizes, personalizes, dramatizes, stages and convinces, it also by extension localizes and concretizes things which are otherwise more abstractly known. Moreover, given that the 'politicization of place' in the face of a range of threats and concerns is one of the more ironic consequences of global modernity (Lash and Urry, 1994: 217) perhaps it acquires a different focus and intensity now. Some 'crime talk' is curiously generic and placeless, simply reiterating common experiences or dominant discourses in readily recognizable and packaged form. But conversely 'crime talk' and 'place talk' frequently infuse one another, as the changing experience of crime becomes a preferred and emotionally charged way of narrating the story of the failures and successes, splendours and miseries of our journeys through modernity. It is in these respects that the media bring it all back home.

Of course in the background of this concern to understand how prevailing public discourses on crime and punishment intersect with the preoccupations of situated actors (Thompson, 1996) there also lies the question of their political deployment – of the mobilization of diffuse anxieties for specific populist uses; of the strange forces of attraction and repulsion between communitarian yearnings and exclusionary practices and so on. The dilemmas and confusions which result feel permanent and intractable but they are very contemporary in their specific forms. They raise, as Taylor (1997) acutely notes, a series of problems involving the protection of particular local forms of life and obstacles to democratic participation. Under conditions where even the 'zones of peace' feel chronically uneasy we face some nagging troubles about where (if indeed anywhere) to locate resources of legitimate political authority (Keane, 1996). In the face of such challenges to the trustworthiness of the 'basic terms of social existence' (Unger, 1987: 62) the tug of nostalgic and demagogic promises of security is easy enough to understand.

New penologies, the media and the diverse faces of risk

Most of those positions which emphasize the advance of certain prospectuses for calculative risk management in the penal realm also acknowledge that this is not all that is going on. Feeley and Simon famously observe the creeping emergence of an actuarial 'new penology' (in their 1992 paper) but also note (in Simon and Feeley, 1995) its apparent lack of headway in *public* representations of crime and punishment – its 'cultural sterility', its lack of connection to 'the more fundamental tasks of government' and its 'blindness to the cultural effects of penality itself'. The motor of public debate lies elsewhere: 'national discourse on crime is populist and centred on fear'.

Ericson and Haggerty also accept the moral character of risk, and the intrinsic relation between the generation of new technologies of risk management and avoidance and the emotional texture of everyday life in advanced liberalism: the awareness of danger, the presence of foreboding, the collective sense of unsafety 'perpetuate insecurity, and feed incessant demands for more knowledge of risk' (1997: 6). The resulting privatism and 'withdrawal from public involvement' ironically create the demand for abstract systems for surveillance and the market in 'securities'. They argue subtly that there can therefore be no 'simplistic dualism between sovereign/disciplinary power and risk management, as if the complexities involved could be reduced to a simple binary opposition' (1997: 12). At the same time, they suggest, there is a marked hiatus between the 'utilitarian morality' that characterizes the actual infrastructure of risk management and the 'very different logic of mass media in public culture' whose 'dramatizations' and 'morality plays' are 'increasingly at odds with those of other institutions that govern people's lives' (1997: 41).

Each of these formulations addresses, I think, genuine cultural contradictions and perplexities of our times. Each also creates some space for the troubled position of the state and for the role of media at least in relaying some aspect, the emotive and affective dimension, of the risk politics of penality. Yet I remain somewhat uncomfortable with the kinds of distinctions being drawn here between on the one hand an underlying and embedded set of institutional logics, and on the other a public arena which is in some sense anachronistic, out-of-kilter with and perhaps subsidiary to it. My suggestion is merely that there remain other questions that can also still be validly posed and which are by no means trivial. These include:

- First, what then are the primary motors of penal politics in their public aspect? – how do we explain the jagged and uneven dynamics of prison populations and other sentencing issues? Why are they so different in diverse national settings now? Why are debates on prison conditions and prisoners' entitlements (for example) so differently constituted in the United States and in Holland or Scandinavia? Moreover what precisely is at stake in the new formations of penality (the 'Boot Camp', 'Three Strikes' and so on) that are also peculiarly phenomena of our time?
- And second, what is it like to live under these conditions? What does it mean to have children, person, property to protect? Or to lack the kinds of resources of security and social position that others enjoy? And hence to be the target of their suspicion and censure? How then is penal culture involved in political culture, such that we are invited to express our sense of membership and commitment in some part through endorsing and emotionally involving ourselves in a certain way of punishing?

These are in some sense old questions. But they have specific contemporary answers. Moreover, they too are questions about risk – or at least about the intersection between a certain set of dispositions towards risk and some rather basic dilemmas of order, authority, legitimacy and justice as these matters are capable of being thought about now.

The point, I suspect, is to avoid counter-posing the calculative face of risk management (the new) to the public, mass mediated representations of risky and fearful topics (old, populist business-as-usual) in binary fashion. Instead we need to readdress the question of the media's role is sustaining our apprehensions (in both senses) of crime in a properly contemporary way – i.e. one attuned both to the kind of 'media-scape' that now exists and to the kinds of consumers, listeners and viewers that we now are; and hence one which can provide some degree of insight into the particular varieties of attention, commitment and emotional engagement in terms of which we can read and respond to them. Amongst the issues that might arise here would be the particular kinds of emotionality that now characterize some of our engagements with crime and punishment (the 'new expressiveness' as David Anderson [1995] nicely says in his book on the Horton case) and, relatedly, the brittleness of some of our social relations and the fragility of the resources of ontological security that we invest in them.

One of the most prescient observations made by Stuart Hall *et al* in *Policing the Crisis* was that in a complex, plural, mobile and mutually anonymous society the 'networks that connect' are crucial. In the case in point it was the mobilization of the respectable, law-abiding nation against the alien intrusion of mugging that such 'connections' made possible. Perhaps then the point might need to be made again now in a somewhat accentuated way. Given the proliferation since the late 1970s of media and channels (and their market segmentation and niche targeting), and the corresponding attenuation in the capacity of the media to function in some sense as a 'public sphere' *only* certain topics will be potent enough, graspable enough, emotive enough, 'visualizable' enough to make connections across publics, markets and sectors.

Some at least (perhaps a disproportionate number) of such connections are likely to be made through the vehicle of crime and punishment. Thus the temptation upon politicians to reach for the common, connecting theme (to make 'the war on drugs' into 'the nation's number one priority', for example-cf. Beckett, 1997) is intense, and is structurally provided for. Meanwhile, whilst it is in no sense any longer the case that we are all watching, reading or listening to the same media at the same time, nevertheless certain names and their emotional associations (William Horton, Kimba Reynolds, O.J. Simpson, Louise Woodward, Jamie Bulger and so on) are known to all, at least for a time. Even in heatedly dividing us they give us something to talk about; they prompt discourse; they engender that form of social communion that only mass media can provide, what Thompson in *The Media and Modernity* calls 'despatialized commonality'.

Viewed in this way the notion of risk simply cannot designate only an objective set of calculations, our commonplace deviations from or misunderstandings of which are merely symptomatic of our irrationality or want of knowledge or our inability to handle statistical concepts. That error is one of the least attractive legacies of modernist criminology. It generates another equally unappealing presumption, namely that because emotive stories catch us on our tender spots the emotions that they invoke in us are only and necessarily regressive. I suggest to the contrary that our interest in and attention to the alarming, outrageous, unnerving and disgraceful happenings in crime news and crime stories are more than the tokens of our gullibility or indicators of our reactionary and punitive dispositions. Instead those interests that we display, and which we enact in various ways (through our consumption of security hardware and services, for example, as much as through our expressions of political preferences) intelligibly summarize our sense of our relations to the objects of our experience. We can engage, emote and evince sympathy with others only in such ways and on such occasions as are culturally produced for and made available to us. In this sense our engagement with crime and punishment is inherently ambiguous. It catches us as much in and through our attempts to express our better (more moral, more sympathetic, more civically responsible) selves as through the hatreds, enmities, prejudices and distortions so much beloved of media scholars, radical criminologists and moral panic theorists. That part of us that feels something in response to the latest media story of this or that enormity may not merely be the mean-minded gossip, or the fearful defender of property and person. It may also be the sentimental altruist in us; the part of us that still aspires to act politically.

Notes

1   In fact Bottoms makes a four-fold distinction which in full comprises 'just deserts/human rights' concerns and an appeal to 'the community' as well as 'system management' and 'populist punitiveness'.

2   Namely, the intricacies that flow from a 'crowded and dynamic political arena' in which many interests and opinions exert 'some small influence on policies' (Canovan, 2000).

3   This part of the argument owes much to work that I have conducted jointly with Evi Girling and Ian Loader on public fears and feelings towards crime in an unexceptional English town. For example, we have explored the ways in which one 'vigilante' episode in which a troublesome local boy was ritually humiliated by some of his adult neighbours related to much more generically-available problematizations of 'youth' and public housing estates (Girling *et al*, 1998; and see generally Girling *et al*, 2000).

4   Recent European work in comparative criminology supports this interpretation and identifies pronounced differences between European countries in social anxiety and preoccupation with 'community' (Lacey and Zedner, 1995), attitudes to violence and support for 'law and order' solutions (Melossi, 1994) and the investment of trust in persons and institutions (Nelken, 1994). For a more general account of the differing routes through modernity of European nation-states, see Therborn (1995a, 1995b).

5   Some observers (Pearson, 1983) regard some such nostalgia as a chronic and venerable dimension of crime talk (and can adduce examples dating back to the Romans to buttress the point). Lash and Urry (1994: 246–7) *per contra* argue that nostalgia is a particularly pervasive sensibility in the late modern world, in response to the speed and violence of social change, as well as being increasingly institutionalized and fostered in the form of the 'heritage' industry (see also Lowenthal, 1985).

6   Such sensibilities are most drastically visible in Davis's (1990) account of the fortress suburbs of Los Angeles, and more generally in his discussion of the 'ecology of fear' (1992). But in less extreme form a high preoccupation with propriety and avoidance

seems endemic, as in Baumgartner's (1988) evocative depiction of the 'moral minimalism' of an affluent surburb. Although he elsewhere acknowledges that 'local nationalisms' (but just how *local* is 'local'?) are themselves stimulated by globalization (1990: 164) and has written feelingly about 'fundamentalism' as a response to post-traditional conditions of life, Giddens at times (1991) writes as if place *could only* matter to one who was a born-and-bred child of one's native soil. *Per contra* Lash and Urry show persuasively that the 'manufactured diversity' of places is now crucial to their strategies for economic restructuring (Lash and Urry, 1994: 284–305; see also Butler and Savage, 1995; Bagguley *et al*, 1990).

References

Anderson, D. (1995) *Crime and the Politics of Hysteria*, New York: Times Books.

Bagguley, P. *et al* (1990) *Restructuring: Place, Class and Gender*, London: Sage.

Bauman, Z. (1998) *Postmodernity and its Discontents*, Cambridge: Polity Press.

Baumgartner, M. P. (1988) *The Moral Order of a Suburb*, Oxford: Oxford University Press.

Beck, U. (1992) *Risk Society*, London: Sage.

Beckett, K. (1997) *Making Crime Pay*, Oxford: Oxford University Press.

Bottoms, A. (1995) 'The philosophy and politics of punishment and sentencing', in C. Clarkson and R. Morgan (eds) *The Politics of Sentencing Reform*, Oxford: Oxford University Press.

Butler, T. and Savage, M. (1995) *Social Change and the Middle Classes*, London: UCL Press.

Canovan, M. (2000) 'Taking politics to the people: populism as the ideology of democracy', paper presented to conference on Populism and Democratic Theory, European University Institute, Florence, January 2000.

Davis, M. (1990) *City of Quartz*, London: Vintage.

Davis, M. (1992) *Beyond Blade Runner: the Ecology of Urban Control*, Westfield, NJ: Open Media Pamphlets.

Douglas, M. (1992) *Risk and Blame: Essays in Cultural Theory*, London: Routledge.

Ericson, R., Baranek, P. and Chan, J. (1991) *Representing Order*, Buckingham: Open University Press.

Ericson, R. and Haggerty, K. (1997) *Policing the Risk Society*, Toronto: University of Toronto Press.

Featherstone, M. and Lash, S. (1995) 'Globalization, modernity and the spatialization of social theory', in Featherstone, M., Lash, S. and Robertson, R. (eds) *Global Modernities*, London: Sage.

Feeley, M. and Simon, J. (1992) 'The new penology: notes on the emerging strategy of corrections and its implications', *Criminology*, 30, 4: 449–75.

Felson, M. (1998) *Crime and Everyday Life* (second edition), Thousand Oaks, Ca: Pine Forge Press.

Gamble, A. (1997) 'Politics 2000' in P. Dunleavy, A. Gamble, I. Holliday and G. Peele (eds) *Developments in British Politics 5*, Basingstoke: Macmillan.

Garland, D. (1990) *Punishment and Modern Society*, Oxford: Oxford University Press.

Garland, D. (1996) 'The limits of the sovereign state', *British Journal of Criminology*, 36, 4: 445–71.

Giddens, A. (1991) *Modernity and Self-Identity*, Cambridge: Polity Press.

Girling, E., Loader, I. and Sparks, R. (1998) 'A telling tale: a case of vigilantism and its aftermath in an English town', *British Journal of Sociology*, 47, 3: 474–90.

Girling, E., Loader, I. and Sparks, R. (2000) *Crime and Social Change in Middle England: Questions of Order in an English Town*, London: Routledge.

Hall, S., Clarke, J., Critcher, C., Jefferson, T. and Roberts, B. (1978) *Policing the Crisis*, London: Macmillan.

Heelas, P., Lash, S. and Morris, P. (eds) (1996), *Detraditionalization*, Oxford: Blackwells.

Keane, J. (1996) *Reflections on Violence*, London: Verso.

Lacey, N. and Zedner, L. (1995) 'Discourses of Community in Criminal Justice', *Journal of Law and Society*, 22, 3: 301–25.

Lash, S. and Urry, J. (1994) *Economies of Signs and Space*, London: Sage.

Lowenthal, D. (1985) *The Past is a Foreign Country*, Cambridge, UK: Cambridge University Press.

Melossi, D. (1994) 'The Economy of Illegalities: Normal Crimes, Elites and Social Control in Comparative Analysis', in Nelken, D. (ed) *The Futures of Criminology*, London: Sage.

Meyrowitz, J. (1985) *No Sense of Place*, Oxford: Oxford University Press.

Nelken, D. (1994) 'Whom can you Trust? The Future of Comparative Criminology', in D. Nelken (ed) *The Futures of Criminology*, London: Sage.

Pearson, G. (1983) *Hooligan: a History of Respectable Fears*, Basingstoke: Macmillan.

Pratt, J. (2000) 'The return of the wheelbarrow men; or, the arrival of postmodern penality?', *British Journal of Criminology*, 40, 1: 127–45.

O'Malley, P. (1992) 'Risk, Power and Crime Prevention', *Economy and Society*, 21, 3: 252–275.

O'Malley, P. (1997) 'Policing, politics and post-modernity', *Social and Legal Studies*, 6, 3: 363–81.

O'Malley, P. (1999) 'Volatile and contradictory punishment', *Theoretical Criminology*, 3, 2: 175–96.

O'Malley, P. (2000) 'Risk societies and the government of crime' in M. Brown and J. Pratt (eds) *Dangerous Offenders*, London: Routledge.

Robertson, R. (1995) 'Globalization: Time-Space and Homogeneity Heterogeneity', in M. Featherstone, S. Lash, and R. Robertson (eds) *Global Modernities*, London: Sage.

Rose, N. (2000) 'Government and Control', in D. Garland and R. Sparks (eds) *Criminology and Social Theory*, Oxford: Oxford University Press.

Sasson, T. (1995) *Crime Talk: How Citizens Construct a Social Problem*, New York: Aldine De Gruyter.

Simon, J. (1995) 'They died with their boots on: the Boot Camp and the limits of modern penality', *Social Justice*, 2: 25–48.

Simon, J. and Feeley, M. (1995) 'True crime: the new penology and public discourse on crime', in T. Blomberg and S. Cohen (eds) *Punishment and Social Control*, New York: Aldine De Gruyter.

Sparks, R. (1991) 'Reason and unreason in left realism: some problems in the constitution of the fear of crime', in R. Matthews and J. Young (eds) *Issues in Realist Criminology*, London: Sage.

Sparks, R. (1992) *Television and the Drama of Crime*, Buckingham: Open University Press.

Stones, R. (1996) *Sociological Reasoning*, London: Macmillan.

Taylor, I. (1995) 'Private homes and public others', *British Journal of Criminology*, 35, 2: 263–85.

Taylor, I. (1997) 'Crime, anxiety and locality: responding to the "condition of England" at the end of the century', *Theoretical Criminology*, 1, 1: 53–75.

Therborn, G. (1995a) *European Modernity and Beyond*, London: Sage.

Therborn, G. (1995b) 'Routes to/Through Modernity' in M. Featherstone, S. Lash, and R. Robertson (eds) *Global Modernities*, London: Sage.

Thompson, J. (1996) *The Media and Modernity*, Cambridge: Polity Press.

11

American television, crime, and the risk society

Phillip Green

The mass media, and especially television, are central to the maintenance of the risk society. 'Individualization' means 'market dependency in all forms of living', but it is television above all that 'isolates *and* standardises', that both 'removes people from traditionally shaped and bounded conversations, experience, and life', and also puts 'everyone in a similar position', consuming 'institutionally produced television programs'.[1] Visual culture (television and movies) in European societies, however, has not always been so relentlessly market-shaped. Whereas the American system of network television has from its inception epitomized the social arrangements of neo-liberalism (*avant la lettre,* so to speak), European television was initially statist and, in most cases, artistically elitist. Not regularly but at least occasionally content producers and creative artists, even avant-garde artists (e.g. Goddard, Fassbinder), formed a creative artistic community together on terms that if not set by the latter, were at least acceptable to them. Here dependency was not on the market but rather on an aristocratic culture to which artists had potential access.

Of all the European mass media systems, British television (and radio) was the most familiar to the world at large, and in many ways the most successful. (BBC's *World Service* is still the most trusted and reliable news report in the world.) Even after the creation of a commercial channel in the 1950s, British television's tone, scope and the BBC, subsidized by Parliament and overseen by a more or less independent public board, set informal standards. Of the two BBC channels, one was designed to be 'popular', and to compete with the commercial channel; the other (BBC 2) was specifically and unabashedly dedicated to promoting artistic and intellectual excellence. Of course, the medium has always been the message, and mass elitism must have its limits. Still, one of BBC 2's leading producers was once able to say, only partly in jest, that if we woke up one morning and found out that the night before everyone's sets had been tuned to Channel 3 (the commercial channel), then to be sure questions would have to be raised about 'the Beeb's' mission. Otherwise though, it was generally understood that 'culture' (in the normative sense) rather than mass popularity was the primary issue for it. Thus BBC 2 was considered to be doing very well by its controllers if it drew an audience share of 15 per cent as opposed to 35 per cent to 40 per cent for the popular channels. So powerful was this ethos that the creation of Channel 4, the first new channel since the 1950s, a semi-commercial channel with the public mission of promoting programming for 'minority interests', actually took place early in the Thatcherite regime; and its audience share was considered to be 'very satisfactory' in the 10 per cent to 12 per cent range.

At the end of the day, Margaret Thatcher, with the help of Rupert Murdoch and the new cable and satellite technologies, was indeed to destroy that ethos. Starved into submission, governed by a board no longer independent of its ideological masters, and facing competition from a world-wide transmission dominated by Murdoch and the American giants, the BBC, and the British system as a whole, is now a shell of its former self. However, for a period of time during the 1980s and even the early 1990s, during which BBC 2 and the new Channel 4 inhabited a dwindling but still protected public space, British television continued to produce programming that the American commercial channels will never emulate. (*The Sopranos* is an exception that proves the rule, in that it is produced not for commercial television but for a paid subscription movie channel, so that no individual programme has to prove its worth in the ratings game in order to survive – see note 3 below). The comparisons between a market and non-market media system that follow, therefore, may be thought of as a snapshot in time. That time is certainly over for as long as the risk society remains the dominant social form; the comparison, however, continues to be instructive.

To set out to compare systems, of course, is implicitly to evaluate them according to some standard. That standard then has to be made explicit: here, the standard to which I advert is one of ideological and intellectual openness and pluralism. The author is always open to question, but it requires no further defence: to be asked to defend it is already to state its justification. In any event, 'openness' and 'pluralism' are exactly what spokespersons for American network television constantly allege that it is delivering, or is at least in good faith attempting to deliver; I merely take that claim seriously.

It is the case, though, that in the contemporary US, cultural arguments are being made that the system *is* open and pluralist. That argument has to be addressed in at least a preliminary way. Among contemporary students of popular culture, a consensus has begun to emerge about American television quite different from the view dominant only a few decades ago. The theorists of 'mass society' criticized commercial television from a standpoint informed both by intellectual disdain for cultural trash, and political fearfulness in the face of cultural conformity. Today, post-modern theorists see the cultural field as a realm of plurality, play, and multiple meanings, where members of different subcultures appropriate cultural commodities for their own purposes.

This appropriation may indeed happen from time to time. The problem with the theory of mass society was not so much its aesthetic snobbery as its understanding of communication as always and only a one-way process. Even obsessive television-watchers are not passive receptacles. Socialization is a two-way process, and we can never predict, for any particular individual, what will happen during that process.

On the other hand, it would be a mistake to make too much of the phenomenon of communications feedback. Because most people do not regularly suffer from false consciousness, one of the effects of ideological discourse is always to call up resistance to itself; and the more so the greater its pretensions to 'realism' – which do reach a kind of apogee in episodic television. There is a difference, though, between cultural artefacts that leave the field of interpretation open and those that attempt, even if sometimes unsuccessfully, to close it. That television's message is often 'seen through' by women or minorities (or audiences generally) should not lead us to mistake its general direction. The pervasive argument that human life makes sense, social forces are comprehensible, 'happy' endings are normal (justice is done), and the meanings of what people say is ultimately unambiguous – all this represents a secular version of sentiment that 'God's in His Heaven/All's right with the world'. As men and women, we are reassured that a fundamental sympathy, recognized in the institution of marriage and the family, binds us together. As citizens of diverse social backgrounds, we are told that only 'whiteness' gives access to the highest level of awards, but that tolerance of differences is a recognized social virtue. And as political/economic subjects, we not only find that our cultural milieu rewards passive consumption, but we are also assured that there is ultimately nothing to be active about; politics on American television is notable only by its absence.

Thus post-modern critics substitute a legitimate insight about the freedom with which ideas circulate – all of us can reinterpret any text for our purposes – for the quite separate truth that there is an enduring material structure of cultural power to which those of us who merely consume cultural commodities are always subject. With this sleight-of-hand, the hope that media of mass communication might encourage moral ambiguity, transformative critique, or the justification of structural change, simply disappears. Why bother; when anyone can generate their own critique in the privacy of their own home by 'appropriating' *Seinfeld* – as though mild amusement had somehow become socially defiant. As though individual acts of consumption had somehow become politically significant. Carried to this point, subjectivist theories of interpretation justify political passivity.

I want to argue instead that 'mass society' theory is still essentially correct, once the confusion between helpless audiences and passive consumers is clarified. To support this argument, I will first draw a few direct contrasts between American television (at its most prestigious) and its quite different British counterpart; and then try to account for the difference.

In a wonderful moment of serendipity, the same story line appeared on two very different television networks one night in 1988. On ABC-TV's *L.A. Law*, Kuzak (unsuccessfully) defended an accused rapist by attempting to show that the victim's conduct could reasonably have led the accused to believe that 'she wanted it'. On BBC-TV's *Blind Justice*, its female protagonist was doing the very same thing. In each episode, the defence attorney apologized to the victim at the end and was told by her to go to hell. There the similarities end; it is the differences that are revealing.

The American episode concluded, after the accused's conviction, with a confrontation between Kuzak and Van Owen, which soon devolved into the familiar sub-ideological conflict between order and constitutional liberty, 'putting a rapist back on the streets' versus 'even a rapist deserves the best defence he can get'. 'Why', snapped Kuzak with the last word, 'don't you just shoot the bastard and not bother with a trial?' Civil liberties wins the argument but the rights of an innocent victim win our emotions. America is celebrated (by Kuzak) for its protection of civil liberties, the rapist goes to prison, and having it both ways wins the day.

Blind Justice moved in another direction entirely. Assigned by her firm to defend the accused man, Catherine Hughes demurred with the uncompromising statement, 'I don't do consent rapes.' Unlike Kuzak, she made us aware of a crucial asymmetry within the accepted standards of 'fair trial' and 'due process of law'. A 'consent' defence to a rape charge actually requires that the character of the victim be blackened, in order to show that the defendant could reasonably have expected this woman to 'consent', despite the possibility that in her own mind she had no intention at all of doing so. However, forced by circumstances into finally taking the case, she did what she had said she wouldn't do – 'just doing her job' – and secured the accused's acquittal. (This is the most likely outcome of all such cases, but one that *L.A. Law* carefully hid from us.) There are no conclusive reflections about 'putting a rapist back on the streets', because for the creators of *Blind Justice* the issue was not one strand of conventional thought versus another. Instead, Catherine resigns to join a radical law collective that she had previously scorned for its marginality; a collective whose members presumably will understand why she doesn't 'do consent rapes'.

Unlike *L.A. Law*, *Blind Justice* recognized that in the law of rape, consent is inferred only on the basis of what a man *as a man* might 'reasonably' have thought a woman 'wanted', even though force has admittedly been used. This doctrine of consent wipes out a woman's perception of her own non-consent, and thus the law's pretence of neutrality and equality is belied in practice.[2] For a lawyer who takes the rights of women seriously, then, the larger question is how she can do her job in an unjust society. It's not that this question could not be answered on American television, but that it could never be raised. Catherine's only possible response, in her own view, is the morally disturbing conclusion that she must change her life.

Serendipity again: in one week of December 1993 it was possible on British television to see episodes of two police drama series, *Prime Suspect 3* and *Between the Lines*, in sequence with an Emmy-winning two-part episode of the American *Homicide*. At first glance there was a superficial resemblance, in that all three concluded with failure. *Prime Suspect 3* and *Homicide* both featured a detailed interrogation of a 'prime suspect', who walked away unscathed at the end. There the resemblance ended, however, and it is again the fundamental difference that was so striking.

Put simply, *Homicide* was a paean to the efforts of those who try on behalf of the rest of us to make 'law and order' a reality. They do not succeed in every case, but as one detective remarks, 'the great thing about being in Homicide is that there's always more of them'. The failure of the police symbolizes their humanity; nobody is perfect, especially when forced to endure the hazards and brutalities of 'life on the street'. This is the strange, inverted version of Hollywood naturalism, beautifully realized in its gritty urban surfaces, but totally unlike the socially conscious naturalism of Zola or Dreiser or Norris. Here, the good guys are us, on this side of the interrogation table; and the bad guys are them, on the other: occasionally supported by bleeding heart judges, evil defence attorneys, and other do-gooders – the only forces that are systematically shown to prevent 'justice' from being done.[3]

Prime Suspect 3 and *Between the Lines* are not about the defence of law and order. Rather, they are about the frightening ambiguity of police work, or of the very concept of the 'police' who, as any picketer or community activist could testify, do not exist only to protect citizens from crime (see Reiner *et al*, Chapter 9 in this volume). The police exist also to protect the state and the elites that staff and run it from having to undergo full democratic accountability for their own often illicit behaviours. The murderer in *Prime Suspect 3* does not walk away simply because Detective Chief Inspector Jane Tennison is unable to break his alibi, as in *Homicide*. Rather, he walks away because the police hierarchy and powerful political forces have combined to make it impossible for her to pursue her case properly from the beginning.

This is also the constant theme of *Between the Lines*, a series about a mythical 'Complaints Investigation Bureau' that investigates alleged (and often real) police crimes. Its ambiguity runs even deeper than that of *Prime Suspect 3*, for the narrative and symbolic manipulation by which ideological narratives lead us to their unique conclusions are entirely absent. There is systematic injustice, and there is police work that ineluctably leads to it, yet seems necessary in its own right. What exactly are we to think?

It is not merely that *Between the Lines* emphasizes the reality of injustice more than the humanity of its characters or that its 'hero' himself engages in cover-ups to 'protect the honour of the force', but that even the humanization of its protagonists is equivocal. The male lead is a philanderer who at one point systematically betrays both women in his life: an ironic commentary on his assigned task of rooting out the same kind of work-related behaviour among his colleagues. American visual culture always politicizes sex, but we learn nothing about 'law and order' itself from the sexual bickering between, say, Kuzak and Van Owen. Watching *Between the Lines*, we are confronted with the real meaning of the slogan, 'the personal is political'.

That Tony Clark betrays his wife and his mistress (herself a policewoman involved in a cover-up), while compromising two of his own cases in the process, does not by itself reveal anything about the alleged politics of personal life to us. What is truly political is the revelation of how thoroughgoing, how all enveloping, is the life of secrecy, betrayal, and anti-social solidarity that the police are forced to lead. A man whose job it is to root out lies is himself constantly telling lies, and does not even notice the contradiction. Watching him negotiating his sex life we wonder not about male philandering, which would be a trivializing response, but about policing as an organised activity: whether 'law and corruption' might not be a more accurate epithet than 'law and order'; and how it is that a good policeman may be not quite a good man.

These British shows do what cannot be done on American commercial television: they challenge the ideology of 'law and order' itself. The case for the police is stated with unequivocal tough-mindedness in all these series. But it remains an argument, rather than, as in American versions of the genre, a conclusion all the more decisive for being implicit.

Although the programs I have referred to here were exceptional rather than typical, even a more general account of the British system makes the same point. What was most decisively different about this system was that it makes possible the destruction of artificial connections – which in the United States have the hard reality of a natural phenomenon – between television genres and viewing-time segments. In one week in England in 1994, for example, at a time when the system was already decaying, the following programmes appeared during the prime time hours of 9 p.m. to 11p.m.:

Two sporting events; two full-length news coverage programmes every night; sixteen documentaries or exposes of various kinds, including three about controversial political issues, two about cancer, one about gay nuns, two of particular interest to women, two about cars, and one about American movies by blacks; two original plays; two series about doctors; six sitcoms, two of them American; nine films, seven of them American, the others Australian and English; one 'true crime'; three comedy programs; four police series (including a rerun of *Between the Lines*); two private eyes (one of them a woman, the other Sherlock Holmes); two programmes of questions directed at public figures; one dramatized best-selling novel episode; one soap opera; three popular-song and culture programmes; one serious quiz show and one game show; one programme of childhood reminiscences of a well-known politician; one appeal from Bosnia, carried in short form every night on the BBC; two segments of an extraordinary, multi-episode documentary film (produced by Channel Four) of daily life in China; an appreciation of the Chrysler Building by John Malkovich; and from a unique and indescribable Channel Four series of short plays, an episode in which the anti-Semite Degas and the leftist Jew Pissarro, both once central members of the Impressionist movement but now no longer talking to each other, are brought to the Channel Four studio to debate the Dreyfus Affair.

In short, the hierarchy of American television, in which (especially on 'prime time') the expensive programming of narrative fiction and Hollywood movies is privileged compared to all other uses of visual technology, was here overturned. The entire range of programming that in the United States would be ghettoized as 'public television', less than and different from the real thing, appeared interchangeably with *Dynasty* and *Roseanne*, *Murphy Brown* and *Home Improvement*, all together making up a metatext that to American eyes is unrecognizable.

Nothing I have said here constitutes a judgement of aesthetic quality. There is one ultimately aesthetic *and political* characterization, though, that can be offered with confidence. American television is made for people who, in the ordinary course of events, will spend their evening passively consuming its cultural commodities. Occasionally this system produces major 'events', recognized by everyone with a kind of astonished reverence, before they disappear back into the metatext from which they so briefly emerge. This television is not designed to compete with other ways of living life, except with its generic cousin cinema. The presumption is that to be immersed in it but not really engaged with it *is* the normal way of living. For delivering the kind of entertainment which, to paraphrase T.S. Eliot, is designed to distract us from distraction by distraction, American television is unexcelled.

It was also possible to 'live with' British television this way, especially its soap operas, which are even more the subject of national attention in all social circles than are their American counterparts. But these all run in the early evening when Americans, whose real nightlife has not yet begun, are watching endless local and national recounting of the same 'news'. British prime-time television, contrastingly, is – or at least was – also and perhaps even equally made for people who might otherwise be spending their evenings reading, or working, or pursuing hobbies, or going out or engaging with the unpleasant material world.

In sum, British television did not colonize the consciousness of its potential audience in the same way or to the same extent as its American counterpart. It was not a total, self-referential world, designed literally to screen out all alternatives to passive consumption. Instead, it offered the passive consumption of culture as one alternative to all those other, less passive modes of linking cultural productions with their material referents. If we must spend some of our nights watching other people's versions of the worlds we live in, this is certainly the most varied, pluralistic, and open way in which those nights can be programmed for us.

How could this be? With the exception of Channel Four's founding, the creators of British television had not the faintest intention of providing either more democracy or more pluralism in visual culture. The BBC was conceived of (by Lord Reith) with a frankly elitist and paternalistic mission, and though it might be barely possible to imagine a similar outcome of some future reform effort in the United States, its explicit justification would have to be totally different. Nevertheless, the various components of the system produced results strikingly variant from those American televiewers are used to, and it is worth considering just how this was accomplished.

There are certainly profound cultural differences between the United States and Great Britain, the one being anarchically and even violently democratic, unequivocally consumerist, and relentlessly progressive; the other being authoritarian and hierarchical, and still marked by strong elements of traditionalism and social deference. By its very terms, though, this cultural account can hardly tell us why the more democratic nation produces a monolithic televisual culture, compared to the variegated output of its more authoritarian counterpart. The tradition of cultural elitism at the BBC probably accounts for the occasional prime-time appearance of Restoration tragedies or sober discussions of post-modernism in the arts. But it cannot have accounted for the political radicalism of *Blind Justice,* the corrosive cynicism of *Between the Lines* and *Prime Suspect 3,* the uninhibited female self-expression of *Absolutely Fabulous,* or (later at night) the musical outrageousness of Frank Zappa, who never appeared on American network television – the first name in what could be an endless roster of creative artists subject to the same negative characterization. Only attention to institutional structures, to the way visual culture is produced and distributed rather than to the cultural ideals it might be presumed to express, can provide the necessary explanation.

American network television can be characterized simply, as we have seen: it is a market-driven industry par excellence. More precisely, it is an oligopoly, in which a handful of producers dominate the bulk of the market and compete with each other for profit. In fact, profit, as is the case for most oligopolies, is guaranteed, in that the worth of the basic asset – the network franchise – is beyond price. Monopolizing a group of channels is not what it once was, now that the UHF band on cable television is almost indefinitely extensible. But other producers, even the pay-for-play movie channels, are mere satellites within this system; the networks are the planets.

But each of the networks must reproduce and expand its value, because the oligopoly is competitive. There is no fixed source of income: theoretically, every programme produced by NBC or CBS or ABC or TNT or Fox could not only lose money but fail to return a single dollar, if every viewer absolutely preferred a competing programme on some other network. Advertisers would go on strike, shareholders would disinvest, the network's stock would collapse, and hundreds of corporate raiders would be competing to buy control and throw the existing ownership and management out on its collective ear. Though profit-seeking is only comparative, it is as desperate and ruthless as if it were absolute. Market share within the oligopoly must be roughly maintained, if for no other reason than to guarantee the power and wealth of its rulers. The ratings game, which measures market share, is a life-and-death matter. Millions of advertising dollars, and more important, dozens or even hundreds of well-paying jobs, can be lost on a single ratings point. Risk is ubiquitous, and pervasive.

The key to the operation of this system is that, as has often been said, networks do not sell programmes to audiences but audiences to advertisers. All the major advertisers on commercial television are in exactly the same position as the networks: they are competitors in an oligopoly, trying to maintain or improve market share. What they know is that if the other oligopolists advertise and they don't, their product will fade from sight. If, less dramatically, their programmes are only marginally less popular than those of their oligopolistic competitors, that may or may not be bad for sales, but it cannot possibly be good: once again, heads will roll. Innovation or originality are therefore, and for good reason, fundamentally suspect.[4] That risk cannot be taken. Commercial television, though its narratives are often predicated on a never-ending tease, must still in the end give the kind of satisfaction that maintains interest in a given programme as a series of meaningful outcomes, the most meaningful of which is the advertising time it sells.

In order to understand the way this system of oligopolistic competition determines the production of cultural commodities, we have to rid ourselves of fantasies about 'free markets'. The notion of 'consumer democracy' describes a system in which producers respond to every shifting demand of the market, and the implication we are supposed to draw is that cultural production shares the most important feature of political democracy, consumer choice being a close analogue to voter choice. This much is true in the sense, and only in the sense, that political parties are also oligopolists, and that party competition is oligopolistic competition. But in the well known analysis of rational-choice theory, competitive parties organised for the winning of elections therefore tend to deliver similarity rather than diversity.[5] Or, as Ulrich Beck puts it, individualization standardizes.

A simple thought experiment will show why this must be so. Let us imagine three companies, A, B, and C, that dominate a particular consumer market and whose products are largely indistinguishable – the condition under which oligopolies arise in the first place. Suppose company A decided to market a distinguishable product; that is, one catering to a part of the market not yet actually satisfied by the oligopoly. This would require a major diversion of resources, but at great and pointless risk. Because similar types of products cannot meaningfully be patented or copyrighted, B and C would immediately copy A if A's innovation were successful, and A's brief lead in marketing a new product would disappear (after one season, if we are thinking of television shows). On the other hand if the innovation were failure, A would have wasted precious resources and lost some portion of market share by being, in effect, a guinea-pig for the rest of the industry. The game is not worth the candle: little to be gained and much to be lost.

Free-market oligopoly cannot produce diversity. It cannot cater to minority or exceptional tastes unless these can be isolated as an identifiable group of potential consumers. This is especially true of television, where the traditional product is so familiar, the costs of production so high, and the risks of failure so great. Network television caters only to the average viewer. The average viewer may be different at different times of day, and for different television genres: children for Saturday morning cartoons, women for daytime television and soap operas, men for professional sports, adult families for prime-time television, adult men for cop shows. Whatever the genre or time, though, only the mass audience – of women, of families, of men, of children – is the advertiser's target. More specifically, only the mass audience of likely consumers is the target.

Television, therefore, is specifically intended to be addictive, like heroin or crack or any other addictive substance; the main goal of any commercial television programme is not to be switched off. Just as, for example the central purpose of visual pornography ('hard core') is to get its audience to watch more pornography (or else the industry would go out of business), so the central purpose of any television episode is to get the viewer to watch more television: the next segment, leading to the next set of ads; the next programme, leading to four new sets of ads; and the same programme(s) next week, leading to a repetitive seeing of the same ads.

This being the case, we can no more imagine American television producers consciously trying to insert into the middle of this schedule a sense of holy terror, unbearable anxiety, Brechtian cynicism, or profound outrage at injustice, than we can imagine the producer of a pornographic film inserting one of Bergman's endless husband/wife dialogues in between two scenes of orgiastic coupling. 'Get on with it!' is their common motto. This is not to say that intellectual thoughtfulness will never be found in fictional presentations on commercial (or public) television, but only that it must be kept in its place, bracketed off from the rest of the schedule and at the same time reintegrated into it by a major publicity campaign, so that it will not lead us to want to do something other than watch television. It is not just that only the average viewer is addressed by this system, but that the average standardized viewer is offered only average aesthetic standardized experiences: nothing that might turn our attention away from television-watching itself, by throwing us into a state of real emotion or intellection. Exceptions stay firmly within the bounds of humanistic naturalism, do not stray far ideologically, and refuse any possibility of formal innovation that might confuse viewers who understand television as a site of relaxation and passive enjoyment.

The caustic wit of *Roseanne*, the quirky multiculturalism of *Northern Exposure*, the sometime feminism of *Cagney and Lacey*, the racial consciousness of *Frank's Place* or *A Different World*, the social satire of *The Simpsons*, the sometimes counter-ideological 'movie of the week' productions of Robert Greenwald and his successors have stretched American television's boundaries slightly. It would be wrong to think that network television always remains the same; the explosion of same-sex weddings in the 1996 season is a case in point. But at no point will network television ever be intellectually independent or aesthetically imaginative in what was once the British sense. Nothing in the United States is equivalent to those challenges to dominant understandings of the world described above. What cannot be inserted into the schedule of commercial television is precisely what was inserted, only occasionally but often enough to be noteworthy, into the British television schedule. In the soap opera *Brookside*, one 1993 episode featured both a political party debate on the National Health Service and a discussion between a teacher and her student about the latter's lesbianism, which concluded with the two going off to make love. Neither real politics nor uncensored female (or male) sexuality is permitted on American network television, for either of those shocks to the system might prevent some element of the audience from being delivered to the advertisers who foot the bill.

Even the occasional originality of Hollywood cinema is beyond the reach of American television. Nothing on network television could possibly equal the visual terrorism of *Psycho*, the nightmarish nihilism of *Jacob's Ladder*, the elegiac look and tone of *Unforgiven*, the unrepentant vengefulness of *I Spit on Your Grave* or *Thelma and Louise*, the sexual transgressiveness of *Basic Instinct*, or the racial transgressiveness of *Suture*.[6] As for those independent but still recognizably narrative films that trail Hollywood's wake, there is no equivalent anywhere within the television system, no matter how many cross-subscription channels cable has added to it.

Instead, the metatext of American commercial television reveals a unique national ideology and aesthetic style that go hand in hand. In this version of storytelling, 'problems' are introduced only to be solved, critiques only to be repudiated. People share gender unity as members of families and class equality as consumers; knowledge of significant social differences among them is suppressed; and developmental needs that cannot be expressed as patterns of material consumption might as well not exist; and visual distraction itself (the source of television's immense profits) is firmly positioned as a central – perhaps the central – communal need. Just as in the midst of bitter divorce we can enjoy a weekly narrative of family unity, in the middle of political crisis we can enjoy a weekly narrative of social integration and political passivity.[7]

American television's addictiveness, and its unending, unimaginative conformity to a narrow range of choices has intellectual consequences. Though there is no evidence that watching television changes minds in any particular ideological direction, there is plentiful evidence of its pacificatory effect; and of its tendency (especially when watched heavily by children) to bring about a confusion between the real and the fanciful.[8] Unlike movies (which seem to emanate phantasmatically from within ourselves), television appears simply as the 'real' upon which we are eavesdropping. It is just there being life. And even though we know that life is not a sitcom or soap opera or police drama, these programmes still seem to be about American people leading American lives; the unalloyed aesthetic naturalism of television positions us as inhabitants of the same world it is bringing into our living room.[9]

Nor is the apolitical character of television without a serious politics. American television series are carefully tailored to fit into genres that are sexually and also nowadays racially coded to find and not to offend a particular primary audience, an audience that can instantly be identified simply by watching the ads. But with the exception of only the most successful 'crossover' programmes (for example, *The Cosby Show, L.A. Law*), they accomplish this via the technique of 'narrowcasting'; that is, quite deliberately structuring and then appealing to a fractured public. This public cannot help but recognize its re-presentation as ghettoized. When a white woman watches a programme for white women she knows what she is watching (if somehow she managed to miss this point, it would be brought forcibly to her attention at the first commercial break). In this way American television's simulacrum of pluralism affirms the divisions of the sexual and racial order even while seeming to appeal to particular subject positions within it. This is not a genuine democratic pluralism, but a pluralism that cancels itself out. So ideological ambiguities of race, class, and gender do occur and reoccur, because the social order itself is immersed in them to a perhaps historically unprecedented degree. But in the television world they are always brought under control in the end (if only via the extreme sanction of cancellation). And the given always reasserts itself as normative. Gay people are interesting because they are gay, female protagonists may be full of rage but they are never unalloyed feminists, and despite the occasional presence of black judges or chiefs of detectives, the most omnipresent image of black men, whether on *Homicide, N. Y. P. D. Blue*, or the pseudodocumentary *Cops,* is that of being shoved up against a car by a policeman, frisked, and handcuffed. The other remains the other; despite the explosion of subjective positions in front of the television cameras, there is only one camera eye on television: the eye of the objective observer who stands in for the standardized social whole.

At this point, then, we are finally in a position to understand how the British public service system, both as I have been idealizing it and as it more or less actually worked for a number of years, managed to sustain itself. The answer is that reversing the structure of American commercial television also reverses its priorities. In the absence of oligopolistic competition, standards of 'success' change drastically. Market competition produces conformity; the elimination of market risk or the attenuation of competitive pressure produces variety. The opposite of competition, of course, is protection; and if we use this word rather than its more particular counterpart, 'subsidy', we can see what it is that makes the difference.

BBC-TV and Channel Four functioned behind a protective wall, and this wall was designed to protect them not only from market competition but from the political process; to treat them as the welfare state once treated health, for example. In the case of the BBC, its financing was traditionally provided primarily by the television licence fee, which was paid annually by every television-owning household in Britain, for every television set owned (or rented). Public television was thus refinanced yearly, without the necessity of asking for any legislative appropriation; as long as the fee could be raised without resistance, the system was stable.

As with other tertiary services, the pressures of globalization destroyed this assurance. As for Channel Four, it is permitted to sell time to advertisers within certain limits agreed on with the commercial channel, but the sponsor relationship is mostly arm's length. Particular products or advertisements are not identified with particular programmes, and the American style of corporate pressure on producers, or of interest-group pressure on corporate sponsors, is unimaginable. Much more crucial, however, is the fact that the main source of protected revenue for Channel Four is still a legislatively mandated set-aside: the commercial channel allocates ten per cent of gross revenues as a subsidy to Channel Four, and this is part of the cost it must bear for being licensed to monopolize public airspace.

Much more so than in the case of the BBC, then, there is no built-in pressure for reducing or eliminating this subsidy, since its ultimate source is the indirect and invisible tax that advertisers impose on consuming viewers (and in any event, the argument that particular licencees have a right to hold this licence in the first place, and to do anything they want with it, is simply incredible). Imagine a new network financed by the existing networks and mandated by the Federal Communications Commission to give special representation to women, gays, African-Americans, and so on, and one can begin to imagine the extent of the difference.

So the most important criterion for maintaining a vitally pluralistic visual culture on the public service model is that its management and its financing are independent of both political and commercial pressures; that they are insulated from the risk society. Thus to call the British system 'elitist' and the American system 'democratic' would be to miss the point. American television is governed by an economic elite and, where public, a non-representative political elite; all decisions on the ground are subject to their imprimatur. The elite that dominated British television (historically) was, contrastingly, an elite drawn in significant part from the creative community. It always lacked appropriate regional, minority, and female representation, but in principle it was open to the claims of those groups, as long as their representatives had the talent to make a contribution – as why should they not? The sub-business class that controls American television may well be more democratic in its composition, but that is irrelevant; its only purpose is to prevent imaginative acts of creation from taking place.

In the future there may be possibilities for democratizing the production of mass culture that will go far beyond the British model. But they will have to start from its basic rejection of the false promises of 'consumer democracy', for the 'free market' can never produce anything but an unfree culture.

Notes

1   Beck 1992: 132–33.
2   See MacKinnon (1989), ch. 9; also Pateman 1989: 71–89.
3   The most notable exception is the HBO movie *Criminal Justice*, with Forest Whitaker as an alleged, and ultimately convicted, murderer whose rights are given scant acknowledgment, and of whose guilt or innocence we are never certain. Here we are left in a genuinely ambiguous state of unease about 'law and order'. However, HBO is an exception only by virtue of its institutional position. Since for any given film it has a guaranteed audience which has already paid to see whatever films it is going to show, its projects do not have to pass the standard marketability tests. Thus HBO is receptive to commercially dubious projects as long as they might get favourable reviews, and not raise the kind of flak that can result in falling subscriptions. In this respect HBO is in a position comparable to that of Channel 4 in Britain, as discussed below.
4   The fate of 'minority [a euphemism for 'black']-oriented' television is a sad case in point. See 'The transformation of the television industry and the social Production of blackness', in Gray (1995).
5   The original and still perhaps the most influential analysis is that of Anthony Downs (1957).
6   *Suture* is about two men, half-brothers, whom we may call A and B. In order to escape a mob-hit, A tries to kill B and – with planted ID, etc. – have him identified as A. B survives and is taken for A. No one ever doubts his identity as A, an outcome which has been presaged by an exchange between the brothers about how much they resemble each other. As it happens, one brother is white and the other black, and they do not resemble each other in any obvious way at all. The movie is not 'about race' in any of the ways that Americans mistake for public conversation about that subject; it is instead about the way in which we, the racialized audience, construct 'race' as a given category to satisfy our own expectations, instead of as the conundrum it actually presents.
7   We should not confuse the stylistic difference of series such as *the X-Files* or

Millennium with the aesthetic imagination. These merely add febrile paranoia to an already unhealthy dose of unreality.

8   See Postman (1987) and Gerbner *et al* (1987); and Kline (1989).
9   An American television watcher would have to see a non-naturalistic product of British television such as *Pennies From Heaven* or *The Singing Detective* even to begin to comprehend what such television might look like.

References

Beck, Ulrich (1992) *Risk Society: Toward a New Modernity.* London: Sage Publications.

Downs Anthony (1957) *An Economic Theory of Democracy.* New York: Harper & Row.

Gerbner, George *et al,* (1987) 'Charting the Mainstream: Television's Contributions to Political Orientations', in Donald Lazere, ed., *American Media and Mass Culture: Left Perspectives.* Berkeley: University of California Press.

Gray, Herman (1995) *Watching Race: Television and the Struggle for Blackness.* Minneapolis: University of Minnesota Press.

Kline, Stephen 'Limits to Imagination: The Marketing of Children's Culture', in Ian Angus and Sut Jhally, eds., *Cultural Politics in Contemporary America.* New York: Routledge.

MacKinnon, Catherine (1989) *Toward a Feminist Theory of the State.* Cambridge: Harvard University Press.

Pateman, Carole (1989) 'Women and Consent', in *The Disorder of Women.* Palo Alto: Stanford University Press.

Postman, Neil (1987) 'The Teachings of the Media Curriculum', in Donald Lazere, ed., *American Media and Mass Culture: left perspectives.* Berkeley: University of California Press.

Index